LITTLE MOSQUE ON THE PRAIRIE AND THE PARADOXES OF CULTURAL TRANSLATION

In 2007, *Little Mosque on the Prairie* premiered on the Canadian Broadcasting Corporation network. It told the story of a mosque community that worshiped in the basement of an Anglican church. It was a bona fide hit, running for six seasons and playing on networks all over the world.

Kyle Conway's textual analysis and in-depth research, including interviews from the show's creator, executive producers, writers, and CBC executives, reveals the many ways Muslims have and have not been integrated into North American television. Despite a desire to showcase the diversity of Muslims in Canada, the makers of *Little Mosque* had to erase visible signs of difference in order to reach a broad audience. This paradox of "saleable diversity" challenges conventional ideas about the ways in which sitcoms integrate minorities into the mainstream.

(Cultural Spaces)

KYLE CONWAY is an assistant professor in the Department of Communication at the University of Ottawa.

Little Mosque on the Prairie and the Paradoxes of Cultural Translation

KYLE CONWAY

UNIVERSITY OF TORONTO PRESS
Toronto Buffalo London

ISBN 978-1-4426-5003-9 (cloth)   ISBN 978-1-4875-2055-7 (paper)

Cultural Spaces

Library and Archives Canada Cataloguing in Publication

Conway, Kyle, 1977–, author
Little mosque on the prairie and the paradoxes of cultural translation / Kyle Conway.

Includes bibliographical references and index.
ISBN 978-1-4426-5003-9 (hardcover)   ISBN 978-1-4875-2055-7 (softcover)

1. Little mosque on the prairie.   2. Muslims on television.   3. Islam in mass media.
4. Cultural pluralism in mass media.   5. Multiculturalism in mass media.   6. Minorities
on television.   7. Situation comedies (Television programs) – Canada – History and
criticism.   I. Title.

PN1992.77.L585 C66 2017   791.45′72   C2016-908102-8

This book has been published with the help of a grant from the Federation for
the Humanities and Social Sciences, through the Awards to Scholarly Publications
Program, using funds provided by the Social Sciences and Humanities Research
Council of Canada.

University of Toronto Press acknowledges the financial assistance to its publishing
program of the Canada Council for the Arts and the Ontario Arts Council, an agency
of the Government of Ontario.

Canada Council **Conseil des Arts**
for the Arts **du Canada**

ONTARIO ARTS COUNCIL
CONSEIL DES ARTS DE L'ONTARIO
an Ontario government agency
un organisme du gouvernement de l'Ontario

Funded by the   Financé par le
Government gouvernement
of Canada   du Canada

Contents

Acknowledgments   vii

Introduction: Muslims and Sitcoms in Post-9/11 North America   3

1 Sitcoms, Cultural Translation, and the Paradox of Saleable Diversity   17

2 Representation between the Particular and the Universal   33

3 The Paradoxes of "Humanizing Muslims"   54

4 Saleable Diversity and International Audiences   80

5 Religion as Culture versus Religion as Belief   99

Conclusion: Identity and Difference in North American Sitcoms   123

Notes   143

References   155

Index   169

Acknowledgments

Thank you:

To Rebecca Weaver-Hightower, for introducing me to Mosab Bajaber, and to Mosab, for introducing me to Zarqa Nawaz;

To Zarqa Nawaz, for her insight into the creation and production of *Little Mosque*, for her kindness and humour, and for introducing me to Mary Darling and Clark Donnelly;

To Mary Darling and Clark Donnelly, for their thoughtfulness about this project, for their exceptional generosity and hospitality, for *Little Mosque* seasons 4 and 6, and for introducing me to the rest of the production team;

To Susan Alexander, Sadiya Durrani, Michael Kennedy, Anton Leo, Mike Mosallam, Al Rae, John Ranelagh, Rebecca Schechter, and Peter Sussman, for their insight into what it takes to produce and distribute sitcoms (and other programs) about Muslims in North America (and elsewhere);

To the University of North Dakota, for the Arts, Humanities, and Social Sciences research grant and the Summer Graduate Research Professorship that allowed me to travel to gather interviews and spend a summer working with graduate students on audience research;

To Lucian Stone, for our conversation about "humanness" and the taboo against showing the full range of emotions on screen, which helped me put the idea of saleable diversity into words;

To Eric Gomez, Kiley Wright, Angela Beason, and Deb Jenkins, for their help with the initial audience research, included in chapter 3;

To Serianna Henkel, for her many contributions to the analysis of the reception of *Little Mosque on the Prairie* in Norway, included in chapter 4;

To my colleagues at the University of Ottawa, for finding my job talk based on this manuscript interesting enough to hire me and for welcoming me so warmly when I arrived;

To the anonymous reviewers of the manuscript, for pushing me to sharpen my analysis and recognize implications of my arguments I would not have otherwise seen;

To Siobhan McMenemy, for guiding me diligently through the editorial process and for offering encouragement when I had to rewrite the book;

And to my family: Ellie, for sleeping in my arms as a newborn as I watched episode after episode of the first three seasons; Ben, for making me stop and read books about turtles while I revised my manuscript; Kristi, for everything. This book is for you.

Earlier versions of portions of the introduction and chapters 2 and 3 appeared in Kyle Conway, "*Little Mosque*, Small Screen: Multicultural Broadcasting Policy and Muslims on Television," *Television and New Media* 15, 2014. Reprinted by permission of SAGE.

LITTLE MOSQUE ON THE PRAIRIE AND THE PARADOXES OF CULTURAL TRANSLATION

Muslims and Sitcoms in Post-9/11 North America

In North America, according to conventional wisdom, situation comedies – sitcoms – are more than mere television shows: they are minorities' ticket into mainstream culture. "One of the ways that new communities gain acceptance into the mainstream is through humour," explains the *Ottawa Citizen*'s television critic, Michael Murray (2007a, K1): "Once you're able to laugh at yourself and your environment, everybody tends to relax, and a sense of security sets in. And there is nowhere people feel more relaxed and secure than in front of the television set. So often the success of new sitcoms signals the acceptance and recognition of a new culture into the mainstream ... Through sitcoms, we've seen black, Italian, gay and Jewish cultures, amongst others, take their place in North America."

In 2007 it appeared that Muslims, one of the most frequently scapegoated communities in North America, would finally have their turn, too. *Little Mosque on the Prairie*[1] premiered on the Canadian Broadcasting Corporation's (CBC) English-language network (as did *Aliens in America* on the American "netlet" called The CW). It told the story of a Muslim community that worshipped in the basement of an Anglican church in a fictional small town in rural Saskatchewan, and it featured the widest range of Muslim characters ever seen on North American television – a lawyer-turned-imam, a feminist doctor, a university professor, a small café owner, and more, but not a single terrorist in sight. Writing about *Little Mosque*, Murray (2007a, K1) said, "It's finally time for the Muslim community to show Canada that they're just another wacky and lovable family living amidst us." The *Toronto Star*'s Sabrina Jalees (2007, D4) wrote, "Based on the principle that tragedy plus time equals comedy," the time had come for sitcoms about Muslims, which held the potential to humanize Muslim "others" for non-Muslim viewers.

This book examines these claims and – more important – the contradictions they cover up. On the one hand, humour does have the potential to transform how we see the world. Jokes are an odd thing. They function through an excess of meaning: we get a joke when we recognize the gap between what it *says* and what it *means*. We laugh because we are surprised, and our surprise has the potential to jolt us into seeing the world a little bit differently, if only for the duration of the joke. But seeing the world differently is a first step to questioning our assumptions about it, including the stereotypes we maintain about people unlike ourselves.

On the other hand, the sitcom can be a conservative genre. For instance, the most successful sitcoms have made their creators money through syndication, when they were sold to local stations or cable networks to air in reruns. Producers had no guarantee that viewers would watch episodes in order. As a consequence, they needed to tell stories that were self-contained and episodic rather than serial. One effective narrative structure followed the pattern of stasis-conflict-resolution-stasis – any changes within the story world, such as character development, risked making later episodes confusing for viewers who had not seen the earlier episodes. Change became an industrial liability.

The sitcom's conservatism works at cross-purposes with the potential of jokes to make stereotypes appear strange. So how has that contradiction played out? In particular, how has it played out in North America in the decade following the attacks of 11 September 2001, during which time Canada's powerful southern neighbour conducted an amorphous war on terror, and the threat of further attacks seemed to loom constantly on the horizon?

In this book I answer these questions by examining *Little Mosque on the Prairie* through the lens of cultural translation, or the acts of negotiation and mediation performed by people – the show's makers – occupying a space between different cultural communities – Muslims and non-Muslims. I say "Muslims" and "non-Muslims" rather than "Islam" and "the West" because the second set of terms hides more than it reveals. Both "Islam" and "the West" name exceptionally diverse entities that overlap and interpenetrate. (For instance, Zarqa Nawaz, *Little Mosque*'s originator, describes herself as both Western and Muslim, not to mention feminist.) For this reason I focus on the play between text and context, between micro- and macro-levels of analysis, in ways that echo producers' and viewers' own approaches to *Little Mosque*. They were reflexive in their production and consumption of the program, and their negotiations over its meaning were at the heart of the process of cultural translation.

I also describe how the sitcom's conservatism, a byproduct of the commercial logic that shapes Canada's television industry, restricted the range of choices the producers of *Little Mosque* could make. In many instances they had to erase visible signs of difference in the name of diversity, a paradox I call "saleable diversity." If cultural translation was a process, saleable diversity was its result, although it too was subject to negotiation. In the end, *Little Mosque on the Prairie* did not break decisively from programs that came before it, but in its novel depiction of Muslims it did break new ground.

Little Mosque on the Prairie

Little Mosque was originally created by Zarqa Nawaz, a feminist Muslim filmmaker who grew up in Toronto and lived in Regina. Before *Little Mosque* she was best known for her documentary *Me and the Mosque*, made for the National Film Board, about the growing conservatism in North American mosques. *Little Mosque* was produced by Mary Darling and Clark Donnelly of WestWind Pictures, who were motivated by their Bahá'í faith to choose programs that promoted the idea of human unity.

It premiered to great fanfare in January 2007, one of a number of scripted comedies to gain prominence in Canadian television in the mid-2000s. As *Variety* observed in 2007, "The sitcom may be on life-support in the U.S. but it's the hottest thing on TV in the Great White North" (Kelly 2007a, 30), where shows like *Corner Gas* (also set in small-town Saskatchewan) and *Trailer Park Boys* (set in Nova Scotia) were attracting a surprising number of viewers. The CBC had heavily promoted *Little Mosque*, going so far as to bring camels to downtown Toronto as part of a publicity stunt. It had also attracted international attention, most notably from the *New York Times*, which sent its religion reporter, Neil MacFarquhar, to write a story while it was still in production. His article, published a month before the premiere, described the balance that the writers and producers wanted to strike between entertainment and the potential for controversy (MacFarquhar 2006). Thanks to this publicity, *Little Mosque* attracted 2.1 million viewers – an exceptional number for the CBC – when its pilot aired on 9 January.

Two things make *Little Mosque* valuable as the object of an extended case study. First, it is Canadian, and scholars of Canadian television, in contrast to their US and British counterparts, have been late to the game in examining popular television content. This is to say not that they have ignored Canadian television, but only that their focus has been on the political economy of the US-dominated international television industry and on policy as a tool for the development of national culture.[2] Only in the late 1980s did people such as Mary Jane Miller begin to examine Canadian shows on their own terms. They have now been followed by a second generation of scholars such as Sarah Matheson and Michele Byers and the contributors to volumes such as *Canadian Television: Text and Context* (Bredin, Henderson, and Matheson 2012). Indeed, such work has marked a "new 'turn' towards textual analysis" (Czach 2010, 175). In this book, I follow their lead and ask, as the editors of *Canadian Television* encourage, about "the potential in moving beyond conventional discourses of cultural nationalism. Rather than entering into a debate over what Canadian television could or should do," I ask what it *is* doing (Bredin, Henderson, and Matheson 2012, 15). What my analysis lacks in breadth, it makes up for in depth as I examine Canadian television in a global context, where the category "Canadian" functions in constant tension with the global forces that affect Canadian TV.

Second, examining *Little Mosque* makes it possible to ask a different set of questions about representation of Muslims on television than others have asked and – importantly – to arrive at a different set of conclusions. Two of the most compelling recent books on Muslims in North America – Evelyn Alsultany's (2012a) *Arabs and Muslims in the Media* and Mucahit Bilici's (2012) *Finding Mecca in America* – identify *Little Mosque* as a show that promised to break from the conventional logic linking Muslims to terrorism in North American media: "Not only do story lines represent a departure from prior tropes, but the characters also deviate from the standard patriot and victim molds. What makes [*Little Mosque*] notable ... is that characters are not measured in relation to terrorism; they are people with varied lives" (Alsultany 2012a, 176).

Indeed, the makers of *Little Mosque* took a deliberate, interpretive approach. One of their goals was to show non-Muslim viewers how Muslims saw the world, in order to challenge the stereotypes upon which other programs relied. In contrast, most other analyses are concerned with shows where the inclusion of Muslim characters is coincidental, or at least not deliberately interpretive. Consider news and drama. Journalists want to present timely, accurate stories told in a balanced way, and they make choices about whom to include in light of that goal. In other words, they discuss or interview people who played a role in an event or who offer a perspective that contributes to a story's balance. Only in the case of certain "soft" or human-interest stories do journalists actively try to explain how a person or community sees the world. Similarly, people who make dramas have many goals other than representation as such: they want to generate conflict between characters to create a compelling, plausible story. One reason to include Muslim characters is they fit viewers' expectations about heroes and villains. Their very identity simplifies the task of generating conflict. Hence the Muslim characters in stereotypical villain roles. Their inclusion solves a structural problem, rather than working towards interpretive ends.

But my focus on *Little Mosque* does not mean I am not concerned with other shows. On the contrary, the people who made (and watched) it were also paying close attention to the broader conversations about Muslims taking place in the news, in dramas, and elsewhere. In fact, we can observe the influence of those other shows in *Little Mosque* itself. The producers of *Little Mosque* used it to comment on other media and current events. They also tried to use it in an anticipatory way to influence the conversations in which they were taking part. Thus, this book is about more than one show: *Little Mosque* is a lens through which we can examine perceptions and arguments about the role of religion, especially Islam, in contemporary North America.

Islam in Canada and the United States

What is the broader context in which *Little Mosque* circulated? In 2009 *Maclean's* magazine reported the results of a survey that found, much to the consternation of the leaders of many of Canada's mainline Christian denominations, that religions "such as Islam and Buddhism ... are growing in Canada at a surprising speed. According to new data from Project Teen Canada, more teens now identify as Muslim than Anglican, United Church of Canada and Baptist combined" (Lunau 2009). The result was surprising for a number of reasons, not the least of which was that it did not reflect Canada's larger religious make-up: in the 2001 census, about 44 per cent of Canadians described themselves as Roman Catholic, 29 per cent described themselves as Protestant, and only about 2 per cent described themselves as Muslim (Canada 2005).

But it seemed to reinforce concerns among some non-Muslim Canadians that their society was changing, and not in ways they liked. The article followed on the heels of a number of high-profile events involving Muslims, such as a proposal in Ontario in 2004 to allow the use of Sharia law to settle divorce or inheritance cases or, more frighteningly, the discovery of an apparent plot to establish an al-Qaeda-style cell in Toronto in 2006.[3] These events, of course, took place against the backdrop of the lingering anxiety produced by the attacks of 9/11.

Part of the explanation for the intensity of these concerns lies in the pace of the growth of Islam in Canada in the 1990s and 2000s. Islam's presence in Canada is a relatively recent phenomenon. Although religious diversity as such is not recent, Kamal Dib (2006, 39) writes, "Since the 18th century, and until the early 1980s, Canadian religious diversity was largely one of a variety of Christian denominations from Orthodox to Protestant, along with a tiny Jewish minority and a variety of Aboriginal customs." The censuses between 1931 and 1961, for instance, found that about 3 or 4 per cent of the population identified as neither Christian nor Jewish (Kalbach 1970, 68), although they did not break the "other" group into smaller groups. But it is still possible to get a sense indirectly of the number of Muslims living in Canada. By 1967, about 35,000 people from the Middle East lived in Canada, according to the Canadian Citizenship Branch of the Department of the Secretary of State, although how many were Muslim is not clear (Canada 1967, 237). In 1971, however, a researcher could write of Lac La Biche, Alberta, that with its 244 Lebanese residents (about 10 per cent of the population) the town "may well be the most Muslim town in either Canada or the United States" (Barclay 1971, 67).

In the past two decades the number of Muslims in Canada has grown dramatically, immigrants in English-speaking Canada coming largely from India, Pakistan, Lebanon, Syria, Iraq, and Iran, and immigrants in French-speaking Quebec coming largely from the francophone Maghreb region of North Africa (McAndrew 2010). In 2001 Muslims accounted for about 2 per cent of the country's population, a rate that was predicted to rise to more than 4 per cent by 2017. This growth has been especially visible in Canada's major cities. In 2001 more than 5 per cent of people in Toronto were Muslim (predicted to rise to more than 10 per cent by 2017), with slightly smaller percentages in Ottawa and Montreal (Dib 2006, 40–1). Muslims' increasing visibility, both in everyday city life and in the high-profile events referred to above, has produced considerable anxiety among many non-Muslim Canadians.

Much of their anxiety stems from their perceptions about Muslims' loyalty to Canada and their willingness or desire to integrate into Canadian society. On the one hand, according to a 2007 poll by Environics Research Group,

> Canadian Muslims expressed simultaneous pride in Canada and pride in Islam, a willingness to participate in and adapt to Canadian norms, and a condemnation of the extremism that is sometimes cast as commonplace in other countries with significant Muslim populations. Although seriously concerned about discrimination and underemployment, Canadian Muslims expressed feelings of goodwill toward Canada and were the least likely Muslim minority in any Western country surveyed to express a sense that the bulk of their compatriots are hostile to Islam. (Adams 2009, 20)

On the other hand, non-Muslim Canadians "expressed moderately positive views of Islam, but were less likely than Muslims to feel that most Muslims wish to integrate fully into the Canadian mainstream." They "placed great stock in symbolic adaptations, such as the abandonment of religious clothing," and they were thus "more inclined than the Muslim minority to favour certain measures geared toward forced adaptation" (ibid., 20–3). For example, one such measure was introduced as part of a bill in Quebec's provincial legislature, and it garnered considerable support. In March 2010 Justice Minister Kathleen Weil introduced An Act to Establish Guidelines Governing Accommodation Requests Within the Administration and Certain Institutions, which would have required women wearing a face veil to remove it when requesting services from the government. It would also have required civil servants to interact with the public with their faces uncovered. An overwhelming number of people inside and outside the province supported the proposal: 80 per cent of non-Quebecers and 95 per cent of Quebecers expressed support, according to a poll taken shortly after the bill's introduction (Angus Reid Public Opinion 2010; see also Conway 2012d). The bill did not pass, but three years after its introduction the governing Parti Québécois introduced a similar bill (the Quebec Charter of Values), this time to enshrine secularism in the province's Charter of Human Rights and Freedoms.

In all of this, of course, Canada cannot escape the influence of the United States. Since the attacks of 9/11 its leaders have tried to strike a balance between acknowledging the diversity of Muslims (inside and outside the United States) and justifying a long military campaign

against countries where Muslims are in the majority. The contradictory messages they send are part and parcel with many non-Muslim
Americans' distrust of Muslims. When asked whether they thought
there was support for extremism among American Muslims, 40 per
cent of the general public thought there was a "great deal" or a "fair
amount" of support, as opposed to 21 per cent of Muslims. Similarly,
24 per cent of the general public thought support for extremism was
rising, as opposed to only 4 per cent of Muslims (Pew Research Center
2011, 1). When asked whether they thought Muslim immigrants wanted
to adopt American customs, 51 per cent of the general public thought
Muslim immigrants wanted to remain distinct from US society, whereas 56 per cent of Muslims thought they wanted to integrate (ibid., 6).

News coverage was one factor that fuelled this distrust. In 2011, for
instance, stories about Islam accounted for more than 30 per cent of all
stories about religion in US mainstream news (newspapers, television,
and radio), and "tensions with Islam [were] becoming a bigger story"
(Pew Research Center 2012, 2–4).[4] Such media coverage is indicative
of a deeper pattern. According to Jack Shaheen's (2001, 19–21) exhaustive list of Hollywood movies, the categories "Muslim" and "Arab"
are treated as if they are the same, and stereotypes prevail: Muslim
(and Arab) women are "bosomy bellydancers leering out from diaph-
anous veils," while Muslim (and Arab) men are "stooges-in-sheets"
or terrorists intent on killing Westerners, especially Americans. The
media perpetuate these stereotypes by using "us-versus-them" stories and, according to Edward Said's (1997) well-rehearsed argument,
the legitimacy of their narrative is ensured by an academic appara-
tus that privileges certain voices over others, through funding and
gatekeeping in publishing and hiring. The resulting consensus has
shaped more than just US media. According to Karim Karim (2003),
the Canadian media system is embedded in a transnational system that
is largely dominated by US corporations, a situation strengthened by
the increasing concentration of media ownership. This is true in news,
and it is true in fiction: after the 9/11 attacks, rentals in Canada of
Hollywood films about terrorist attacks committed against Americans
spiked (Ramji 2005).

These were the factors that motivated the people who made *Little
Mosque*. They saw humour as a way to encourage non-Muslims to question their preconceptions and understand Muslims as more like themselves than unlike. They sought, in effect, to "translate" Muslims for
non-Muslims.

Scope and Approach

Here is where the idea of cultural translation proves its value. One way to understand it is by analogy with translation in a linguistic sense: it is the act of making a foreign object or text intelligible in a new context. In the case of *Little Mosque*, it is a question of making a minority community perceived as "foreign" intelligible to the majority community. The task was not – and is not – straightforward. The diversity of Muslims meant that, despite their efforts to the contrary, *Little Mosque*'s writers and producers could not depict everyone, and "representation," such as it was, was not necessarily representative: the characters in *Little Mosque* could not stand in for all Muslims everywhere. Some were bound to feel left out.

Thus, as an analytical lens, cultural translation reveals a range of conceptual challenges, which scholarship in two fields – cultural studies and translation studies – can help us unravel.[5] For this reason I see this book's audience as belonging predominantly to these two fields, which offer complementary tool sets. Cultural studies, especially in the subfield of media studies, has developed powerful tools for talking about the conditions of media production, circulation, and consumption, tools that would benefit translation studies scholars who want to understand the factors that shape media translation. Similarly, translation studies has developed tools for describing the changes texts undergo when they leave one locale for another, tools that complement those of cultural studies scholars interested in global media-, techno-, and ideoscapes (Appadurai 1990). These fields operate on different sets of assumptions, which I will make explicit. Each considers some matters settled that the other does not, and because there is little dialogue between them, without my explanation each is likely to find some aspects of my analysis puzzling. Hence, when I raise points readers see as going without saying, I ask them to bear with me: they do not go without saying for everyone.

My particular approaches include critical production studies and agent-oriented translation studies. Both ask how structural factors (economy, politics, and so on) exert pressure on program-makers and how program-makers in turn manoeuvre within their circumscribed horizons. The first – critical production studies – is concerned with the way "many film/television workers ... critically analyze and theorize their tasks in provocative and complex ways" (Caldwell 2008, 2). It is grounded in political economy and ethnography, which provide the analytical tools to reveal what I am calling saleable diversity.

The second – agent-oriented translation studies – draws special attention to program-makers' role in mediating between communities. It broadens the definition of "translation": rather than a form of rewriting or transcoding, it treats translation as a "mode of participation in a semiotic economy where signs are exchanged for other signs, on a basis not of equivalence but of negotiation" (Conway 2012b, 587). It examines acts of negotiation in the broadest possible sense – inquiry, explanation, and clarification, in ways that give shape and contour to the relationships between communities. It seeks to understand such negotiation "from the viewpoint of those who engage in it, in particular (social, cultural or professional) settings," which include a broad spectrum of mediating actors, including "politicians, military personnel, publishers, educators" (Buzelin 2011, 8–9) or, in this case, people who make television.

My evidence comes from a series of interviews I conducted between 2011 and 2014 with people involved in the production of *Little Mosque*. I spoke with the show's originator and executive producers as well as the most frequent director and writers from all six of the show's seasons. I also interviewed the CBC executive instrumental in green-lighting the show.[6] I corroborate and extend their accounts with others provided by trade journals and CBC reports. I pay attention to points of contradiction and ambiguity that characterize how *Little Mosque*'s makers created meaning in the show: the contradictions between sources reveal gaps in the narratives the media industries – and program-makers – tell about themselves. They also reveal the contradictions within the environment where program-makers worked and their approaches to resolving them.

Hence, I hope to provide cultural studies and translation studies scholars with insight into the complex processes of mediated intercultural communication. But if along the way I also provide analysis that is useful for religious studies scholars – my third potential audience, although I am merely a sympathetic outsider – then this book's conclusions will be all the more felicitous.

Chapter Overview: Cultural Translation and Saleable Diversity

My purpose in this book is twofold: to provide a careful account of *Little Mosque*'s production, circulation, and final textual form and to develop a theory of cultural translation and test it against an empirical case. To be clear, when I say "theory," I mean it in the sense that literature scholars use the term, as a mode of writing and analysis that is interdisciplinary, speculative, reflexive, and critical of common sense (Culler 1997, 14–15). But theory is valuable only in so far as it describes the world: the world is the conceptual limit that theory must confront. If one must yield, it will not be the world, which is stubbornly material. As Anthony Pym (2010, 1) says, "the practice of translation" – not to mention cultural translation – "exceeds its theory, thus requiring an ongoing empirical attitude."

"Cultural translation" describes a set of practices shaped by a series of ideas – in short, a theory – about how people act as intermediaries between different cultural groups. In the specific case of North American television these practices result in depictions of saleable diversity. Both terms – "cultural translation" and "saleable diversity" – operate on a practical plane and a conceptual plane. In a practical sense, saleable diversity is what acts of cultural translation produce. In a conceptual sense, it is cultural translation's limit, the stubborn empirical fact we must confront when putting forward ideas about how people act as intermediaries. But this distinction is only heuristic. I cannot ask how television performs the work of representation without asking how people who make programs understand the tools at their disposal; I cannot ask how these same people conceive or explain the nature of interpretation without examining the images they produce. The images themselves provide a focal point for my analysis, and, at the same time, they serve as a point of empirical resistance, a grindstone on which to sharpen the tools of theory.

I have divided the book into five chapters and a conclusion. Chapter 1 develops a theory of cultural translation by exploring the two aspects of *Little Mosque* that made it different from other programs scholars have considered: its interpretive impulse and its use of humour. It begins by describing producers' understanding of how humour works; in that respect, it describes their implicit theories about the sitcom's role in television and society more broadly. Second, it questions and supplements those theories, which attribute transformative power to humour without always acknowledging its potential to support the status quo. Cultural translation is a process, a form of negotiation or exchange structured like a multilayered, wide-ranging conversation, where utterances take many forms. They might be spoken exchanges (e.g., when the producers and network executives consider production choices they might make), but they might also be episodes of *Little Mosque* itself, which the network and production team collectively address to viewers and to which viewers respond either in discussion among themselves or through more public venues such as letters to the editor. One outcome of this negotiation is the paradox of saleable diversity. It imposes limits on the range of characters that can be represented and the range of emotions characters can experience, and it also affects international syndication.

Chapters 2 through 5 put this theory of cultural translation to the test. They are ordered chronologically, and they provide a thick description of the interactions between the CBC, the show's originator, executive producers, and production team (including writers, actors, and directors), and the viewers. They identify points where the relationship between actors or the factors external to their relationship changed. Chapters 2 through 4 focus on the first two seasons, while chapter 5 focuses on the final four, an imbalance that reflects the evolution of the logic of saleable diversity.[7] It was built into the show from the initial point of conception, and during the first two seasons, as *Little Mosque*'s makers negotiated with the CBC, it came to take a stable form.

Chapter 2 establishes a baseline for comparison by describing *Little Mosque*'s genesis. It begins by describing where the conversation about "Islam" and "the West" stood when *Little Mosque*'s originator and producers wanted to join. It considers the multiple factors involved: Zarqa Nawaz's personal experience and perspective as a feminist Muslim, the CBC's various mandates and its interpretations of them, and Mary Darling and Clark Donnelly's religious convictions, which shaped their choices about which programs to produce and how.

Chapter 3 describes *Little Mosque*'s first two seasons. It asks what happens to the process of cultural translation when the industrial model changes. Season 1 was short (only eight episodes in 2007) and marked by careful attention to detail. Season 2 was much longer (twenty episodes in 2007–8) and, because of the increased pace of production, it relied more heavily on sitcom conventions and lost the attention to detail of the first season.

Chapter 4 begins by noting another paradox that shaped *Little Mosque*. Its domestic production and distribution depended on WestWind Pictures' ability to syndicate it internationally to make up for a recurring funding gap. Thus, *Little Mosque*'s producers were thinking about more than just Canada. This chapter examines the conversations they carried on with US viewers and critics as they worked (largely without success) to export the show to the United States. US critics were interested in *Little Mosque* because of its striking differences from US media, and Canadian critics read their feedback and responded to it. Canadian critics also watched *Aliens in America*, a US sitcom about a Muslim exchange student in Wisconsin, and they drew inevitable comparisons with *Little Mosque*. Although WestWind had trouble syndicating *Little Mosque* in the United States, it had better luck in France and Norway, the two other countries this chapter examines. But there, networks struggled to attract an audience.

Chapter 5 describes the third through the sixth seasons. It continues to test the theory of cultural translation by asking what happens when people in positions of authority (in this case, CBC executives and the executive producers) have a different vision of the form a show should take. Season 3 (twenty episodes in 2008–9) represented a turning point – the executive producers, in consultation with CBC executives, decided to abandon the sitcom's conventional return to stasis because they wanted to show characters changing over time. Season 4 (eighteen episodes in 2009–10) represented another turning point. CBC executives thought *Little Mosque* had grown too pat and no longer addressed current events or critical issues in the "real" world, and the executive producers decided to generate a more "realistic" conflict by replacing a well-loved character (the priest of the church hosting the mosque community) with one who was abrasive. They thought his distrust of Muslims better reflected the attitude of many Canadians.

Seasons 5 (thirteen episodes in 2011) and 6 (eleven episodes in 2012) returned to the questions of faith that had motivated Darling and Donnelly in the first place. The producers wanted to distinguish between religion as culture, an idea that was dominant for the first four seasons, and religion as belief, which was dominant for the last two. And one of the most striking aspects of the show's finale – the choice by a convert from Anglicanism to remain Muslim even after her divorce from her Muslim husband – resulted from a disagreement between WestWind and the CBC over the culture/belief divide. As such, it is the clearest example of a compromise resulting from the give and take of cultural translation.

The concluding chapter returns to the question of theory by asking about the assumptions underlying the interpretive impulse that led to *Little Mosque*. Chapters 1 to 5 ask about the means of interpretation; the conclusion asks about the ends. When *Little Mosque*'s originator and producers talk about the show, they see interpretation as an end in itself: explaining Muslims to viewers means "humanizing" them by combatting stereotypes. But something greater is happening, at least potentially. Bilici (2012), for instance, sees the emergence of Muslim comedy as an index of the increasing incorporation of Muslims into the North American imaginary. What does *Little Mosque* reveal in that respect? Has the interpretation performed by show's makers made Muslims appear less foreign? I consider this question in light of a theme that emerges over the course of the show's run, that of interfaith understanding or ecumenism.[8] In *Little Mosque* the idea of ecumenism appears to take on a narrow meaning, that of the unity of the Abrahamic faiths (especially Christianity and Islam). In the context of the show this idea made possible the "translation" or transformation of Muslims into North Americans; it represented the realization of that process. It also encouraged the gentle humour that characterized the show. But, I argue, other options exist. Other shows suggest different approaches to humour, many of them more agonistic than that of *Little Mosque*. A broader notion of ecumenism that did not shy away from thornier questions of disagreement would encourage a different type of humour and lead to a different type of conversation, one whose scope would reach beyond that of *Little Mosque*.

What this extended case study illustrates is that cultural translation as a process and saleable diversity as an outcome were two sides of the same coin. In their efforts to humanize Muslims for non-Muslims the people who made *Little Mosque* had to make choices that did not exceed certain bounds. But those bounds were not fixed: they, too, were subject to negotiation. *Little Mosque*, despite its limitations, combatted stereotypes by allowing characters to define themselves on their own terms, rather than in relation to terrorism, the dominant frame in North American media. They could be doctors, contractors, imams, parents, children, or friends, without the question of terrorism being raised. In the end, at least in the short term, the show's impact was less pronounced than its makers had hoped – the conversation described in chapters 2 to 5 might have convinced some viewers to reject their stereotypes about Muslims, which are pervasive and ingrained in North American society, but it certainly did not convince all of them. But *Little Mosque on the Prairie*, because of its interpretive goals and use of humour, suggests that incremental change is possible if television producers engage in sustained and creative efforts to encourage people to think differently about Muslims.

Chapter 1

Sitcoms, Cultural Translation, and the Paradox of Saleable Diversity

Two things make *Little Mosque on the Prairie* both different from other shows and valuable as an object of sustained study. First, its creator and producers took a deliberately interpretive approach, in contrast to most shows where the value of Muslim characters – if there are any at all – is the role they play in the structure of the plot. Muslims frequently are villains or, as has been the case since 9/11, innocent victims of people who believe the stereotype that Muslims are villains (Alsultany 2012a). In these programs Muslims have replaced the bogeymen of the past (such as the Russians during the Cold War) and, as bogeymen, their beliefs are beside the point. Rare are the shows that talk about what Muslims think or acknowledge the fact that Muslims belong to a diverse community. *Little Mosque*'s makers wanted to do just that. According to executive producer Mary Darling, "We have [a] reaction [to] people saying, 'You're trying to make people understand Islam.' And I say, 'Yeah yeah, why not?'" (quoted in Kelly 2007b, 20). Or, in originator Zarqa Nawaz's words, *Little Mosque* "shows Muslims being normal. It humanizes Muslims. I want the broader society to look at us as normal, with the same issues and concerns as anyone else" (quoted in Bilici 2010, 204–5).

Second, *Little Mosque* used humour to talk about Muslims.[1] Humour differs from other modes of representation in that its polysemic qualities unsettle the relationship between images and what they purport to represent. Jokes work by saying two things at once: words' literal meaning is contradicted by their connotative or ironic meaning, and we laugh (or squirm) because we recognize that gap. But that gap calls into question images' ability to stand in for what they depict. Many of the characters in *Little Mosque* were Muslims, but they were also works of fiction, a fact that jokes helped bring into the foreground.

To understand how these two traits worked together, we could ask producers about their work. The people involved with *Little Mosque*, from the originator and producers to the writers, directors, and actors, were reflexive in their work. But their explanations show the influence of contradictions within the television industry. Although they wanted to humanize Muslims, they were careful not to appear didactic for fear of alienating viewers. Nawaz explains, "I don't feel like there was ever any real attempt to educate or to teach anyone, but because it happened to be about Muslims, the stories revolved around Muslim issues" (interview with author, 2011). Darling echoes Nawaz: "I see *Little Mosque on the Prairie* as a show which should have been able to air on any of the channels ... we went in with a very strong interest in the content for our own reasons, but those reasons couldn't become preachy or didactic, or it wouldn't have gotten 2.1 million [viewers] on its first airing" (interview with author, 2011).

In other words, the people who made *Little Mosque* wanted to counter stereotypes about Muslims by helping viewers understand them better, but they also wanted to create a successful show. The pursuit of commercial success restricted their choices about how to interpret Muslims to a wider audience. This contradiction appears in their accounts of the show: they described both goals – improved understanding and commercial success – as primary, but they often elided those points where they came into conflict. Thus, we must go beyond their accounts to understand how *Little Mosque* performed the work of representation. What are the implications of this contradiction? How did it shape the interpretive work *Little Mosque*'s makers wanted to do? How did humour help resolve the contradiction?

We need a different analytical lens. The contradictory forces that shaped *Little Mosque* also created a series of paradoxes, variations on the theme of the erasure of difference in the name of diversity. But these paradoxes were not absolute, and they allowed for a certain give and take among producers, network executives, and audiences. To ask questions about the limits of the interpretive impulse, in this chapter I draw from the field of translation studies, which has been examining these limits for four decades. I use the lens of cultural translation, or the negotiation that takes place when people try to substitute a sign in one semiotic system for a sign in another. I begin by describing why such substitutions are necessarily imperfect. I then identify the people involved in the specific negotiations that led to *Little Mosque* and examine how these negotiations played out during production, how they became manifest in the program itself, and how audiences reacted.

What I demonstrate is that two things make jokes valuable. First, by saying two contradictory things simultaneously, they create a set of formal conditions for change: they present people with alternatives to the stereotypes they usually see. Second, by making people laugh they act as a potential catalyst for causing them to question their prior assumptions. Whether this potential is realized – that is, whether viewers question their assumptions – depends on the viewers, but the value of identifying the formal and affective dimensions of humour is the insight we gain into the mechanics of sitcoms and cultural translation.

What Is Cultural Translation?

One of the key insights in translation studies, a field that began to develop in its current form after the publication of George Steiner's *After Babel* in 1975, has been that movement and transformation are two sides of the same coin. Consider translation in a conventional sense, as a form of rewriting: when translators take a text from one locale and move it to another, they must also change it by substituting one language's words for another's if their purpose is to introduce something intelligible to a new set of readers. (I can buy a book in Arabic and bring it to my home in Canada, but if I don't know Arabic, I still am unable read it.)

This movement-transformation has a paradoxical effect. On the one hand, many people read the translation because they have no other access to the work; for them, the translation comes to stand in for the original.[2] On the other, the act of rewriting denatures the text it makes available to new readers because to make sense in a new context, it must do so on the new readers' terms. The author of the original can write with the knowledge that readers will share a set of unspoken assumptions about the world, assumptions that shape how they interpret what they read. These assumptions are part of the foundation on which the text is built. Translators work with the knowledge that their readers will likely share a *different* set of unspoken assumptions. Thus, they must build a text on a new foundation. They must substitute one set of cultural assumptions for another, and the resulting resemblance between original and translation is approximate at best. This paradox has a direct influence on their strategies for managing this resemblance. They can maintain an original text's cultural specificity, but they do so at the cost of confusing readers unfamiliar with the culture that is not their own. Conversely, they can substitute cultural references relevant to the new readers they reach, but they do so at the cost of moving further away from the text they are claiming to represent.

The substitution of cultural references raises a similar set of issues, ones that British cultural anthropologists began to address under the rubric of *cultural* translation in the 1950s. Godfrey Lienhardt (1954, 97), for instance, explained in a 1953 lecture that the "problem of describing to others how members of a remote tribe think [appears] largely as one of translation, of making the coherence primitive thought has in the languages it really lives in, as clear as possible in our own." In a 1958 essay, Ernest Gellner (1970, 24) described the anthropologist's task in similar terms: "The situation, facing a social anthropologist who wishes to interpret a concept, assertion or doctrine in an alien culture, is basically simple. He is, say, faced with an assertion S in the local language. He has at his disposal the large or infinite set of possible sentences in his own language. His task is to locate the nearest equivalent or equivalents of S in his own language."

This substitution has a similarly denaturing effect. Anthropologists who ask how the people they are studying interpret the world must recast their subjects' interpretations in new terms. In effect, their subjects' interpretations are to cultural translation what conventional texts are to linguistic translation, the material that undergoes transformation as it moves from one locale to another. Anthropologists, after all, bring what they learn back to their own communities after transforming their subjects' lived experience (and resulting interpretation of the world) into books or articles.

This paradox has important implications for understanding *Little Mosque* and its makers' desire to "humanize Muslims." Frequently, what they meant when they spoke of humanizing Muslims was demonstrating that they were "like" non-Muslims. A lot hinges on what "like" meant. To highlight similarities between groups, they emphasized certain identity traits and de-emphasized others. For instance, as the next chapter describes, they created two zealously conservative characters, one Muslim and one non-Muslim, to emphasize "right wing" and de-emphasize "Muslim" and "non-Muslim." Similarly, they frequently described the show as being about immigrants and outsiders, rather than Muslims as such, to explain its appeal to non-Muslims. In effect, they were making an implicit claim that, at least in one respect, two apparently unlike people are interchangeable. This claim underpinned the notion of ecumenism that grounded the series, as I discuss in the concluding chapter.

In short, they were creating equivalences that allowed them to "translate" Muslims for non-Muslims through a form of substitution. This substitution denatured the identity of the people being "translated"; it erased difference in the name of diversity. By emphasizing the universal, they obscured the particular, and many Muslim critics felt left out. When these critics in turn disparaged *Little Mosque* as whitewashing Muslim identity, what bothered them was precisely this erasure.

Cultural Translation-as-Negotiation

In an absolute sense, then, translation-as-substitution is impossible: the denaturing transformation is the price anthropologists – and mediamakers – pay for the movement they bring about. But in a relative sense, such substitutions take place all the time, in the most quotidian circumstances. Imagine two people from different backgrounds who meet by chance and are curious about each other. The first might ask about an object the second carries, and the second might try to explain its cultural significance. Through a series of exchanges – "We use it to celebrate a holiday." "Oh, that sounds like what we do when ..." "No, not quite, it's more like this ..." – the first refines his or her notions of the object, which becomes less and less foreign. The two people come to understand each other's view of the world through a series of approximate substitutions that, although imperfect, help them understand each other better, too. As Shirley Ann Jordan (2002, 98) writes, "To produce cultural translation is not a question of replacing text with text ... but of co-creating text ... and it is in this sense that it can be powerfully transformative for those who take part."

The makers of *Little Mosque* participated in similar give and take. It is in this sense that I use the term "cultural translation": a negotiation over meaning where one group of participants tries to understand how the other group sees the world. I want to be clear because in recent years, cultural translation has become one of those ideas "that at a certain point in time achieve such a broad circulation that they seem able to name just by themselves the main determinants of the epoch" (Ribeiro 2004, 2). It is what W.B. Gallie (1962) would call an "essentially contested concept" that evokes a range of relatively coherent yet contested ideas for which no one single "correct" definition can be established.[3] Uses that differ from mine, to give one example, come from everyday, common sense ideas about culture and translation, articulated by people who reason by analogy with translation but do not carry through with their analogy. They talk, for instance, about the need for "'DJs ... [or] skilled human curators' who can speak the language of the West and of other cultures at the same time" (Ethan Zuckerman, founder of the Global Voices blog, quoted in Mayberry 2010). This analogy leaves important questions unanswered. Which words make up these languages? How do they operate syntactically, semantically, or pragmatically? Still other uses come from postcolonial literary studies. They are associated with the work of people such as Homi Bhabha (1994), Tomislav Longinovic (2002), and Boris Buden and Stefan Nowotny (2009), and they emphasize the disruption the foreign causes when it is introduced in the realm of the familiar. For my purposes, the idea of negotiation sheds more light on *Little Mosque* than the idea of disruption, although some viewers' reactions to the show did indicate they found it upsetting because it did not conform to their assumptions about Muslims.

If we examine *Little Mosque* through the lens of cultural translation-as-negotiation, we can see the space through which its makers manoeuvred as they pursued the goals of humanizing Muslims while making a successful show. Figure 1 traces the shape of this negotiation, whose principal participants included Zarqa Nawaz, the CBC (in particular, Anton Leo, head of English comedy), WestWind Pictures (the production company run by Mary Darling and her partner Clark Donnelly), the production team (writers, actors, directors, show-runners, and so on), and, finally, viewers and critics.

Arrows indicate the direction of influence: they show who spoke to whom in an effort to explain or persuade. They also describe the form that utterances took. In most cases utterances were spoken or written, but when the production team addressed viewers, it did so through *Little Mosque* itself. Arrows also indicate forms of indirect influence: the executive producers at WestWind Pictures interacted directly with the production team and, through them, indirectly with viewers. The figure illustrates how the relations between everyone involved with *Little Mosque* – the CBC, the show's originator, the executive producers, the production team, and viewers – were reciprocal: everyone could respond to everyone else, although in some cases, they did so indirectly.

This negotiation was both reactive and predictive: not only did participants respond to what others said, but they actively anticipated the

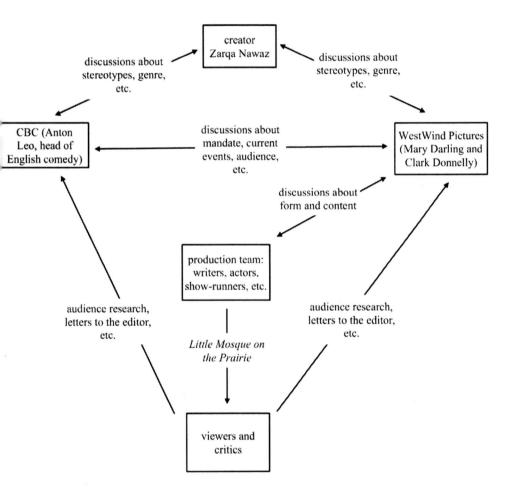

Figure 1. Map of negotiation in the production of *Little Mosque on the Prairie*.

responses their utterances might provoke. What Mikhail Bakhtin (1986, 95) suggests with respect to more conventional conversation was true here, too: "The utterance of the person to whom I am responding (I agree, I object, I execute, I take under advisement, and so forth) is already at hand, but his response (or responsive understanding) is still forthcoming. When constructing my utterance, I try actively to determine this response. Moreover, I try to act in accordance with the response I anticipate, so this anticipated response, in turn, exerts an active influence on my utterance (I parry objections that I foresee, I make all kinds of provisos, and so forth)." In the case of *Little Mosque* the network and producers anticipated viewers' responses through formal means such as audience research and informal means such as hunches about what they wanted to see. Viewers, for their part, were savvy about the industry and frequently interpreted the show in light of their perceptions of its logic or their ideas about the CBC.

In the next sections I consider the negotiation mapped out in figure 1 as it relates to sitcoms, in particular *Little Mosque*, and the interpretive work they perform. The people on the top half of the map – the originator, the executive producers, and the network itself – had clear but often unspoken ideas about how cultural translation should work, ideas that did not always match the expectations of the people on the bottom half of the map – the viewers. The focal point of the negotiation was *Little Mosque* itself. It was the analogue to the target text in literary translation studies and thus occupies a position of analytical privilege.[4] Its role was double in that it was one utterance among others, but it also gave structure to what was otherwise a more diffuse conversation. People talked broadly about what it meant to be Muslim in North America, but they also talked more narrowly about *Little Mosque* itself. The show's makers designed it to be polysemic,[5] in the hope that the contradictory meanings would prompt viewers to reconsider what they thought they knew about Muslims; that polysemy allowed viewers a wide range of interpretive latitude, and they did not always respond as the show's makers might have hoped.

Formal and Affective Dimensions of Cultural Translation

The people responsible for *Little Mosque* made assumptions about humour's effect on viewers that guided their production choices, although they did not always put their assumptions into words. As they saw it, humour's transformative power came through the physical or psychic reactions it provoked. For instance, Zarqa Nawaz, who originally created *Little Mosque* after producing the documentary *Me and the Mosque*, explains: "You can do so many more things with humour than you can do with straight documentary work. I mean I got way more attention with *Little Mosque* than I ever did with my documentary work because it manages to unite people and make them laugh. I remember an American told me that when he saw Baber [an irascible but lovable conservative Muslim character], he just couldn't look at Muslim men in the same way again, and that really surprised me. Because I never really thought that it would have that type of impact on people" (interview with author, 2011). Laughter is not the only response that can be transformative, as Mary Darling explains. Discomfort works, too, because it causes people to examine and question how they understand their relationship with people they see as "other": "[To be successful, *Little Mosque*] had to be about relevance, relatable character comedy with some real laughs in it that come from a place – I hope – not only that the jokes are funny but ... a place of, 'Can you say that?' or, 'Is that – can you say that about those people?' Which sort of came up in some of our focus tests, where the Muslims were laughing their heads off, but ... [white] Canadians were kind of like, 'Can you say that about those people?' And [our reaction was] this is why we're making the show, folks, right?" (interview with author, 2011). At first glance, these theories are compelling. Others have shared them, such as Katie Couric, who in 2010 suggested that a "Muslim *Cosby Show*" might be what the United States needed to overcome stereotypes about Muslims ("Katie Couric Speaks" 2011).[6] But these theories do not explain humour's potential to influence people to question stereotypes of Muslims, because they elide several steps in the logic of change. What are the steps that lead (potentially) to change?

Jokes function "by simultaneously opposing meanings against each other" (Fiske 1987, 86). They say two things at once, something literal and something ironic.[7] Irony then loosens the grip the image has on the thing it depicts. Consider one of the first scenes in *Little Mosque*'s pilot. An imam dressed in a *kurta* (a traditional shirt from Pakistan) and a *kufi* (a skullcap) is addressing the members of the mosque seated in front of him. His cadence and tone are reminiscent of what viewers might see on the evening news in a story where a radical imam calls on his followers to do violence against the West. But his words are not what they might expect: "As Muslims, we must realize, the enemy is not only out there. The enemy is much closer than you think. The enemy is in your kitchen. My point is this: *wine* gums, *rye* bread, *licor*ice – Western traps *designed* to seduce Muslims to drink alcohol!" He wags his finger to punctuate his lesson. The humour derives from the gap between what he says – his assertions are silly – and the way he says it, especially those aspects of his delivery that likely remind viewers of far more serious news stories. Through this double discourse jokes create a set of formal conditions for change. The joke is funny because viewers recognize its two competing meanings. The ironic meaning draws the literal meaning into question, leading viewers to a moment of epistemic doubt (would an imam who looks like that say such silly things?), even if that moment is fleeting. Irony raises the possibility that the person viewers see, who on the surface appears so different, might have more in common with them than they think.[8]

But this is only half of the work the joke performs. As Nawaz and Darling intuit, it also acts as a potential catalyst for causing viewers to question stereotypes about people unlike themselves. Mucahit Bilici (2010) provides insight here. By his account humour operates as part of an economy of affect, where cause and effect are a function of prox-imity between emotional (or affective) states. He explains that "what is common to both conditions" – the phobic, manifest in the stereo-type, and the philic, manifest in humour or laughter – "is their dis-tance or alienation from reason/normality." When people fall from reason into fear,

> it is much easier to go from fear to laughter than back to reason. There is a reason for that: while fear and reason belong to different spheres, fear and laughter (or pity, or love) share the same world of emotions. To restore reason, one emotion has to be undone by another emotion. This process of undoing the fall from reason requires catharsis (purification, purging of negative emotions). A bit of laughter can undo your fears and bring you back into the fold of rationality. This is the therapeutic function of comedy (and tragedy) that Aristotle argued for in his Poetics. Both tragedy and comedy, the philosopher argues, have a cathartic effect. They purify the soul and restore the balance of reason. (Ibid., 204)

Of course, nothing guarantees that jokes will have this effect. Their po-tential to cause viewers to question stereotypes goes unrealized more often than not, precisely because they provide two competing mean-ings. Viewers might favour one meaning over the other, and they make their choices in the broader context of the relationships described in figure 1. So what are the factors that shape their interpretive process?

Sitcoms and Hegemonic Clawing Back

There are two points at which humour's transformative potential goes unrealized. The first occurs at the moment of production. If our concern is interpretation through humour, we must ask what type of humour is possible in a conventional North American sitcom. What restrictions does the industry's commercial imperative impose on producers' choices, and to what effect? The second occurs at the moment of reception. When viewers find their familiar points of reference – the ground upon which they stand, and have always stood – drawn into question, some become disoriented. Instead of turning to negotiation as a means to establish a new footing, many dig in their heels and hold even more firmly to familiar social norms, especially when those norms afford them a place of privilege.

The sitcom's potential for change pivots on a point of precarious balance; like other genres, it can operate to shore up conservative forces, too. As Todd Gitlin (1979, 263) writes, "In liberal capitalism, hegemonic ideology develops by domesticating opposition, absorbing it into forms compatible with the core ideological structure." In the sitcom this clawing back operates at the moment of production through a double movement: an opening and a closure. The opening consists in a gesture of space clearing, an attempt to make room for representations of "others" who had previously been excluded because they did not conform to hegemonic notions of "mainstream" (or national) identity. The closure consists in an act of containment, where the outlet for opposition is marginalized or neutralized. Gitlin's example is *Mary Tyler Moore*. On the one hand, it opened a space for new depictions of femininity by featuring single women. On the other, he wrote, "The single-women shows following from *Mary Tyler Moore* acknowledge in their privatized ways that some sort of feminism is here to stay, and work to contain it with hilarious versions of 'new life styles' for single career women" (ibid., 257).

This double movement is observable in a wide range of sitcoms, especially from the United States. Gays and lesbians, for instance, became more visible in the early 1990s as over-the-air broadcast networks sought "edgy" programming to draw viewers away from cable (Becker 2006).[9] For example, the main character on *Ellen* (ABC, 1994–8), played by Ellen DeGeneres, revealed she was a lesbian in 1997. DeGeneres herself was open about her sexual orientation, which contributed to the buzz surrounding the show, as Valerie Peterson (2005, 165) writes: "As the first television show to depict the coming out of a lead character, the episode was viewed and discussed by many people outside the show's usual audience. This combination of subject matter, authenticity, and popularity made Ellen's coming-out episode a media event with the potential to persuade many viewers." But this potential was closed down in the episode itself. The industry conditions that made the episode possible, namely, networks' desire to attract affluent, socially liberal viewers, also imposed a limit on what *Ellen* could show: networks risked alienating those same viewers, who were predominantly heterosexual, if they pushed them beyond their comfort zones. As a result, the notions of lesbian identity conveyed by the coming-out episode were essentialized and depoliticized, implying "lesbianism is a largely nonthreatening sexual identity" (Peterson 2005, 173). Paradoxically, erasure of difference became a necessary condition for the depiction of a more diverse image of US (and North American) society.

A similar clawing back affected *Will & Grace* (NBC, 1998–2006), whose main characters included two gay men. The need to present nonthreatening images to heterosexual viewers kept writers from showing the gay characters in romantic relationships. Similarly, the relationship between Will (one of the gay characters) and Grace (his straight roommate), whose apartment was one of the main settings, frequently came to stand in for heterosexual marriage. Stories brought them into situations where, for comedic effect, their dialogue followed the conventions – fighting, making up, declaring their (platonic) love for each other – that are usually identified with married heterosexual characters (Provencher 2005).

In *Little Mosque* the erasure of difference happened in a similar way. The show's makers wanted to humanize Muslims, but they also wanted to produce a commercial success. They wanted to explain Muslims' beliefs, but they did not want to be didactic or alienate viewers. They wanted to illustrate diversity – and, as the next chapter shows, they created the widest range of Muslim characters ever featured in a sitcom – but to be successful, they had to make characters recognizable within the shorthand of the sitcom's conventions. In other words, they had to be "strategically essentialist," to adapt a phrase from Christopher Cwynar (2013): to show diversity they had to lean on stereotypes, even as they challenged them. They wanted to make Muslims more "human," but in the language of contemporary television, "human" meant approachable and non-threatening. They had to shy away from a range of human emotions, such as anger and indignation, even when characters had to face situations of discrimination that, outside of a sitcom, would make people angry. To be sure, the people who made *Little Mosque* had room to manoeuvre within the bounds of these competing forces, and they were able to find ways to challenge audiences rather than make them comfortable. Over the course of the show's run, for instance, they worked to develop characters and undo the effects of the "strategic essentialism" necessary in early seasons.

What viewers saw reflected these contradictions. As the following chapters describe, some saw *Little Mosque* as challenging stereotypes, while others saw it as perpetuating them. Rather than "right" or "wrong" interpretations, their divergent reactions were made possible by the polysemy that had been deliberately worked into the show. Hence the second point where humour's transformative potential frequently went unrealized. Whether *Little Mosque* prompted viewers to question their preconceptions about Muslims depended on a range of factors external to the show itself. George Posner et al. (1982, 212), for instance, observe that "inquiry and learning occur against the background of the learner's current concepts. Whenever the learner encounters a new phenomenon, he [or she] must rely on his [or her] current concepts to organize his investigation." People interpret new phenomena in light of older concepts, where they appear nonsensical precisely because they violate people's pre-existing conceptions of the world. Before people can interpret such phenomena, they must first recognize their current understanding as inadequate. But when their views are well formed, when they provide explanations without loose ends, and when they grow out of their broader political philosophy, viewers have no reason to see them as faulty (Dole and Sinatra 1998).

This was the challenge producers of *Little Mosque* faced. Viewers might be swayed by the ironic meaning and the challenge it posed to the literal meaning, but they might reject it, too. Humour as a catalyst for change went only so far, and viewers were savvy about the relationship between themselves and the other people depicted in figure 1. In some cases, for instance, their objections to *Little Mosque* were as much about the CBC, which many perceived as elitist, as about the show itself.

Viewers shared their reactions through various public forums such as letters to the editor (and, to a lesser degree, blogs). Professional critics reviewed the show in their respective publications. *Little Mosque*'s producers and CBC executives took these letters and reviews, coupled with their own in-house audience research, into account when making decisions about the show. When audiences responded and producers and executives listened, they completed a circuit, as described in figure 1. At each step in that circuit producers, executives, viewers,

Muslims, and non-Muslims were asking what it meant to be Muslim in post-9/11 North America. The negotiation in which they engaged was dynamic and changing, and over the course of *Little Mosque*'s run their answers to that question evolved.

Producers and network executives originally conceived the program in reaction to the stereotypes they saw in other media. In this respect, they were entering into a conversation that was already in progress. They created a show in response to those stereotypes, but also in anticipation of viewers' expectations. Viewers, in turn, saw the show and responded to it. They agreed with the depictions of Muslims, or they disputed them. Because the producers had deliberately built in a rich form of polysemy – jokes always said at least two things at once – viewers had a range of interpretations open to them. They arrived at theirs by drawing on their impressions of the CBC, their beliefs about the role of religion (especially Islam) in North American society, and what they saw in other media, in addition to *Little Mosque* itself. Producers, in turn, responded (or not, depending on similar forms of social knowledge) by changing the show or maintaining it, depending on the case. They participated in this conversation much as they did when originally conceiving the program, fashioning it in ways that anticipated audiences' responses. The concurrent conversation they entered when they created *Little Mosque* continued after the show ended as an object of discussion not only among viewers and critics, but among academics in books such as the one I have written here.[10]

Conclusion: The Paradox of Saleable Diversity

In working through the contradictions between interpretation and entertainment (or between "humanizing Muslims" and attracting viewers and advertisers), I have described a paradox that arises when producers, in response to the commercial imperative that permeates Canada's broadcasting system (and even its public broadcaster), must privilege their audiences' expectations over the work of interpretation. I propose to call the resulting erasure of difference in the name of diversity *the paradox of saleable diversity*. If cultural translation is a process, then saleable diversity is one of its results. In short, "humanizing Muslims" by emphasizing "universal" traits makes a program saleable.

I am not the first to identify a paradox along these lines. What I describe here operates in other genres in different ways. It is akin to what Evelyn Alsultany (2012a, 14) describes as "simplified complex representations," or the "representational mode that has become stan-dard since 9/11 [that] seeks to balance a negative representation [of Muslims] with a positive one." This mode, which characterizes many television dramas, appears to broaden the range of depictions, but it does not escape the logic according to which "all Muslims are assumed to be bad until they perform and prove their allegiance to the U.S. na-tion" (ibid., 15). It is also akin to what I describe elsewhere as "cultural resistance" in television news (Conway 2010b). When reporters try to explain a foreign idea or cultural object, they must do so on their audi-ence's terms, in the context of which such an idea or object might ap-pear nonsensical. Such has been the case, for instance, when journalists have tried to explain Muslim women's choice to wear a veil to their audiences who value secularism and gender equality (Conway 2010a, 2012c, 2012d).

The paradox of saleable diversity operates differently in sitcoms. Because of their specific form of built-in polysemy, sitcoms are shaped by two opposing forces, one conservative, the other transformational. The need to privilege viewers is the first: it reins producers in and limits the range of choices open to them. Humour's potential as a catalyst for change is the second: it holds the promise to jolt viewers into seeing the world differently. Humour becomes a way to appeal to and challenge viewers; it invites them in (by providing a pleasurable experience) and pushes them at the same time. It is held in check by viewers' willing-ness to go along or their openness to being persuaded to see the world (and Muslims) in a new light.

There are four dimensions of saleable diversity I examine in the fol-lowing chapters. The first three relate to limitations it imposes, while the fourth relates to efforts to overcome those limitations.

Saleable diversity limits the range of characters (chapter 2). Expanding the range of characters is an interpretive act, but the range is still lim-ited by the logic of synecdoche (where a part stands in for a whole). When a person stands in for a group, his or her identity will not match up entirely with the identities of the other group members. The act of standing in obscures the diversity of the group the person represents. Producers and writers can expand the number of characters, but no matter how much the range of depictions is increased, some traits will not be represented.

Saleable diversity limits the range of emotions characters experience (chap-ter 3). Explaining aspects of Islam – how people observe their religion – is also an interpretive act, but such explanations are limited as to how they can address characters' emotions. The sitcom is governed by a logic according to which negative emotions such as anger must be attributed to personal character flaws, while the underlying social structures – such as racism and other forms of inequality – remain largely unaddressed.

What makes diversity "saleable" is culturally specific (chapter 4). Through syndication WestWind could share the results of its interpretive efforts, but notions of diversity – what counts as "diverse," what marks diversity – are not the same from one national (or cultural) context to the next. WestWind struggled to export *Little Mosque* to the United States, despite extensive coverage of the show by US media. When it exported *Little Mosque* to France and Norway (among other countries, although these are the two I examine), it was a moderate success, but it did not find an audience as large as in Canada. France and Norway have different televisual traditions, different social and historical concerns (even if they are related), and different spokespeople for their respective minority groups. As a result, *Little Mosque* and the diversity it depicted were less saleable.

The paradox of saleable diversity is not absolute (chapter 5). Nor is it unassailable. The producers of *Little Mosque* were constantly seeking to get around the limitations imposed by notions of saleability and address more difficult, less saleable themes. They broke intentionally with certain sitcom conventions, such as the return to stasis, and they created long story arcs, such as the one about a character, for instance, who converted to Islam to marry her husband and decided to remain Muslim even after her divorce.

This fourth dimension is made possible by the fact that people acting as cultural translators adopt a reflexive approach. *Little Mosque*'s producers and network executives were constantly evaluating the program and its effects in the context of changing political and social circumstances. When necessary, they adjusted their approach. In other words, the evolution of circumstances brought about an evolution in the program, as its producers sought to overcome the limits they recognized in their need to make a commercially successful program. To observe that evolution it is necessary first to observe the point where *Little Mosque* began. That description is the subject of chapter 2.

Representation between the Particular and the Universal

The first episode of *Little Mosque on the Prairie* opens with a shot of a small country church. The camera pans down to reveal a sign that says "Mercy Anglican" and lists times for services. The background music shifts from something slow, picked on a guitar, in a major key to something faster in a double harmonic scale that is frequently used to evoke notions of "Arabness" for North American viewers. The shift occurs as a series of people dressed in stereotypically non-Western clothing (e.g., men wearing a kufi and women wearing a hijab) walk past the sign and are ushered quickly into a side door of the church by a Lebanese man in black pants and a button-down shirt. One of the men in traditional dress stops and says, "Alhamdulillah! Finally, our own mosque! No more shuffling around from one basement to another. Well done, Yasir! We can hold our heads high!" As he says this, Yasir looks around nervously and pushes him through the door, saying, "Yes, let's get inside, *let's get inside.*" Yasir closes the door, and the camera tilts up to show a crooked wooden sign that says "Parish Hall."

The scene establishes the setting – a mosque within a church – and two of the program's principal conflicts. The first is between non-Muslims and Muslims, signalled by the shift in music and the juxtaposition of people wearing Muslim caps and headscarves walking in front of a sign advertising Anglican services. The second is between liberal and conservative approaches to Islam, signalled by the difference in dress between Yasir Hamoudi (played by Carlo Rota), the Lebanese man, and Baber Siddiqui (played by Manoj Sood), the man who congratulates him on finally finding a mosque. Viewers will soon learn that Yasir is a contractor who has rented the basement of the church on the pretence of using it as an office and that Baber is a conservative imam who has been serving

The opening shot of the pilot episode of *Little Mosque on the Prairie*.
Image courtesy of WestWind Pictures.

the community while it waits for its new leader to arrive from Toronto. The third principal conflict, pitting rural, western Saskatchewan against urban, central Toronto, will become apparent when the new imam arrives and proceeds to tell the townspeople that Mercy, Saskatchewan, is not at all like the cosmopolitan city he has just left.

These conflicts reflected the themes *Little Mosque*'s makers wanted to address. They grew out of a collective, ongoing conversation whose central question was what it meant to be Muslim in post-9/11 North America. Both Muslims and non-Muslims joined the conversation when they posed that question among friends, on social media, on television, or elsewhere. Their contributions took a range of forms from spoken words to television shows like *Little Mosque*. They were frequently responding to what they heard, read, or saw in other places, and in some cases, they spoke with the people around them rather than those whose contribution to the conversation prompted their own. (How does a viewer respond when the people who made the program she is watching are not present?) Their participation ranged from casual to engaged, and they left and rejoined the conversation as they saw fit. In other words, this collective conversation contained many smaller conversations. It was – paradoxically, perhaps – a cacophony with focus, heterogeneous and diffuse, but always revolving around the question of Islam in contemporary North America.

In this chapter I describe the state of this conversation when *Little Mosque*'s makers entered it. I ask what issues appeared salient to them and why they felt compelled to act. I begin with an overview of *Little Mosque*'s production timeline. Then I describe how four people – Zarqa Nawaz, the show's originator, Mary Darling and Clark Donnelly, its executive producers, and Anton Leo, the creative head of CBC television comedy in the mid-2000s – perceived two key relationships. The first was between non-Muslims and Muslims. The second, which was really a more generalized case of the first, was between majority and minority Canadians. It was between these communities – non-Muslim and Muslim, majority and minority – that they acted as cultural translators.

Three factors shaped their decisions about the show. First, they wanted to be topical: they wanted to talk about the influx of conservative imams into Canadian mosques, the prejudice against Muslims in North America, and the broader geopolitics of Islam in the world. The second factor related to policy: the CBC and its executives worked to follow the public broadcaster's policies of regional and multicultural representation. The third factor was that of Canada's television industry itself: CBC executives and *Little Mosque*'s producers had to devise programming strategies and find funding. Unlike the first two factors, the third was not the product of a relationship where the makers of *Little Mosque* were acting as cultural translators. Instead, it functioned by placing restrictions on the decisions they could make.

In the second half of the chapter I describe how *Little Mosque*'s creator, executive producers, and production team designed the show to respond to the issues they saw as salient. They chose a sitcom because they felt humour would allow them to broach difficult issues and put viewers at ease. They worked within the framework of the sitcom's conventions to create a setting and characters that would allow them to generate conflicts related to those issues. They were deliberate in their choice to set the show in a mosque within a church and to create a wide range of characters to represent the diversity of Muslims in Canada. But they did not escape the paradox of saleable diversity. To humanize Muslims for viewers, they translated the particularities of Islam into "universal" themes they thought would appeal to people in an immigrant society like Canada, but many Muslim critics found that this approach resulted in depictions in which they did not recognize themselves. This tension between the particular and the universal would shape the show and its depictions of Muslims over the course of its six seasons. The show's makers had to manoeuvre through a field shaped by contradictory forces, including the need to attract viewers and the desire to inform them about Islam, and the program they produced reflected the complexity of their negotiations.

Timeline: *Little Mosque* from Beginning to End

Zarqa Nawaz pitched her initial idea for *Little Mosque on the Prairie* at the Banff World Television Festival in 2005, to which she had travelled to promote her documentary *Me and the Mosque*. At Banff she met representatives from WestWind Pictures, including Mary Darling, who liked the fish-out-of-water concept she presented.

After meeting with WestWind, Nawaz was in Regina when she learned that Anton Leo from the CBC was travelling through Canada looking for programs with a regional perspective. She and a WestWind representative met with Leo when he came through Regina. By Nawaz's account, "I had sort of written up a one-pager, with various characters, and a concept or idea, so then I pitched it to Anton Leo. I remember it wasn't a great pitch, but later on I had asked him why he had decided to go with it, and he said at the time Muslims and Islam were sort of in the *Zeitgeist*" (interview with author, 2011). Leo brought the idea back to CBC headquarters in Toronto, where executives asked for a pilot and for an initial short-run season. WestWind paired Nawaz with a number of different writing partners, who produced a pilot script in time to begin production in the spring of 2006. In what Leo describes as "a very compressed period" (interview with author, 2011), WestWind produced a pilot and eight episodes, and the show was set to premiere in January 2007.

Little Mosque's pilot attracted more than 2.1 million viewers, rivalling the ratings of popular US imports such as *CSI* or *Grey's Anatomy*. The show continued to do well, attracting more than a million viewers for all but one of the eight episodes in its abbreviated first season. It also performed well during the strike by the Writers Guild of America in 2007–8, when the CBC's commercial competitors had to find programs to replace the imported US programs they usually aired. (Because it was a Canadian production, *Little Mosque* was not affected by the strike.) It continued to attract a respectable number of viewers throughout its six seasons, although the average number was closer to half a million by the end of the show's run in 2012 (MacDonald 2012).

Relationships and Salient Issues

The desire to humanize Muslims was influenced by factors closely tied to questions of identity and people's perceptions of where they fit in the relationship between non-Muslims and Muslims or, more broadly, majority and minority Canadians. Nawaz, for instance, was as interested in addressing her own mosque community (and Canadian Muslims more broadly) as speaking to non-Muslims. Their desire to humanize Muslims was also shaped by extrinsic factors, such as the effects of global geopolitics on North Americans' perception of Muslims. The choices they made were constrained by other extrinsic factors, such as the economic pressures of the Canadian television industry. Together, these factors formed a web of influences out of which *Little Mosque* developed as a complicated, frequently contradictory program.

Zarqa Nawaz

The factors shaping Zarqa Nawaz's creation of *Little Mosque* were both intrinsic (related to identity) and extrinsic (related to global geopolitics). Nawaz's identity as a Muslim and her convictions as a feminist provided an initial impulse, which was shaped in turn by factors deriving from global geopolitical events as well as her experience in Canada's broadcasting and film industries.

Nawaz was trained as a journalist but turned to film-making after moving to Regina, Saskatchewan, in the late 1990s. In 1996 she made a five-minute comedy called *BBQ Muslims* as part of a summer workshop at the Ontario College of Art. It was about two brothers whose backyard grill explodes, causing their neighbours to think they are terrorists, and it was an indirect statement about the suspicion cast on Muslims after the Oklahoma City bombing in 1995.[1] Nawaz recounts watching people laugh when it was screened at the 1996 Toronto International Film Festival and realizing the value of humour for talking about sensitive topics. It was a serendipitous beginning: "That's how my career started – by accident. They [the film festival organizers] told me later – they said there are going to be a lot of people who watch your film and say, 'We got rejected for this?' because it wasn't the most technically proficient film ... But they said that this was the first ... indication of someone who was experimenting with comedy and Muslims and terrorism, and they had never seen anything like this before" (interview with author, 2011).

Nawaz's next film was *Death Threat* (1998), a comedy about a struggling writer who tries to garner publicity for her novel by getting someone in her mosque community to put a fatwa on her. After that, she wrote a script for a comedy titled *Real Terrorists Don't Belly Dance* about a Muslim actor cast as a terrorist intent on blowing up an airplane, but after the attacks of 9/11, no producer would take it. At that point she was approached by the National Film Board of Canada, which asked her to make a documentary for its Reel Diversity competition. Nawaz wrote and directed *Me and the Mosque* (2005), in which she makes the case that imams who have immigrated to Canada from conservative parts of the Muslim world are changing the face of Canadian Islam, in particular by forbidding women to pray in the same hall as men. The idea for *Little Mosque* grew out of the documentary: "I started thinking we could solve this problem ... if we had imams that were trained in Canada, that were not trained overseas ... What would happen to a mosque community if the imam was raised here in Canada? ... I thought it would be fascinating if the imam had had a different job, so he came from a secular world, so he understood how the world operated from a secular background, and then decided to become an imam. So that's where the idea [for *Little Mosque*] came from" (interview with author, 2011).

WestWind Pictures: Mary Darling and Clark Donnelly

The factors influencing *Little Mosque*'s executive producers, Mary Darling and Clark Donnelly of WestWind Pictures, were also intrinsic (related to identity) and extrinsic (related to global geopolitics and the Canadian television industry). As was the case for Nawaz, questions of religious identity played an important role. Darling and Donnelly are Bahá'í, a faith based on the idea that "humanity is one single race and that the day has come for its unification in one global society ... The principal challenge facing the peoples of the earth is to accept the fact of their oneness and to assist the processes of unification."[2] (This idea of oneness underpins the conception of ecumenism in which the show was grounded, as I write in chapter 5 and the conclusion.)

The influence of their faith was apparent in WestWind's first major hit, *Designer Guys*, which Darling describes as "a ridiculously popular show, embarrassingly popular. It was two designers who ... we saw make over a room in every episode. But the principle behind the show [came from] a Bahá'í writing that talks about how through the conflict of differing opinions, a spark of truth will come to light. And so we used that principle in making that show. So it was two designers who were very in sync and very unified, but they would disagree about certain things in design in a way that would bring about a better solution" (interview with author, 2011). The same line of thought informed the decision to produce *Little Mosque*:

> We're always sort of looking for the underlying principle that will resonate because we think that if these fundamental principles are addressed or acknowledged, it brings about kind of a universal attraction in people. And I'd say that it's proven out in the shows where we've really focused down like that, that those shows have consistently broken out, and *Little Mosque* is no exception. And really there we wanted to explore what happens when two faiths are forced together, the underlying thought being the oneness of humanity, the oneness of religion ... oneness in general. (Interview with author, 2011)

In this way the intrinsic factor of religious identity dovetailed with the extrinsic factor of global geopolitics, especially as such politics affected relationships between Muslims and non-Muslims in North America.

Another extrinsic factor related to funding strategies. In the mid-2000s, when WestWind was pitching *Little Mosque* to the CBC, Darling and Donnelly were keenly aware of the strategies necessary for funding production in Canada. Part of the funding for *Little Mosque* came from fees paid by the CBC to license the program. WestWind also relied on federal tax credits, money from the Canadian Television Fund (later the Canada Media Fund), and credits from Saskatchewan and Ontario. Each of these sources brought its own set of complications. For instance, working with provincial governments posed certain challenges, as Darling explains: "we were able to do an interprovincial co-production, and that comes with its own set of rules, including how many actors are from there, and how much money are you spending there" (interview with author, 2011). To qualify for Saskatchewan funds, WestWind maintained an office in Regina. WestWind's headquarters were in Toronto, which allowed it to qualify for Ontario funds.

Even with these subsidies, rebates, and other forms of financing, WestWind still had to make up for a shortfall of as much as $1 million each year. The company put up its own money because Darling and Donnelly thought they could reach an underserved audience – not just Muslims but people who were curious about Islam and its place in the world (Darling, interview with author, 2011). As chapter 4 describes, this approach led to a paradoxical situation: WestWind made its money back through international syndication, meaning *Little Mosque*'s domestic production and circulation were dependent on licensing fees from abroad.

Anton Leo and the CBC

For Anton Leo, the creative head of CBC television comedy in the mid-2000s, extrinsic factors (the CBC's regional and multicultural mandates) outweighed intrinsic factors (identity). However, the question of the CBC's regional and multicultural mandates was inflected through – and gained its relevance from – that of identity.

Two mandates influenced Leo's decision to take Nawaz's pitch back to CBC executives. The first was the public broadcaster's mandate to "reflect Canada and its regions to national and regional audiences, while serving the special needs of those regions" (Broadcasting Act, 1991, sec. 3.1.m.ii). The second was its mandate to "reflect the multicultural and multiracial nature of Canada" (sec. 3.1.m.viii). With respect to the first, Leo explains that in 2005, when Nawaz and WestWind were developing the idea for *Little Mosque*,

> I was travelling the country looking for programming that could come from Saskatchewan. It was part of a practice that predated me and one that I embraced when I got to the CBC ... I would take a couple of days ... and I would go across the country and meet as many people as I could in a little tour from time to time during the year. And in addition to that, whenever I would go to something like the Banff Television Festival, I would make sure that the only meetings that I took were meetings with people from regional parts of the country as opposed to Toronto because they were the ones who had less access to the network in Toronto and therefore needed to be served better by my visit. (interview with author, 2011)

The CBC's mandate to represent Canada's regions was one factor influencing Leo's decision, but, he explains, "there was far more to it than its prairie location that piqued my interest." There was also his sense that Nawaz was telling a "very contemporary immigrant story" that would

– indirectly, at least – also help the CBC meet its mandate for multicultural programming (interview with author, 2011).

However, the influence of the multicultural mandate was only that: indirect. As Darling recounts, "When we pitched [*Little Mosque*] to Anton Leo ... we wanted to do a show and tell some stories we really loved. Anton didn't say to us, 'Hey, that really fits our mandate beautifully, let's do that.' He said, 'You know what? ... My parents came straight from Sicily' ... His parents came from Italy ... and Anton was a first-generation Canadian, but he really got the cultural context in the universal characters that we tried to create. He never went off about, 'Doesn't this hit the mandate beautifully?' and, 'This is what Canadians need ...'" (interview with author, 2011).

Leo's account echoes Darling's, but he adds a bit more nuance. Leo explains that, when he took Nawaz's pitch, Nawaz told him "about a show that she wanted to do that was rooted in her life experiences in Regina as a Muslim woman. And as she was talking to me, what I was thinking about was that Zarqa was telling a story of immigration and immigrants, and that she was telling a story about how immigrants are embraced or feared as they come into the country ... Zarqa was telling a very contemporary immigrant story that I believed would resonate with a country of immigrants" (interview with author, 2011). In other words, he thought that *Little Mosque* had promise because it told a universal story, that of the immigrant experience, in a country where everyone (except First Nations) came originally from someplace else. Multicultural programming, in his view, was programming to which a country of immigrants could relate.

Leo advocated for *Little Mosque* in the context of ongoing budget cuts at the CBC, which were forcing the broadcaster to adopt an increasingly commercial orientation. The CBC's programming strategy in the late 2000s grew out of an idea first proposed in the 1990s that, if television networks (commercial and public alike) were going to attract viewers from among the increasingly fragmented Canadian audience, they would have to carve out an identifiable programming niche. For the CBC, that niche would be Canadian programming (Veilleux 1993). When *Little Mosque* was under development, the CBC was focusing on scripted programming. Drama was one focus: "Given that storytelling, especially drama, is the single most pervasive catalyst of popular culture," the corporation asked, "how do we create a critical mass of drama that is first-rate and inimitably Canadian?" (CBC/Radio-Canada 2007, 3). Comedy was another: "we were deeply engaged to try and develop our narrative comedies at the time [in 2005]," explains Leo, "and that was part of the appeal" of *Little Mosque* (interview with author, 2011). This emphasis on scripted programming helped the CBC pursue its strategy of carving out its Canadian niche by positioning the CBC and its out-of-house producers well in the competition for funds from the Canadian Television Fund (Canada Media Fund as of 2009), which subsidized the production of Canadian television. In this way the CBC's concerns converged with those of others involved in *Little Mosque*'s creation: Darling and Donnelly wanted to tap into the federal funds, and Nawaz wanted a show that could reach the wide audience the CBC could provide. And the genre of the sitcom appeared to provide them with the vehicle to reach their goals.

Little Mosque and Sitcom Conventions

In other words, the sitcom as a genre provided tools that allowed the show's makers to address the issues they saw as salient. Its conventions, including its setting, characters, and problem/resolution structure, provided the flexibility not only to address the conflicts playing out in the larger geopolitical realm, but to tell stories in which conflicts between Muslims and non-Muslims were resolved, at least within the world of Mercy, Saskatchewan. The sitcom format also allowed the show's makers to address industry-related topics and, at the same time, issues of policy. Scripted comedies such as *Corner Gas* and *Trailer Park Boys* had gained prominence within Canadian television in the mid-2000s, and as a result, *Little Mosque* was all the more attractive because it would build on the genre's success and provide the CBC with evidence that it was upholding its regional and multicultural mandates.

The makers of *Little Mosque* conceived it as a fairly typical example of the North American sitcom. Its episodes were a half-hour in length, it relied on conflicts between stock characters, and it had characteristics of both the workplace sitcom (in the interactions that took place at the mosque within a church) and the family sitcom (in the interactions that took place in the household headed by Yasir Hamoudi). Its episodes tended to follow the pattern "familiar status quo → ritual error made → ritual lesson learned → familiar status quo" (David Marc, quoted in Feuer 2001, 69), especially in the first two seasons. According to Michael Kennedy, who directed more than thirty episodes, "It was my belief, and the network executives' strong recommendation, that the show would benefit best by being shot in a very clean and simple, straightforward manner, deliberately without any trendy contemporary stylish aspects such as handheld camera, etc. They wanted it to look very much like 'a traditional sitcom.' It would be a traditional sitcom, with a very edgy topic. If it had been possible, I am sure they would have shot it with three or four cameras in front of a live audience, like many successful American sitcoms" (interview with author, 2011).

Another aspect marking it as a sitcom was its frequent intertextual references to other sitcoms, including *Corner Gas*, another comedy about rural Saskatchewan that ran for six seasons (2004–9) on the commercial network CTV. In some cases *Little Mosque*'s references to *Corner Gas* were explicit, if a bit obscure, such as in a first-season episode when the Anglican archdeacon comes to Mercy after having shut down a church in Dog River, the fictional town in *Corner Gas*. *Little Mosque* also evoked other sitcoms in places where its intertextuality operated at a more subtle level, such as that of the relationships between characters, where the 1970s show *All in the Family* was a frequent touchpoint.

However, *Little Mosque* also deviated from the typical sitcom formula. In fact, the ability of its producers to adapt a genre that historically has been identified as American was one of the reasons for its popular success. As Christopher Cwynar (2013) points out, Canadian-made sitcoms have not occupied a large space in Canadian television for a number of reasons, one of which is that they often appear derivative in comparison with their US counterparts. Cwynar, borrowing from Mary Jane Miller (1993), argues that *Little Mosque* successfully inflected the genre in part through the way it structured its central conflicts. Of the three central conflicts, the first to be developed was the one between conservative and liberal Muslims, but CBC executives were hesitant to limit the show to that one theme. Rebecca Schechter, a writer who worked with Nawaz to develop the initial idea for the show, explains, "The first version of the show that Zarqa had developed was basically very insular in the Muslim community ... The CBC wanted it to ... stand out a little bit and pushed us to ... not get rid of that internal conflict, but also depict strongly the conflict between the small community of Muslims and the non-Muslim Prairie community around them" (interview with author, 2011). According to Nawaz, CBC executives, including Anton Leo, also asked her to draw on her own experience as a displaced Torontonian living in Saskatchewan (interview with author, 2011). The effect, writes Cwynar (2013, 49), was to play the Muslim/non-Muslim and centre/periphery conflicts against each other: "As that premise [Muslim/non-Muslim tension] provides an opportunity for national identification through the metanarrative of multiculturalism, so the tension [between the centre and the periphery] constitutes a similar opportunity through a discourse about inter-regional dynamics in Canada."

Sitcom conventions provided at least three devices the producers of *Little Mosque* could inflect to stage and symbolically resolve these conflicts. First, when episodes relied on culture clash narratives, they tended to depict people "settling conflicts in ways that emphasize compromise and suggest that a greater sense of understanding has been achieved" (Matheson 2012, 164). Second, they provided fertile ground for "narratives that flip the dynamics of dominance and subordination that typically underpin Us-Them oppositions" by addressing issues that caused characters to form alliances of convenience, for instance when conservative Muslim and non-Muslim characters would make common cause about social issues unrelated to religion (ibid., 165). Finally, especially in the case of *Little Mosque*, they allowed for demystification: "Each episode offers information about various aspects of Islam, using its culture clash premise to display Muslim culture and to engage with questions surrounding it, especially as they relate to women" (ibid., 166). This contributed to what might be called *Little Mosque*'s "pedagogical effect": when aspects of Islam were central to the conflict, characters would discuss them as they argued with each other, effectively informing viewers.

Thus, these devices served a dual function. They set up the situation that provided the show's humour, and they made it possible to address issues related to the conflicts animating post-9/11 geopolitics. In this way they opened a space for representations of previously excluded Muslim "others," as the next section describes.

Characters, Setting, and Conflict

To address the issues they saw as salient, Nawaz and the executive producers created characters who came from a wide spectrum of cultural backgrounds and approaches to Islam. Nawaz was very deliberate in this, and she had a dual audience in mind: she wanted to talk to Muslims about the growing conservatism of Canadian Islam, and she wanted to talk to non-Muslims about stereotypes. She wanted a diverse range of characters in order to call into question both conservative imams' prescriptive notions of how Islam should be followed and non-Muslims' notions of who Muslims were and what they believed. Expanding the range of representations was one strategy for translating Muslims, and

Partial cast of *Little Mosque on the Prairie*, seasons 1 to 3. From left to right: Fatima Dinssa (Arlene Duncan), Amaar Rashid (Zaib Shaikh), Sarah Hamoudi (Sheila McCarthy), Yasir Hamoudi (Carlo Rota), Rayyan Hamoudi (Sitara Hewitt), Baber Siddiqui (Manoj Sood), and Ann Popowicz (Debra McGrath). Image courtesy of WestWind Pictures.

the idea grew out of Nawaz's (and the executive producers') interpretive impulse: viewers, they thought, would understand Muslims better if they saw the diversity that characterized them.

To this end, Nawaz (and the writers with whom she developed the show) created five principal Muslim characters. The first two were Yasir Hamoudi and Baber Siddiqui, whom viewers met in the scene that opened the pilot. Yasir's wife Sarah (played by Sheila McCarthy), was a local woman who converted from Anglicanism in order to marry him, and their daughter Rayyan (played by Sitara Hewitt) was the town's doctor and had a strong feminist voice. Amaar Rashid (played by Zaib Shaikh) was the young lawyer-turned-imam who arrived from Toronto to serve the Mercy mosque. Secondary characters included Fatima Dinssa (played by Arlene Duncan), a woman from Nigeria who owned a local café, and Layla Siddiqui (played by Aliza Vellani), Baber's teenage daughter.

Nawaz's desire to present a wide range of characters extended to the non-Muslims in the show: "I wanted to balance the show, so if there was a right-wing non-Muslim, there was a right-wing Muslim, and they were equally as racist and extremist, so ... there wasn't the sense that I was picking on one community more than the other." In that vein, she created the character of Fred Tupper (played by Neil Crone), the local radio shock jock who "represent[ed] the media and its misrepresentation of Islam and Muslims" (interview with author, 2011). Tupper acted as a counterpart to Baber, who voiced the conservative views about women that Nawaz wanted to critique. The town's other non-Muslim residents included Rev. Duncan Magee (played by Derek McGrath), the minister at Mercy Anglican church, Joe Peterson (played by Boyd Banks), a local farmer whose dim-wittedness provided comic relief, and Mayor Ann Popowicz (played by Debra McGrath), an opportunistic politician who was also Sarah's boss.

This range of characters allowed Nawaz to provide multiple competing perspectives, both between communities and within them. For instance, several Muslim characters, such as Rayyan and Amaar, provided liberal counterpoints to Baber. There was also Fatima, who owned one of the town's cafés: Nawaz describes her as "the more traditional ... Muslim woman, but she was still an independent businesswoman, like the wife of the prophet had been" (interview with author, 2011). On the non-Muslim side, Rev. Duncan Magee represented the liberal view and served as a counterpoint to Fred. Over the course of the first three seasons Magee approached Mercy's Muslim community with a sense of generosity, becoming Amaar's friend and informal mentor. In the fourth season, however, Magee was replaced by Rev. William Thorne (played by Brandon Firla), whose conservatism reintroduced the Muslim/non-Muslim conflict to the show, a conflict that centred around Thorne's relationship with Amaar.

Nawaz was also keen to include characters whose level of religiosity differed: "they didn't all have to be these 'good' practising Muslims, so you could have every spectrum, so you could deal with all the different nuances of the Muslim community." Baber's teenage daughter Layla, for instance, refused to wear a hijab, but her acts of rebellion provided an opportunity for the show's writers to "[bring] out the human side of Baber" when Baber, whose love for his daughter is clear, would soften his hard-line approach. Similarly, Rayyan's parents, Yasir and Sarah, "were not very devout, even though [Rayyan] was sort of a hijab-wearing feminist. Her ... mom was a convert, sort of 'in name only,' didn't really practise, did it mostly to appease Yasir's mother ... Yasir was one of those Muslims [who was] sort of the fence-sitter – he would only practise as much as it would help his business" (interview with author, 2011). In the non-Muslim community, the town's mayor, Ann Popowicz, served a similar "fence-sitting" purpose, although she was far more cynical and self-serving than Yasir, especially in her willingness to pander to Muslims to get their vote.

The writers used this diversity to generate the conflict on which *Little Mosque* was based. During the first season, for instance, as writer Susan Alexander explains, the writers would give Fred racist dialogue as a "device" for "getting uncomfortable things on the table" and then use Amaar to navigate through the controversy, enabling each character to express one of a spectrum of perspectives (interview with author, 2011). Baber served a similar purpose, giving voice to stereotypes about non-Muslims. At the same time, however, the writers sought to make Fred and Baber sympathetic. Writer Al Rae, for instance, compares Baber to an archetypal lovable bigot with whom many viewers would also be familiar: "Anton [Leo] had tasked us with making the satire in line with *All in the Family*, so Baber [was] based a little bit on the kind of Archie Bunker model, you know, where ... there's always a heart, and [he] always loves his daughter, like Archie loved [his son-in-law] Mike and [his daughter] Gloria" (interview with author, 2011).

The setting of the show – a mosque within a church – provided a place to stage this conflict. Sandra Cañas (2008, 200) observes, "The mosque functions, in part, as an allegory of the marginality of the Muslim community in western society and the struggles they face to build spaces of their own in a non-Muslim country such as Canada." Her observation is in line with the vision articulated by executive producer Mary Darling, who extends her discussion to the realm of global geopolitics. She mentions "Eid's a Wonderful Life" (season 2, episode 10), in which Rev. Duncan Magee and Amaar get into a dispute about parking at the church when Amaar plans a meal to celebrate Eid al-Adha that conflicts with the church's annual Christmas sing-along. Darling explains, "So through the conflicts that can happen over an argument over a parking lot where we can see in that show that ... in some ways we're talking about Israel. Who was here first? We're talking about Israel and Palestine, but we don't actually talk about Israel and Palestine – we let the comedy do it for us. So Magee and Amaar get in a fight over which religion came first and who should get the parking for the Ring-Ding Sing-Along" (interview with author, 2011).

Saleable Diversity and the Tension between the Particular and the Universal

But this approach to characters was an imperfect way of overcoming stereotypes about Muslims. Despite the range of characters, *Little Mosque*'s makers faced two challenges. First, they had to balance depictions of Islam's particularities with themes they thought non-Muslim viewers would find more universal. Second, even more fundamentally, no matter how diverse the range of characters, they could not represent all Muslims. As a result, they produced a form of what I called in chapter 1 "saleable diversity": they had to erase markers of difference in the name of diversity, a process of containment or closure that was the inverse of the space clearing described above. One place where the tension between the particular and the universal was clear was in the audience research WestWind Pictures (and the CBC) performed before the pilot aired. WestWind wanted to make a show in which Muslims could recognize themselves, as Mary Darling explains:

> The audience research happened in an actual focus group the CBC pulled together, and the focus group included first- and second-generation Muslims. So some [were] Canadian-born, not all related, though some were related, and they watched the [pilot] episode together ... When the show finished, the second-generation Muslims were laughing and ... the main thing that the first-generation Muslims wanted to know was that it was okay, that it wouldn't hurt them, and the second-generation assured them [of] that. So there was a lot of actual talk amongst themselves, which we saw as a good sign, in that it created that dialogue inside of the Muslim community in addition to what we always imagined would be a cross-cultural, cross-faith dialogue. (Interview with author, 2014)

The concern for specificity took a number of different forms. The executive producers thought that many non-Muslims had a healthy curiosity about Islam and that if the show could answer their questions, it could help build trust between Muslims and non-Muslims. To that end, they used the character of Sarah, the convert from Anglicanism, "to facilitate the voice of the viewer ... [who] had questions about Islam – why do women pray behind men? What is a barrier? How do you date? We used Sarah's voice as that voice that can ask those questions" (Darling, interview with author, 2012). Members of the production team, especially the writers, wanted to write jokes that were culturally specific. They wanted to avoid jokes that could be about any minority group, according to Al Rae: "I don't like anything where it's about something that I know nothing about but I could have written all the jokes" (interview with author, 2011). Thus, cultural specificity had another, more practical value. Even though they hoped viewers would learn from the show, the writers and producers knew viewers were looking to be entertained, not educated, and Islam provided new material for jokes: "The non-Muslim writers would have their *Islam for Dummies* books out and would be constantly going through trying to find details and things we could spin off into stories. And it was great, because with comedy it's harder and harder to make fresher and newer stories because it's been done so much. What can you say that hasn't been said already? Otherwise it becomes a cliché. So we were really fortunate to have a whole fresh subject matter that *nobody* had ever exploited before for comedy" (Nawaz, interview with author, 2011).

In her earlier work, Nawaz's approach was to take the elements of Islam that caused anxiety for many non-Muslims (through their associations with the threat of terrorism, for instance) and make them funny. She maintained that approach in *Little Mosque*, too. But she placed limits on jokes' subject matter, in ways that differed from the other writers: "I find for the writers that come from the Christian background that there's never anything that's too much for them. Anything could happen. And so for the Muslims ... the way I draw my line is I don't want to make fun of religious figures ... I don't want to make fun of faith, because that's sacred to me ... When it comes to Muslims, I have no problem taking risks ... going after racism, and extremism, and sexism, I have no problem at all [because] those things have nothing to do with faith – they have to do with culture and patriarchy, and they deserve it, and we should go after that, and I go after it all the time on the show" (public forum, University of North Dakota, 2011).

So what concretely did the makers of *Little Mosque* mean when they spoke of cultural specificity? Writers wanted to explore particular religious tenets as well as ways people – at least in Nawaz's assessment

– misinterpreted them to prop up a patriarchal culture. They also wanted jokes that were not stale. In short, they wanted jokes that helped viewers understand Islam better and placed them in a position to laugh *with* Muslims, but not *at* them, to generate feelings of solidarity among both Muslims and non-Muslims, who were in on the joke.

But many Muslims, as the following chapters show, saw *Little Mosque* as misrepresenting their faith. Faiza Hirji (2011, 44), for instance, noted that "if there are Sunnis and Shias, who would differ in their understanding of how an imam is appointed, or in the specifics of their prayers, this is not made apparent." Similarly, Tarek Fatah and Farzana Hassan (2007) thought the show provided a "completely false picture of the Muslim community": "Although the characters are meant to reflect the diversity of Muslim society, a closer examination reveals the show is not about liberal or progressive Muslims competing with conservatives. Rather, the writer has created a false dichotomy of 'conservative' Muslims vs. 'ultra-conservative' Muslims, the former being disingenuously passed on as feminist and progressive."

What prompted these reactions? Part of the answer has to do with the fact that much of the show grew out of Nawaz's personal experience, especially in the first season, when the greatest number of critics were paying attention. Until Sadiya Durrani joined the writing team as an intern in season 3, Nawaz was the only Muslim writer: "I drew a lot on experiences I had growing up. Because all the writers are white ... they don't have any experience going into the show, so it's hard for them. The first episodes were really difficult because we didn't know what the show was, or who the characters were, so we did a lot of issue-based shows ... [and as] the show grew and we got to know the personality of the actors and how the characters of the show were growing, we started moving more into the character-based stories" (public forum, University of North Dakota, 2011).[3]

Part of the answer also relates to the contradictions inherent in the synecdochic mode of representation, where a part stands in for the whole. The problem posed by representation as standing in is conceptually simple: if we wanted to assemble a group of people to speak on behalf of others with whom they share similar traits, what traits would be important? Any list we came up with would expand as soon as someone felt their interests were not represented, and consequently, so would the need for representatives. If we represent Muslims, for instance, we should also represent Muslim women because their perspective is different from that of men. By the same logic, we should also represent minority Muslim women, and minority Muslim women who are also immigrants, and so on (see Eid and Khan 2011). Taken to its logical extreme, such a list would end by including everyone, making representation as the act of standing in unnecessary.[4] This paradox highlights the asymmetric relationship synecdochic representation creates. No person's identity matches up exactly with the identities of the members of the group he or she represents, but as a stand-in for a group, a person still comes to define its public face. The act of standing in creates a power differential between the representative and the other group members, whose diversity is obscured in the process (Galewski 2006).

This logic has important implications for *Little Mosque on the Prairie*: although Nawaz wanted "each character [to] represent a different aspect of the Muslim community" (interview with author, 2011), the choice about which traits were important (liberal/conservative, native-born/immigrant, and so on) was also a choice about which traits would be left out. One result was that "the Muslim group [on *Little Mosque* had to] practise a form of strategic essentialism in order to protect its interests" (Cwynar 2013, 43). Certain characteristics that would mark a difference between Muslim characters were obscured.

This "strategic essentialism" helped make *Little Mosque* a show to which a country of immigrants could relate, as suggested by Anton Leo. Its makers wanted to create equivalences to translate Muslims by showing how they were like non-Muslims, as I write in chapter 1. Thus, they wanted characters who were recognizable archetypes for people from other origins and faith traditions. Nawaz describes being approached by Christians who say to her, "'Oh my god, my church is exactly like that!' ... [I came to] realize everyone has the Babers, the extremists, ... the fence-sitters, the teenager who doesn't want to go – every religious and non-religious community has these archetypes, and they're universal, and that's part of the reason the show was so successful, that if it hadn't been so relatable and universal in that way, it would not have translated ... out of the Muslim community" (public forum, University of North Dakota, 2011). Similarly, Zaib Shaikh, the Muslim actor who played Amaar Rashid, told Katie Couric on the CBS show *60 Minutes* that people said they liked the show because they found it relatable: "It doesn't mean they're speaking from a faith place. They're going, oh yes, an outsider – I've always felt like an outsider looking in, and then I've learned how to become assimilated. In whatever, whether it's socioeconomic, whether it's a clique in high school."[5] Mary Darling even explains that as WestWind looks to sell the format of the show, now that it has finished its run, "We don't even think in every case that it would necessarily have to be Muslims in the minority role, for example. The universal characteristics of those unasked questions that people are afraid to ask" are what matter (interview with author, 2014).

Of course, this reliance on character archetypes also helped make *Little Mosque* commercially successful. Archetypes provided a shorthand viewers recognized and made the story-telling more efficient: "If you take the seven or eight figures of comedy," explains Darling, "you will be able to correlate those in [*Little*] *Mosque*, as to who's playing what role" (interview with author, 2014). They also gave viewers a reason to continue watching, as writer Rebecca Schechter contends: "What the best multicultural programming ... should do ... is it should have in part an opening up of things that the rest of mainstream culture doesn't know and opening it up to them so that they learn about it in a way that doesn't feel like a lesson. And you only do that by making something that has kind of a mainstream appeal to it and yet is at the same time ... a window into cultures that you normally don't get a window into" (interview with author, 2011).

In the design of the show there was no way around the reductive logic of synecdoche, and the people responsible for *Little Mosque* had to make strategic decisions about which traits were important and, by way of that decision, whom to include (and exclude). They had to balance depictions of diversity with an appeal to "mainstream" viewers' sense of human universality. They had to make that appeal at least in part on viewers' terms, even if it meant transforming Muslim characters in a way that some Muslim viewers found lacking.

Conclusion: Synecdoche, Saleable Diversity, and Humour's Unsettling Potential

The effect of the paradox of saleable diversity is clear in the initial conception of *Little Mosque* as a sitcom. In their development of the show the originator, producers, and production team emphasized certain traits such as characters' outsider or immigrant status as a way to create equivalences between Muslims and non-Muslims. Although they treated these equivalences as a reflection of universal human experience, this act of cultural translation had the effect, in the eyes of some Muslim critics, of denaturing Islam. The need to appeal to broad audiences muted depictions of Muslims to the point where such critics did not recognize themselves in them.

But the paradox of saleable diversity (not to mention the logic of synecdoche that underpinned it) was not insurmountable. Nor were *Little Mosque*'s makers blind to the paradox. In fact, Al Rae suggests that specificity and universality are two sides of the same coin and that, by digging deeper into Islam (or any belief system), writers find not only more potential subject matter for jokes but also more points of commonality:

> The deeper you get into something, the better the comedy is always going to be because then you get subtlety, and once you get subtlety – the more subtlety you have, the more likely you are to hit pay-dirt in terms of finding common ground, because it seems like initially you have, "They took our land," you know, and, "No, it's our land and we deserve it because the Bible says so," ... but then as you go down, "Wait a minute, aren't you the same people?" And then, "[Aren't] there commonalities between the language?" And then, "Hey, this food tastes exactly the same," and then by the time you all go around, it's down to that – even if it's just, "Hey, we all love our children." Whatever it might be, there's just something where you're grounded enough that there's a little thing they do, some ritual, some little thing between mother and child, that's very similar to something you do. They do it like that, but it's just like the way we do something else. They both mean the same thing, you know, and that's where you find the comedy. (Interview with author, 2011)

Rae's suggestion draws attention to the ambivalence of the sitcom form that is due in part to its built-in polysemy. *Little Mosque*'s makers worked to take advantage of the way humour unsettles the relationship between images and what they purport to represent. At various points over the show's six seasons different forces prevailed: during the first two seasons the production team hewed closely to the sitcom's conventions, but they had abandoned certain conventions (especially the return to stasis) by season 3. They wanted to move beyond the essentialism observed by scholars and critics by demonstrating that, regardless of where they begin, characters (and people) change.

Chapter 3

The Paradoxes of "Humanizing Muslims"

As chance would have it, I was at the CBC's headquarters in Toronto on 10 January 2007, the day after *Little Mosque on the Prairie* premiered. I had spent a few weeks in the CBC's archives over the previous year working on a different project. Even though I was in the news department, where people had no direct connection to *Little Mosque*, I sensed an excitement I had not felt before. *Little Mosque* had generated tremendous interest, not just in Canada but also in the United States, thanks to coverage by the *New York Times*, CNN, and other news outlets. It promised to provide an antidote to what viewers had been seeing about Islam on the news – suicide bombings and beheadings in Iraq, the arrest of eighteen men and youths at a training camp in Ontario inspired by al-Qaeda's Anwar al-Awlaki, the ongoing search for Osama bin Laden, and so on. In short, viewers wanted to see what the buzz was about, and 2.1 million of them tuned in to *Little Mosque*'s premiere, making it one of the CBC's biggest hits in recent memory.

In this chapter I examine the first two seasons of *Little Mosque*, when attention to (and debate about) the show was greatest, in no small part because of the early buzz it had generated. The first season, which ran from 9 January to 7 March 2007, had only eight episodes, and it was not immediately clear whether the CBC would renew it. The second season was longer (twenty episodes), and it ran from 3 October 2007 to 5 March 2008. Throughout these seasons the show's makers were trying to find their footing: they had to discover who the characters were so they could find the right balance between issue-oriented episodes and character-driven storytelling. Critics published more reviews of the show during these seasons than during those that followed, and viewers were more vocal than in later seasons, when they had largely made up their minds whether they liked it or not. By the sixth season Zarqa Nawaz could say that "the newness and the rawness has passed, and ... [viewers] just take it for granted. It's just this show on the CBC, and there's a generation of Muslim kids who are going to think it's normal to see themselves on television and don't think it's a big deal. Which is great – they watch TV and there's a representation of everyone and it takes away the 'otherness' factor" (public forum, University of North Dakota, 2011). But in 2007 and 2008 the show was still new, and people were eager to talk about it.

I examine these two seasons for a second reason: at that time *Little Mosque* hewed most closely to the conventions of the sitcom. Its production team took this approach to build an audience by meeting viewers' expectations. Thus, it was during these seasons that the negotiation between viewers and the show's makers over meaning was most vigorous. (Later the site of negotiation would shift as Mary Darling and Clark Donnelly sought to persuade the CBC that the show should abandon certain conventions, such as the return to stasis.) It was also when the effects of the paradox of saleable diversity were clearest: the sitcom's conventions imposed a limit on the situations writers could explore and the emotions characters could experience.

I begin by examining the interaction among members of *Little Mosque*'s production team, especially its writers, including Zarqa Nawaz (who was a writer in addition to the show's originator). In the first two seasons, they had to find ways to talk about what it meant to be Muslim in post-9/11 North America within the constraints of the sitcom's conventions. Much of their negotiation related to character development, although it also related to plot structure and other formal elements. I then ask how ideas about what it meant to be Muslim circulated among viewers, both Muslim and non-Muslim. They watched *Little Mosque*, but they were not blank slates, and they interpreted the show in the context of their pre-existing notions of Islam. The implications of *Little Mosque*'s built-in polysemy, not to mention its makers' efforts to strike a balance between the particular and the universal, were clear in Muslims' responses. Some were satisfied that *Little Mosque* expanded the range of depictions of Muslims, while others thought it did not expand them enough. Non-Muslims, on the other hand, were more concerned with the CBC and its place in Canadian broadcasting as well as with *Little Mosque*'s status as a sitcom. Some liked its "hokey" humour, while others thought it whitewashed what they saw as the threat Islam posed.

I conclude by describing one place where the limits of these negotiations – and of diversity's saleability – were clear. Although writers sought to humanize Muslims, sitcom conventions and the need to appeal to viewers kept them from exploring a range of human emotions, in particular, perceived "negative" emotions that risked alienating viewers. "Humanizing Muslims" effectively meant making them appear to be just like "regular" non-Muslim viewers, which writers accomplished by erasing visible markers of difference. In other words, they had to flatten out the complexity of characters' beliefs, especially when they conflicted with those of "regular" viewers. And certain feelings were entirely out of bounds: despite the fact that anger and indignation are as human as love and generosity, "humanizing Muslims" meant avoiding these so-called negative emotions. When writers put characters in a situation where they might experience anger, for instance, they had to attribute it to their personal shortcomings rather than to larger structural factors such as racism or the institutionalized war on terror. Writers were faced with a paradox: "humanizing" these characters meant cutting them off from much of what it means to be human.

Season 1: Negotiations in Production

When members of *Little Mosque*'s production team began to work on the show, they faced two challenges. First, as the last chapter explained, they wanted to write character-driven stories, as is typical of sitcoms, but they did not yet know the characters. Second, their potential viewers did not know Islam well enough to understand jokes about it. To make a successful show, they had to give viewers the tools to understand not just the jokes but the different ways the characters were rooted in Islam. The writers addressed these two challenges through plot structure and, as the show progressed, character development.

Complicating matters further was the fact that Zarqa Nawaz was the only Muslim writer. She had to educate the other writers about Islam, even as they sought collectively to educate viewers without becoming didactic. They wanted viewers to get the jokes, not change the channel; as Nawaz explains: "Nothing ever really came out of education as much as it came out of plot points ... all the comedy always came through character, and what each character was motivated by." The first episodes, however, "were very much issue-oriented more than character-oriented, and gradually as we got to know the sitcom characters better ... we moved to character-based stories ... It's fascinating because most of our writers were non-Muslim, so I think we could never take anything for granted. If they didn't understand it, we had to get it in there" (interview with author, 2011). During the pilot episode, for instance, characters argued about how to determine the beginning of Ramadan, and viewers watching their arguments came away knowing different ways some Muslims observe the season. Similarly, a later episode focused on an attempt by the mosque to host an open house to educate townspeople (and viewers) about the five pillars of Islam and other theological points.

This issue-oriented approach shaped how the writers structured episodes. Susan Alexander notes that writers relied on A-plots to address Muslim-specific themes and B-plots to address themes relevant to a broader Canadian audience (interview with author, 2011). For example, in "Swimming Upstream" (season 1, episode 4), the A-plot concerned Fatima's need, as a Muslim woman who maintained the traditions of modesty from her native Nigeria, to have a female swimming instructor, while the B-plot concerned Baber's conflict with his teenage daughter, who wanted to participate in Halloween activities with her friends, against her father's wishes. Of course, the Muslim-specific themes of the A-plots likely appealed to non-Muslim viewers, too, just as the B-plots addressed "mainstream" themes of interest to the Muslim community. In "Swimming Upstream," for instance, the A-plot addressed a controversy with at least one identifiable precedent in recent Canadian history: many viewers were surely aware of the rancorous debates in Quebec after a Hasidic Jewish synagogue in Montreal asked the neighbouring YMCA to frost its windows so its members could not see women in the swimming pool (see Bouchard and Taylor 2008). Similarly, while the focus of the B-plot was on one father's attempts to influence his rebellious teenager's actions, the source of the conflict was culturally specific.

Because the season had only eight episodes, non-Muslim writers were able to explore Islam carefully and deliberately, not only for themselves but within the show, too. Al Rae, a Christian and one of the principal writers during the first season, explains that, when he began, "I had very little understanding of Muslim culture [and] society. I mean I knew a little bit about the Middle Eastern conflict but other than that I really didn't know that much about it. I didn't have a really good understanding of what was in the Quran, or how Islam worked as a religion." As a result, during the first season Rae and other writers could explore the facets of Islam that interested them, adding "gilt ...

layer by layer because we [had] the time and the flexibility" (interview with author, 2011). Fellow writer Rebecca Schechter also explains that during the first season they made constant efforts to be sensitive in their representation of Muslims (and Anglicans), for instance, by having scripts vetted by Muslim (and Anglican) consultants (interview with author, 2011).

Nonetheless, through a process of give and take between the writers and the actors, writers eventually found ways to tailor characters to fit the actors. Nawaz describes this process from the point of view of a writer:

> When shows first start out ... the first couple of episodes of a series are a little wobbly [because] the writers are trying to figure out the actors. They bring their own personality into the show ... Certain actors are able to act certain types of roles better than other actors, and then you write for that. So Yasir has a certain kind of way of speaking, and we ... started writing dialogue for the way he spoke and the way he acted ... And the actress who plays Rayyan, she's very serious, and we realized we should make her an A-type personality ... because that's how she is as a person, and she's playing that very well on the show. And Baber – Baber was always like a little nuts, and Baber was very ... strong willed. (Public forum, University of North Dakota, 2011)

Zaib Shaikh, the Muslim actor who played the imam Amaar, described this process from an actor's point of view in an interview with the CBC's George Stroumboulopoulos (2011). *Little Mosque*, he explained, was "about outsiders looking in, wanting to be inside, and then kind of assimilating and becoming part of the community. And I think that's what Amaar does too, right? He's kind of the big shot – or so he thinks – from the big city, but then he learns to assimilate in a new community. And I think that's what the show's about ... The thing is that when you're doing the show, as an artist or an actor, you're just in it, not thinking you're really – you're worried about the character, your responsibility to the character, to the show itself." Shaikh related this process back to questions of representation, too:

> But what's happened is, from that first debut, it really has taken on a life of its own. You do find yourself becoming a representative of something larger than yourself. It's really cool for an artist, as you know, you get to be part of something bigger than yourself ... That's what you strive for – it

comes upon you, especially in the Muslim setting, which is primarily ... some Muslims are living in the Victorian ages ... where we're very shaky about admitting things ... so I think to be that representative, of course, you want to make sure you're respecting the religion, and at the same time, you want to make sure you're representing it to people who aren't of the religion in a really good way. (Ibid.)

As a result of this give and take, the first season was educational in effect, if not necessarily in intent. But the limitations of the synecdochic mode of representation were already clear. For one thing, although the first season increased the range of depictions of Islam on North American television, this diversity was held in check by writers who felt the need to subordinate "Muslim" themes to "universal" themes (as made evident by the use of B-plots to demonstrate that Muslims' concerns were no different than those of "mainstream" viewers). For another, writers had to rely on character types, at least until they got to know the actors and write the characters in ways that allowed them to grow into their roles. Many Muslims were critical of the show early on precisely because they objected to the writers' reliance on character types, as the next sections describe.

Historical Audience Research and Its Challenges

When Muslims responded to *Little Mosque*'s first episodes, they tended to react to the idea, as Shaikh suggests, that the show's characters stood in for "something bigger than themselves." Whether they liked the show depended largely on whether they thought it expanded the range of depictions of Muslims enough. In other words, it depended on whether they felt the characters did – or could – stand in for them. In the following section, I examine their responses.

As noted in chapter 1, I use as my theoretical lens Mikhail Bakhtin's ideas about dialogue, or the reactive and anticipatory exchange of ideas that characterizes cultural translation. This approach grows out of a large body of research that describes viewers' modes of engagement with TV, how they "think through television," in Ron Lembo's (2000) phrase. They watch it in ways that range from engaged to distracted, and in many different social situations, and they make sense of what they see "by debating, arguing, mulling over, and working through that which television provides" (Jones 2010, 36). TV acts, as Horace Newcomb and Paul Hirsch (1983) famously observed, as a "cultural forum," a focal point for conversation. So, just as *Little Mosque*'s makers shaped the show in part based on how they thought viewers would respond, viewers and critics (both Muslim and non-Muslim) responded not only to the show but also to each other, and they anticipated each others' responses in turn. Collectively, their reactions were dynamic, and they evolved through conversation with each other. Presumably, most of this conversation took place privately, but much took place publicly, too, in broad-circulation publications such as newspapers and magazines and in blogs, both of which I consider here.

The newspaper and magazine articles come from a keyword search for "Little Mosque" in the ProQuest Newspapers database, which yielded about 200 hits.[1] The dates searched ran from December 2006 to February 2007 (leading up to and following the premiere) and from March to April 2012 (leading up to and following the finale). An author search for the names of critics who wrote about *Little Mosque*'s premiere yielded a dozen follow-up reviews between March 2007 and February 2012. Some content was superficial, such as mentions of *Little Mosque* in entertainment columns about other shows with *Little Mosque* stars or a sentence or two in columns about upcoming programs. Others were substantive and expository, such as Neil MacFarquhar's (2006) profile of the show in the *New York Times*. Still others were substantive and evaluative, such as letters to the editor or reviews by TV critics. Of the 200 initial hits, 43 fell into this third category, and they serve as the basis of my analysis here.

I also examine blogs about *Little Mosque*. Blogs, however, are unruly objects of study (boyd 2006). Some authors identify themselves and give their professional or personal background, but some remain anonymous (or pseudonymous). Most readers who leave comments probably write what they believe, but because some people troll internet comment boards – especially those related to sensitive topics – merely to provoke others, researchers have to face nagging questions about commenters' sincerity (Schwartz 2008).

For *Little Mosque* I worked with a group of research assistants to examine seventy-two blogs during the summer of 2012, immediately after *Little Mosque* ended its run. These blogs were the top hits in Google, and they covered the show from its beginning to its end. We collected blogs until the hits repeated themselves and it appeared we had exhausted the supply. They ranged widely across authors, content, and intent. Some were personal blogs (such as abbaskarimjeeweblog.com, run by Abbas Karimjee, a fan who wrote about nearly every episode and was even featured on CBC news), while others were professional (such as those hosted by the CBC or newspapers such as the *Guardian* [UK] or the *Jerusalem Post*). Some were political, while others were run by fans who treated the show as entertainment. Some focused exclusively on *Little Mosque*, while others discussed it in the context of the broader themes that were their real focus. There was even a mention of the show on a blog about Muslim women's fashion: an entry about Rayyan's hijabs. These blogs addressed themes similar to those in wide-circulation newspapers and magazines, but with less polish and fewer filters. People were more willing to express thoughts at the extremes of the political spectrum, especially when it came to linking Islam with terror (and criticizing *Little Mosque* for failing to do so).

Before I turn my attention to those publications, I want to justify and assess the limits of my approach. My purpose here is to understand the cultural translation *Little Mosque*'s makers performed by describing the conversation they carried on with viewers. As noted in chapter 1, I mean "conversation" in the broadest possible sense: the show's originator and executive producers spoke with each other and with the production team, whose members then addressed viewers through the program they produced. Viewers, in turn, responded in various ways to the show's makers. This conversation took place contemporaneously with the production of the show, and executive producers, writers, and so on adjusted their strategy as a result. I want to capture the effects of this dynamic relationship over the course of *Little Mosque*'s run.

But I do want to note the ways historical audience research is epistemologically fragile. First, the audience as such is not a given entity: "Quite obviously, before there was television, there was no such thing as a television audience. The television audience then is not an ontological given, but a socially constructed and institutionally produced category" (Ang 1991, 3). This aspect makes such research different from the focus groups producers and networks perform: although focus groups reveal something of the complexity of viewers' interpretations (see, e.g., Karim et al. 2011), they do so in an artificial environment. Besides, *Little Mosque*'s producers were not addressing *focus groups* – they were addressing *Canadians* (and, once they had syndicated the show, citizens of other countries). In fact, after a handful of initial focus groups run by the CBC, they did not use focus groups at all (Darling, interview with author, 2014).

Second, contemporary research about past viewing must account for the influence of recent events on people's interpretations. If I asked people now how they interpreted *Little Mosque* when they first saw it, their recollections would be coloured by the events that have taken place in the time since the episodes aired. For instance, viewers in 2007 or 2008 did not know, as we know now, that the "Arab Spring" would take place in 2011, challenging many North Americans' assumptions about the potential for democracies in the Arab world. When we watch *Little Mosque* now, we do so through a lens shaped by such events.

Hence my approach here. I examine people who self-identified as audience members by publishing responses to *Little Mosque*. To identify themes I use a strategy of refinement through recursive reading (i.e., constantly re-evaluating earlier responses in light of later ones), and I pay special attention to places where critics responded to each other. What makes these responses valuable is their public visibility. My interest is not in identifying a representative sample of viewers but in examining the double role a range of people played in the show's reception: they were viewers in their own right, but they also were in a position to influence other viewers' responses. Television critics adopted this double role consciously and explicitly. People who wrote letters to the editor played it, too. Their letters had to pass through a selection process that gave them a certain legitimacy precisely by making them public. Blog posts did not necessarily have to pass through a selection process (a fact that accounts for bloggers' ability to take more extreme positions), but they, too, played this double role.

Thus, even though the responses I examine do not capture viewers' reactions in their entirety, they do provide a record of the public circulation – over time and in constant tension with *Little Mosque* itself – of ideas about the meaning of Islam in post-9/11 North America.

Muslims' Responses to *Little Mosque*

As the last chapter described, a contradiction inheres to synecdoche as a mode of representation. When individuals stand in for a group, they come to define its public face. But their identity never matches up completely with the identities of the people they represent, and that mismatch obscures the diversity of the group. No matter how much the range of representation expands, certain group members will feel unrepresented.

When Muslims[2] published responses to *Little Mosque*, they talked about its accuracy, by which they frequently meant its ability to represent their experiences. Those who found it accurate tended to be those who felt represented; those who did not tended to be those who felt left out. Sheema Khan (2007, A19), for example, wrote, "Many of the situations are rooted in reality. For example, North American Muslims have failed to unite in the determination of the start of Ramadan," one of the plot lines from the pilot episode. Aisha Sherazi (2007, A15) went further:

> The sitcom was actually a fairly realistic look at some of the challenges that Muslims face in Canada and around the western world. It also showed that Muslims are not always the typical stereotypes that one sees in the media.
>
> There were Muslims from various countries and cultures, each arguing typically about what food would be best to serve for *iftar* (the opening of the fast), and how the moon should be best sighted for the start of Ramadan. There were Muslims who had adopted the faith of Islam through conversion as well as Muslims who were fairly secular in their approach, and Muslims whom one might describe as "straight off the boat."
>
> Yes, the script was exaggerated. But good humour usually is.
>
> We were to see scenes that displayed paranoia, where a young Muslim male argues with his mother just before boarding a plane about how taking a job in the Prairies is not an act of "suicide" – and a fellow passenger reports him immediately. We were to witness scenes of prejudice in which immigration officials assumed the man had terrorist tendencies because he spent a year in Afghanistan, and scenes of discomfort and misunderstanding when a Muslim man finds people praying in congregation while bowing their heads as Christians do.

If anyone should be offended, she wrote, it was non-Muslims, who were depicted as "ignorant and paranoid."

Sherazi's review, published originally in the *Ottawa Citizen*, elicited a wide range of responses in letters to the editor. Many of those who agreed did so on the basis of an equivalence they observed between the experience of Muslims and that of non-Muslims. For instance, Anjum Jaleel (2007, A11) wrote, "This sitcom should also reveal that we Muslims are just like any other humans on this planet, possessing the full range of emotions and feelings, and are merely trying to live a normal life in the Western world and should not be stereotyped or punished for the actions of a few in our midst" (see also Reta 2007). But other parts of her review touched a nerve with non-Muslim readers. Sherazi suggested, "There are perhaps two take-home messages from the show. For non-Muslims: Educate yourselves about Muslims. For Muslims

Table 1 Structure and content of the dialogue generated
by Muslims' responses to *Little Mosque on the Prairie*

Theme	Summary of dominant position taken	Summary of responses provoked (if any)
Accuracy	*Little Mosque* presented a realistic view of Muslims because its characters had a range of cultural identities and levels of religiosity, although it did exaggerate for effect.	Agreement among Muslims: "We Muslims are just like other humans on this planet, possessing the full range of emotions and feelings."
		Disagreement among non-Muslims: *Little Mosque* was offensive because it stereotyped non-Muslims.
		Agreement among non-Muslims: People of all types need to develop a sense of humour about themselves.
Inaccuracy	*Little Mosque* presented a distorted image of the Muslim community by sanitizing what happens in Canadian mosques and by presenting conservative approaches as progressive.	
Potential for mutual understanding	Muslims gain insight into non-Muslims' anxieties while non-Muslims gain insight into the day-to-day life of one of Canada's cultural minorities.	

came the perhaps harder message to swallow: We do not communicate with ourselves well enough to educate others about us." An atheist wrote about being offended by being told to learn about yet another religion, concluding, "The one thing I marvel at is humankind's limitless capacity for self-delusion" (Ertmann 2007, A11). Sonia Zakrevsky objected to an assertion made by Sherazi (2007, A15) according to which "[because they are] politically correct, non-Muslims will not complain about their unfair portrayal in the sitcom." Zakrevsky (2007, A9) wrote, "Discrimination goes both ways. If you want to make fun of yourself, go ahead. To make fun of someone else's religion, that's not quite OK ... with a lot of us, I'm sure ... We have to pretend it's OK to be put down because it may not be politically correct to complain? This is my home, and I would certainly like to feel comfortable in it, and I would appreciate it if we all portrayed ourselves the way we really are." She took particular offence at a joke that seemed to equate Protestants with prostitutes. Zakrevsky's letter in turn prompted others, such as that of Jennee-Lee Thorne (2007), who agreed with Zakrevsky, and that of Jill Young (2007, A11), who wrote, "Let's stop analysing every word spoken. Soon we will spend so much time pausing, searching for the right words that we will all be left speechless" (see also Hingorani 2007).

This exchange reveals the way writers reacted to and anticipated each other. In her reaction to Sherazi, Zakrevsky revealed her anxiety about her home changing and tried to head off counterarguments by adopting language similar to Sherazi's, framing her concern as one about respect for people as they are. How could people like Sherazi disagree if she was, in effect, making the same argument that people should "reflect a little on how we need to reach out to each other and where we can improve" (Sherazi 2007, A15)? Notably, Young (2007), who agreed with Sherazi (and disagreed with Zakrevsky), made a similar point, echoing Sherazi's sentiment: "if we do not take a look at what is happening in the world, and stop to laugh at ourselves, we are in grave danger of taking ourselves far too seriously" (2007, A15).

Those who criticized the show tended to find that, despite its range of characters, they did not recognize themselves in it. For instance, on the "Little Experiences" blog, where "readers can relate their real-life experiences to the focal points in [*Little Mosque*]," a viewer who self-identified as a convert made the following comment about the first episode: "I'm not sure about the convert character, 'Sarah.' She is ok, but it bugs me to think non-Muslim viewers may think the majority of us white Muslim converts are like her. We are so different from one another."[3] In broad-circulation media the Muslim critic who was interviewed most frequently and was given the most column space was Tarek Fatah, founder of the Muslim Canadian Congress, an organization that promotes "a progressive, liberal, pluralistic, democratic, and secular society where everyone has the freedom of religion."[4] Along with Farzana Hassan, Fatah published a scathing review of *Little Mosque* in the *Toronto Sun* shortly after its premiere. They thought the first four episodes, which focused on issues related to Islam, provided a false picture of Muslims in Canada. They also thought conservatism was being passed off as progressivism, and the effect, they said, was insidious: by "sanitiz[ing] what really goes on in the typical Canadian mosque [including the] hijacking of our religion, Islam, by politicized clerics affiliated with Saudi Arabia or Iran," the show's makers were advancing "an Islamist agenda that seeks to justify inequities that

There were too many linguistic differences, and they thought I was making fun of the faith, and not the situation ... I think the show resonated
most among Muslims who were born and raised in North America, who
grew up with a diet of North American television, and that was our audience. (Public forum, University of North Dakota, 2011)

In her interactions with Muslim viewers Nawaz found that those who
were born outside Canada fixated on jokes' literal level of meaning,
whereas those who were born in Canada were more open to irony's
polysemy: "It was hard for some Muslims who were like that, that we
were making a sitcom, that we weren't replicating reality, it had to be
larger than life, the people had to be larger than life, the situations were
bigger" (ibid.; see also Nawaz 2014, 184–6).[5] In short, irony produced
multiple, competing meanings. Synecdoche as a mode of representation – the idea that characters stood in for real groups of people – had
to compete with it when it used exaggeration to imply that characters
did not (indeed, could not) stand in neatly for real people.

Non-Muslims' Responses to *Little Mosque*:
The CBC and the Sitcom as Genre

When non-Muslims responded to *Little Mosque*, their point of departure was different. In general, the show's fans wanted to talk about the
CBC and the sitcom genre. On the other hand, as I discuss in the next
section, the show's detractors wanted to talk about religion, either their
own or that of the characters, although their debate about "authentic"
Islam took place in parallel with that of Muslim viewers and critics.

Although discussions of the CBC and the sitcom might appear to be
only tangentially related to questions about Islam in post-9/11 North
America, people's thoughts about the CBC – whether it served to unify
the country, for instance, or whether it was elitist – influenced their
sense of the intents of network executives and the show's makers.
Similarly, their thoughts about the sitcom – what types of humour suited it, or whether religion was an appropriate topic – influenced their
interpretation of the relationships between characters (and between the
story world and the world it was meant to depict). People who thought
that the CBC helped unify the country and that religion suited the sitcom genre were more inclined to approve of *Little Mosque*'s positive
depictions of Muslims than were those who thought the CBC was elitist
or that sitcoms should focus on family dynamics.

Most critics writing about the CBC applauded the network for airing *Little Mosque*. Brigitte Pellerin (2007, A10), for instance, expressed concern about the potential fallout of the program, given the controversy that had surrounded the publication in Denmark of cartoons depicting the prophet Muhammed as a terrorist, but she then said, "I am impressed that CBC will broadcast a sitcom chronicling the tribulations of a small Muslim community trying to live in peace with its neighbours." John Doyle (2007a, R1) was outright enthusiastic: "Today, we celebrate a triumph. What arrives tonight on CBC is the smartest thing the broadcaster has done in years ... And the important thing is this – popular, consequential Canadian TV is a vigorous demonstration of our difference from the United States in our attitudes and national character" (see also Kohanik 2007; McKenzie 2007a). Not all assessments were positive, of course, especially when critics were predisposed to think that the CBC was patronizing and elitist. For example, Margaret Wente (2007, A15), writing in the *Globe and Mail*, took a sarcastic tone: "*Little Mosque* is the most-hyped new CBC show in years, though not exactly the most true to life. Like all CBC shows, it has a mandate to instruct and uplift.[6] Here is the moral lesson: Muslims are people too! And guess what! They're harmless! ... *Little Mosque* is a show only the CBC could make. It is so risk-averse, so painfully correct, it makes your teeth ache."

Those who were critical of *Little Mosque* spent more time discussing its qualities as a sitcom. They picked up quickly on the show's "wobbliness," in Nawaz's words, as writers put flesh on the characters' bones. After the first episode they reached something of a consensus, namely, that despite the show's potential to be cutting edge, its producers preferred a more temperate approach: "*Little Mosque on the Prairie* taps into the xenophobic ignorance that exists across the religious spectrum, but then it cautiously pours out sanitized silliness. In other words these hijinks in hijab are, above all else, placid" (Menon 2007a, D5). One of the most common adjectives to describe the show was "hokey." In a frequently quoted line Doyle (2007a, R1) described it as "hokey as hell," but went on to say that "it's terrifically good-natured, has a few terrific jokes and its mere existence is a grand-slam assertion that Canadian TV is different and that the best of Canadian TV amounts to a rejection of the hegemony of U.S. network TV." Their disappointment derived in part from their uncertainty about whether the writers would have time to develop the characters: "It remains to be seen if Nawaz and her talented cast can sustain *Little Mosque*'s early promise and base a long-running series on the concept of a Muslim community in small-town Saskatchewan. If CBC is happy with the numbers over the long term, the broadcaster may spring for another season, with more episodes next time. For now, the jury is out on whether *Little Mosque* can thrive" (Strachan 2007a, E8).

Critics became much less tentative after the CBC announced it had picked up *Little Mosque* for a second season, especially once the second season had begun. The renewal had a direct influence on the show's mode of production, as Darling explains: "Season 1 was ... about issues, it was thoughtful, we had a lot of time to develop it. [In] season 2 we went ... from a cottage industry [to] a factory model, and we brought in a show-runner who didn't quite understand what it was we were trying to do." As a result, "we had a couple of decent episodes, but we lost our way in that season, trying to be funny and relying too much on the jokes instead of the ... relevant ... conversation that's happening in the world." The producers (and network executives) were disappointed with this shift: "if you just sort of forget about the rest of the world and just make funny episodes ... then it's just a bunch of funny people, some of whom are wearing a hijab" (interview with author, 2011).

Critics, on the other hand, liked the shift: "it now seems the idea is to generate gently provocative humour from the internal dynamics of the small Muslim community and then play up the ordinary family oddities" (Doyle 2007c, R3). The new emphasis on characters – and less on religion as such – suited their sense of what a sitcom should be. Alex Strachan (2007d, F6) wrote, "The gentle-spirited tale of culture clash has overcome its initial stiffness to become a confident, often witty TV parable, with believable, easy-to-like characters and confident, skilled performances ... [This] season it has struck the right combination of whimsy and wisdom." Michael Murray (2007b, K1) agreed: "The writing is tighter and more contemporary this season."

What accounts for the divergence between how the producers and how the critics saw this shift? Here the critics' use of words such as "ordinary" is key. The word works to exclude visible religious character traits that differ from those of "mainstream" viewers. In other words, it subtly strengthens the idea that "Muslim" and "mainstream" are incompatible categories. This difference is further suggested by the fact that, by the third season, critics could write: "In hindsight, controversy over *Little Mosque*'s content was the proverbial tempest in a Moroccan teapot – look past the accents, the kufis, caftans and cultural rituals, and *Little Mosque* is just another comedy, family-friendly and funny in an underhanded, disarming way. It plays like a traditional sitcom, but without the laugh track" (Strachan 2008, C12).

Non-Muslim Responses: The Place of Islam in Post-9/11 North America

During *Little Mosque*'s first two seasons non-Muslim viewers talked about the show in relation to religion, in addition to the CBC and the sitcom genre, but they did so differently than Muslim viewers. Their point of departure was not Muslim identity but their own. Some, like Sonia Zakrevsky, whose response to a joke about Protestants and prostitutes I alluded to above, felt Christians were singled out for ridicule. That impression was not a coincidence, although the production team, especially the writers and executive producers, took pains to mock not faith so much as the trappings of religion. Mary Darling explains: "In comedy ... if you're going to make fun of something, you're supposed to 'kick up.' In other words, you're only going to kick what can be kicked ... and so in our case, because Christianity in Canada is so known and established ... in some cases, you would kick up and Christianity would be more made fun of than Islam, because you're trying to establish a sympathetic view of Islam, while still exposing its warts, right?" (interview with author, 2012). They tried to gauge their jokes informally by consulting Christian friends: "In terms of using our network of friends, acquaintances, people in the biz ... and getting reads on episodes, we've got some neighbours who are Catholic, and on the other side, Dutch Reformed ... so we would call on them to see [whether we were] kicking up too hard ... Our writers were always prone to kick up to Christianity and leave Islam a little bit less called out ... so we tried to make sure we were balancing that ... [while] making sure the Christian community never felt we were making fun of it" (interview with author, 2014).[7]

More common, however, were non-Muslims' responses to the depiction of Islam. In this respect, the show had a number of prominent detractors, especially conservative writers, who made frequent claims about "authentic" Islam without any reference to the debates Muslims themselves were having, despite the fact that many of those responses appeared in the same publications. The harshest critics presumed they knew Islam's "true" nature, as made evident by their many a priori statements about how Muslims were or should be. They thought the show insulted viewers by denying the connection between Islam and terror (Coren 2007) or they worried that, as one blogger wrote, the "point of the show seems to be to take over the society entirely – not just to complain about it. To supersede Canadian culture with Islamic or Arabic language, holidays and cultural behavior" (Asrat 2008).

They were also critical of the CBC, which they felt was too timid about speaking the "truth" for fear of offending its liberal viewers, who had what they saw as a misplaced sense of fairness. Mark Steyn (2007) was among the most critical. He described *Little Mosque* as "a surreal latter-day PC version of the old vaudeville act 'The Hebrew and the Coon,'" and he saw the CBC as pandering to viewers' "smug conviction that [Canadians are] the most progressive people on the planet." The purpose of *Little Mosque*, he wrote, was "to make Islam, like homosexuality [as depicted in 1990s television], something only uptight squares are uncool with." Because of the show's pandering, its depiction of Muslims was sanitized, while its depiction of non-Muslims was filtered through a lens of political correctness:

> Never mind that, in the real Canada, the talk-radio guy [Fred Tupper] would be off the air and hounded into oblivion by the Saskatchewan Human Rights Commission; and that, instead of looking like Rick Mercer after 20 minutes on a sunbed and being wry and self-deprecating and Toronto-born, your typical Western imam is fiercely bearded, trained in Saudi Arabia, and such linguistic dexterity as he has is confined to Arabic; ... and that, in the event they do bust up a terrorist plot, the Mounties inevitably issue statements saying this in no way reflects on any particular community in our glorious Canadian mosaic, particularly any community beginning with "Is-" and ending with "-lam."

Barbara Kay (2007, A19) was equally convinced that she knew the true nature of Islam and Muslims. Like Steyn, she found *Little Mosque* too politically correct, a throwback to 1950s sitcoms where "all conflicts are resolved within 12 seconds of their being aired, and everything works out the way you knew it would: ... a little compromise here, a little coaxing there, an explanation, a smile, a handshake, a sigh, a shrug and even though nobody explains why the beautiful daughter wears a hijab and the mum doesn't, everyone is cool with whatever." The show fell victim to the relativism that she saw as characteristic of Canadian multiculturalism: "This Islamophilia is urged upon us by omission and commission, and in ways both benign and wicked: from CBC's intelligence-insulting series, *Little Mosque on the Prairie*, to the singling out of Muslims from

other religious groups for government outreach programs, to – most per-
niciously – indulgence by our human rights commissions of hate-filled
anti-Western rhetoric by imams, while demonizing heritage Canadians
who 'offend' Muslims with facts and statistics" (ibid., A24).

Both Kay and Steyn structured their critiques following a well-worn
rhetoric that equates multiculturalism with political correctness and
political correctness with pandering. This logic is part of a more pervasive sense among critics of multiculturalism that it fosters moral
relativism, excessive individualism, cultural separatism, and divided
loyalties (Ryan 2010, 41–2; see, e.g., Bissoondath 1994; Cohen 2007). Kay
and Steyn themselves participate in it (and draw on its persuasiveness)
by recrafting the critiques of multiculturalism to apply to *Little Mosque*
in particular. In that respect it is useful to note that Rob McKenzie responds to Steyn's (2007) comment about making Islam "something
only uptight squares are uncool with" by calling that very logic into
question: "The reason many people are uncool with Islam is its association with terrorism. But the more important issue is not the manner in
which squares and other shapes perceive this association, but the extent
to which it exists. And in its own hokey way, *Little Mosque* diminishes
the risk of home-grown terrorism" (McKenzie 2007b, TO38).

Other critics appeared to give Muslims more credit, only to reverse
themselves as their argument advanced. For example, Margaret Wente
(2007, A15) said that she would not "take issue with" the idea that
"Muslims are people too." But then, much like Steyn, she explained
that, if *Little Mosque* really were accurate,

> the cute imam would have to go. The redneck radio host would be shut
> down by the [Canadian Radio-television and Telecommunications
> Commission], and the townsfolk, instead of reacting to the mosque with
> fear and loathing, would invite everyone in it to join an interfaith group.
> Instead of calling the terror hotline, the village idiot would chuck a rock
> through the mosque's window. A Muslim from Egypt would be tossed
> into jail indefinitely on secret evidence. The convert to Islam (here played
> by Sheila McCarthy who only wears her head scarf in the mosque) would
> be dressed in black from head to foot. And the Muslim versions of Archie
> Bunker and Meathead would have a hilariously incorrect debate over the
> existence of that pesky state of Israel.[8]

Her openness towards Muslims was limited by her contempt for multicultural relativism, which in turn drew her openness into question.

Some viewers avoided such a priori statements altogether and approached *Little Mosque* with the idea that Muslims might be different than stereotypical depictions of them suggest. Most of the reviews expressing this idea were by Muslims (e.g., Ally 2007; Gardee 2007; Sherazi 2007), but not all. After *Little Mosque*'s premiere Michael Murray (2007a, K1) wrote: "Many of us in the West, even the most curious and best intentioned, know virtually nothing about Islam. We get occasional glimpses from the news, where we're bombarded by blunt expressions of rage, unmediated by any objective filter. What we see, and what we understand, is narrow and lacking in nuance. Indeed, the creators of *Little Mosque on the Prairie* have a massive challenge in persuading a mainstream audience to free itself from prejudices."

In short, non-Muslims' responses to *Little Mosque* in its first seasons ranged from approval to contestation, and their responses correlated to their perceptions of the CBC and the sitcom genre. Those who thought that the CBC should encourage Canadians to talk to each other (i.e., those who agreed with the premises underpinning the CBC's mandate as spelled out in the 1991 Broadcasting Act) also tended to think that sitcoms' "hokeyness" helped put viewers at ease. They agreed with *Little Mosque*'s makers that stereotypes about Muslims were short-sighted, that Muslims were more diverse than the media usually acknowledged, and that a sitcom was an appropriate vehicle for making that point. Moreover, they agreed that *Little Mosque* had the potential to be the sitcom to do it. They responded to the show's use of irony with an openness to the idea Muslims might be other than the stereotypes they were used to seeing. Those who contested the premises of the CBC's mandate or who thought that the CBC was elitist and out of touch also tended to view *Little Mosque* – and by extension its depictions of Muslims – with suspicion. They responded to the show's use of irony by linking ironic distance to elitism at the CBC, and they dug in and held to their preconceptions about Muslims. They saw *Little Mosque* as propagating the idea that Islam was harmless – an idea they challenged – and they claimed to speak on behalf of "average" Canadians who shared their "common sense" notions of Islam as a threat.

Saleable Diversity, Plot, and Character Development

Earlier I described certain of *Little Mosque*'s formal qualities by placing them in the context of a circuit of influences. Producers' perceptions of their audience limited the choices they could make, especially as they privileged "mainstream" viewers. The effects of those limits were apparent, for instance, in the range of characters depicted. And viewers in turn responded either by embracing the show or by criticizing it for being "inaccurate," although what they meant by "inaccurate" depended largely on whether or not they were Muslim.

I want to return in this final section to the effects of this interaction and negotiation on the show's formal qualities. Specifically, I want to focus on the effect of the logic of character-driven stories on representation of Muslims. In their book on US sitcoms with majority-black casts Sut Jhally and Justin Lewis (1992) argue that if the character is the locus of the sitcom's action, the social context in which characters act is useful in so far as it provides context for understanding their actions, but structural factors of inequality, for instance, are not addressed. This pattern held true in *Little Mosque*, too, especially in the first seasons. The production team wrote scenes where characters faced discrimination and they allowed characters to express indignation, as long as it was funny. But in each case they resolved the plot by directing attention away from the structural factors (such as racism and the institutionalized war on terror) that made such discrimination possible and focused instead on characters' personal shortcomings. In other words, there was a limit to the "negative" emotions characters could express and, to resolve the plots, characters had to take personal responsibility for the problems they faced.[9] This neglect of structural factors occurred despite efforts by *Little Mosque*'s makers to use parody and satire to talk about events in the world beyond television. The show drew heavily on viewers' assumed familiarity with other genres, but the logic of personal responsibility – at least in the show's first seasons – overrode that of other possible narrative modes. Any attention paid to structural factors would have risked making viewers uncomfortable to the degree it implicated them in the problems characters faced. In other words, it would have made the diversity *Little Mosque* depicted less saleable.

The pilot episode illustrates this pattern well, although it appeared throughout the show's run. In the pilot viewers first meet Amaar, the new imam, as he is standing in line waiting to check in at the airport. He is talking on his phone with his mother, and he says about his father, "It's not like I dropped a bomb on him. If Dad thinks it's suicide, so be it. This is Allah's plan for me. I'm not throwing my life away – I'm moving to the Prairies!" The humour relies on the juxtaposition between the sinister-sounding beginning of his statement ("bomb," "suicide," and "Allah's plan") and the more mundane explanation for his comments, namely, that he's leaving the cosmopolitan city of Toronto for the hinterlands of the Prairies. After he finishes his line, a security guard carts him away, saying, "Step away from the bag. You're not going to paradise today."

This scene is followed a couple of minutes later by one in a small office in the airport. A security officer is sitting behind a desk interrogating Amaar. The scene toys with a familiar script, that of the interrogation scene in a police procedural. The officer presumes that Amaar is guilty. When he asks Amaar why he left his father's law firm, Amaar answers, "While I was in Egypt doing my Islamic studies, I found my true calling." "Explosives?" asks the officer. "Yeah, explosives," Amaar replies as he rolls his eyes. In a conventional police procedural such a scene would resolve with the suspect's confession or denial of guilt, but in this case Amaar's "confession" results only in the officer's simpleminded misunderstanding. Amaar finally tells the officer he's going to be an imam, and he can prove it: "I have the ad I answered for the job. You can call the mosque if you like. If the story doesn't check out, you can deport me to Syria." The officer answers, "Hey, you do not get to choose which country we deport you to."

To discuss the type of intertextuality at play here, Chris Cwynar (2013, 52–3) distinguishes between satire and parody: "satire is concerned with moral, social, and political dimensions while parody is concerned with the aesthetic elements of another discursive text ... Satire thus reduces the stature of dominant entities, while parody often refers to shared cultural materials and frames of reference." The tension between satire and parody is apparent in this scene. Many viewers surely recognized the reference to Syria as a reference to Maher Arar, a Canadian-Syrian dual citizen whom the United States deported to Syria in 2002, on suspicion of belonging to al-Qaeda.[10] But the edge of that potential critique is dulled by the parodic nature of rest of the scene. The scene even ends with a clever one-liner, although neither Amaar nor the officer delivers it. Instead, it is Yasir Hamoudi, the contractor whose answering machine the officer reaches when he calls the number Amaar gives him: "Hello," says the machine. "You've reached Yasir's construction and contracting at our new location. We'll *blow away* the competition!" Thus, the tension between satire and parody illustrates the taboo against showing Muslim characters' indignation by brushing up against it and backing away.

That backing away occurs more definitively in later scenes. When Amaar arrives in Mercy, he is treated with similar suspicion. A two-bit reporter accosts him when he gets out of his car and asks whether he is a terrorist. Finally, the local radio shock jock, Fred Tupper, invites him on air and baits him:

> FRED: Are you a terrorist?
> AMAAR: No, I'm –
> FRED: Do you object to the term?
> AMAAR: Of course I do!
> FRED: Or do you prefer mujahedin?
> AMAAR: Yes! No! I mean, look, Fred, I came here to clear the air. You're not letting me get a word in.
> FRED: Oh, please feel free to give as good as you get. That's the privilege of living in a country with freedom.
> AMAAR: Freedom? To do what? Fan the flames of hatred?
> FRED: Oh, isn't it Muslim preachers like yourself who do that, huh? I got news for you, Johnny Jihad –
> AMAAR: That's –
> FRED: Folks around here will not sit back and let that happen. You can bet your falafel on that!

Here, too, the writers draw on (and parody) familiar scripts, in this case those that characterize conservative talk radio. Fred's refusal to let Amaar finish a sentence, coupled with his insinuation that Muslims squelch free speech, echoes a wide range of conservative talk show hosts, especially those on Fox News.[11] His "common sense" appeal to "folks around here" who "will not sit back and let that happen" is also a common rhetorical device commentators use to build a sense of solidarity (and self-righteousness) among their listeners. (Notably, it characterized the responses by people such as Mark Steyn and Barbara Kay.) The scene's humour comes from the contrast between Fred's aggressive tone and the silliness of his epithets, such as "Johnny Jihad," above, and "Bedouin buckaroo," in the sequence that follows:

> FRED: I call on Rev. Magee to turn you and your gang out of the church hall by sundown. (Cut to Magee.)
> MAGEE (on the phone): Yasir, this is Rev. Magee again. We need to talk about this lease.[12] (Cut to Fred's studio.)
> AMAAR: Sundown? What is this, the wild west?
> FRED: You got that right, my little Bedouin buckaroo.

The genre parodied here is the western, as Amaar's comment indicates. The shift from conservative talk radio to the western also brings about a shift in the plot's logic. Up to this point, Amaar has expressed anger about the unfounded accusations he has faced from Fred (and the reporter at his arrival and the security officer in the airport), but he can go no further. In the lines that follow, Amaar comes to appear to be responsible for his own unhappiness:

> FRED: You're not in the big city any more. (Cut to radio in café.)
> AMAAR (exasperated): Oh, I've noticed. Doesn't anyone in this town know how to make a cappuccino?
> FRED: Oh, you're saying we are ignorant? (Cut to café patrons.)
> AMAAR (over the radio): Some of you, yes. In fact, I've never seen so much small town ignorance in my life.
> CAFÉ PATRON: Well if he hates it here so much, why doesn't he go back to Toronto?

At this point, the camera cuts to Amaar in his office, holding a telephone and saying, "Yes, a one-way ticket back to Toronto."

The concluding scenes reinforce the idea that Amaar is unhappy because he cannot imagine himself living so far from cosmopolitan Toronto. In his concluding lines with Fred, he admits to feeling superior to the small-town residents whom he has come to serve. He thinks he has made a mistake and, tail tucked between his legs, he is ready to return home. He stays only after Rayyan Hamoudi speaks to him in his office:

> AMAAR (on the phone): A one-way ticket to Toronto. (Pause.) Amaar Rashid. (Pause.) Yes, I'll hold. (Rayyan enters the office.) Can't a Muslim book a one-way flight these days without someone having to call their supervisor?
> RAYYAN: Oh, you poor thing! Racial profiling, making it very difficult for you to *run away*.
> AMAAR: What am I supposed to do?
> RAYYAN: I don't know. Let me ask the imam. Oh, wait! He's *running away*!
> AMAAR: Look, I screwed up, okay?
> RAYYAN: No, it is not okay.

This exchange, especially Rayyan's emphasis on running away, clearly subordinates the questions of social injustice to those of personal failings. In the episode's penultimate scene, Amaar even uses his very public failings as a starting point for his sermon on humility, during which he announces his plan to stay. This provides the resolution that brings the episode back to the status quo, thus conforming to the sitcom's conventional return to stasis.

This pattern was repeated in other episodes that raised questions about discrimination. For instance, in "No Fly List" (season 2, episode 9) Baber Siddiqui is scheduled to give a talk at a conference in Chicago, but his name appears on a no-fly list. The episode revolves around Baber's interactions with a US border guard indifferent to his plight, but in the end, Baber reveals that his name is not on any list – the "list" was a story he told to cover up his fear of flying. Similarly, in "Smooth Hate Criminal" (season 5, episode 6) it appears that someone has committed a hate crime against the mosque, but the "perpetrator" actually is the town's mayor, and the "crime" is the result of a misunderstanding attributable to the mayor's ineptitude. Finally, in "Mosque of Dreams" (season 6, episode 7) Baber buys fertilizer and other materials that suggest he is making a bomb, in an effort to show he can get himself arrested. But the police officer lets him go because he bought cheap fertilizer that "wouldn't blow up a dollhouse," and Baber is forced to admit that he concocted the plan because he was sad that his familiar and comfortable life was changing.

Conclusion: *Little Mosque* and the Give and Take of Cultural Translation

In chapter 1, I described cultural translation as a form of ongoing negotiation between two groups performed by intermediaries such as media-makers. My analysis here of *Little Mosque*'s first two seasons has brought to light one of the challenges of cultural translation: television production reduces the potentially open-ended give and take of negotiation to a text with a fixed form. However, *Little Mosque*'s makers tried to incorporate the broader negotiation into the program through various forms of polysemy and strategic representation, and critics and other viewers treated *Little Mosque* as one more element in the broader exchange. The show occupied a privileged semiotic position by virtue of its fixed form and its wide public circulation on a national public broadcaster, but it did not put a stop to the conversation.

In this position *Little Mosque* advanced a number of ideas about what it meant to be Muslim in post-9/11 North America. First, Muslims are diverse, where diversity is a function of identity traits such as religiosity, political views, and immigrant status. Second, Islam is compatible with North American society. Third, the ability to overcome conflict between communities resides in individuals and is a function of personal will.

Viewers in turn made strategic use of a constellation of ideas about the CBC and sitcoms, as well as social and policy issues such as multiculturalism, in their responses to the show. They found *Little Mosque* persuasive when they agreed with the show's premises. They found it unpersuasive when they disagreed. Detractors argued, for instance, that its producers and fans were besotted multiculturalists. They also argued that Islam is incompatible with North American society because it involves people not included among *Little Mosque*'s characters, such as bearded, Arab-speaking imams who, one presumes, preach lessons that encourage harm against North American society.

In other words, viewers' agreement or disagreement with *Little Mosque*'s depiction of Islam stemmed largely from their pre-existing world views. (And in their published responses they sought to persuade others to share those world views.) The next chapter directly addresses this idea of world view by looking at efforts to syndicate *Little Mosque* outside Canada. The show's producers could not count on viewers' sharing the same unspoken assumptions on which they had based *Little Mosque* in the first place. The diversity *Little Mosque* portrayed was less saleable outside Canada, and *Little Mosque* did not find the same audience abroad as it had at home.

Chapter 4

Saleable Diversity and International Audiences

In December 2010, as part of a discussion of the year's biggest news stories, news anchor Katie Couric of the US network CBS said she thought "the bigotry expressed against Muslims in this country [the United States] has been one of the most disturbing stories to surface this year. Of course, a lot of noise was made about the Islamic Center, or mosque, down near the World Trade Center, but I think there wasn't enough ... careful analysis and evaluation." As a solution, she proposed, "Maybe we need a Muslim version of *The Cosby Show*. I know that sounds crazy, but *The Cosby Show* did so much to change attitudes about African-Americans in this country, and I think sometimes people are afraid of things they don't understand ... Maybe if it became more a part of the popular culture," attitudes towards Muslims would change.[1]

Shortly after she made her comment, Couric expressed surprise to learn that such a show – *Little Mosque on the Prairie* – already existed in Canada. Two weeks later she invited Zaib Shaikh, *Little Mosque*'s only Muslim actor, onto her show. She asked him whether viewers had embraced *Little Mosque*, and he responded, "It was received beautifully by all faiths ... It doesn't matter what age you are, what gender you are, what faith you are, what socio-economic status you come from, anyone that comes and speaks to the people that are on *Little Mosque* – they're always talking about how it makes sense to them, they felt those same reactions ... [It's] a place where people laugh, and it's a gentle comedy ... It's irreverent because it has to be – we have to poke fun at our stereotypes because ... if we are proactive about those things, then we can actually negotiate and monitor and hopefully kind of lead the way as opposed to constantly being reactive."[2]

Shaikh's answer reflected more than just his feelings about *Little Mosque*, of course: its positive spin made for good PR, especially since WestWind Pictures had long been trying to syndicate the show in the United States. It also reflected a number of ideas that Canadians and Americans have about each other. For many Americans Canada serves as an idealized (or vilified) national "other," an exotic land of multiculturalism and progressive politics, an idea to which Shaikh made a clear appeal.

In this chapter I examine those ideas and the other factors that influenced WestWind's efforts to syndicate *Little Mosque* internationally. These efforts were paradoxical. Each season WestWind faced a funding shortfall of up to $1 million. International syndication allowed WestWind to make up for it and, in so doing, made production and circulation in Canada possible. Mary Darling explains: "With *Mosque*, we really felt like it was a decent gamble because we believed in it so much, and we felt like it was speaking to ... people who had questions about what's going on in the world. So we felt like it was a decent gamble, so we put in that last amount of money every year. Then we take the distribution rights on it, and we go out and distribute it. And what [self-distribution does is it make it possible] when you make that sale ... to take your distribution advance – the money you've put in – you're able to take out on a first-tier basis" (interview with author, 2011). Happily for WestWind, *Little Mosque* attracted a lot of interest before and after it premiered. When representatives from WestWind went to the MIP television trade show in Cannes in 2007, Darling says, "we literally took appointments from the entire world ... We lined up appointments on the half-hour. We didn't even schedule lunch – we just couldn't – and then we had people breaking into the appointments [who were] interested in the show" (interview with author, 2011). Consequently, WestWind had many early syndication successes in Europe and in 2008 even sold format rights to the Fox network in the United States, although Fox never made the show.[3]

In other words, to understand *Little Mosque*'s production and circulation in Canada, as I have tried to do in the preceding chapters, it is necessary to consider the role of international syndication. For that reason, in this chapter I examine the conversation that *Little Mosque*'s makers carried on, both directly and through the program, with viewers outside Canada. I focus on the first two seasons; this conversation took place parallel to (and occasionally overlapped with) the one described in chapter 3.

One challenge WestWind faced was that what makes diversity "saleable" is culturally specific. The questions Canadians were asking about the meaning of Islam in a society where Muslims were in the minority were similar to questions people were asking elsewhere, but they built the show upon a cultural foundation – a set of unspoken assumptions about the world – that viewers outside Canada did not always share. Thus, in some cases, such as the United States, WestWind did not find a network until after *Little Mosque* had finished its run. In other places, such as France and Norway, the producers were able to find networks to license the show, but it was not the success it had been in Canada. In other words, even when WestWind could sell the show (figuratively and literally) to networks, the networks could not always sell it to viewers.

I begin by examining the conversation about *Little Mosque* and Islam in the United States. US journalists covered *Little Mosque* before and after its premiere, and Canadian critics paid attention to that coverage. Canadian critics also watched and wrote about US television, including the short-lived sitcom *Aliens in America*, which was based on a similar premise. Finally, viewers and critics in the two countries read each other's critiques, and their back-and-forth exchange frequently focused on differences in how each country approached its Muslim minority.

I then examine WestWind's early successes in licensing *Little Mosque* in France and Norway.[4] Both countries have significant Muslim communities, and people in both were asking questions about the place and meaning of Islam in contemporary European society. The networks that took *Little Mosque* – Canal+ in France, TV2 Zebra in Norway – thought the show would help with their branding efforts, but few viewers watched it when it aired. For them, watching the show must have felt a bit like reading an interesting book over someone's shoulder. The themes it addressed were familiar, but the approach was different: in exporting *Little Mosque*, WestWind was transposing the act of translation its originator and producers performed. What makes WestWind's efforts interesting is the conversation Mary Darling and Clark Donnelly carried on in a literal sense with viewers abroad: they travelled to both countries to talk about religious pluralism. Although fewer viewers watched *Little Mosque* than in Canada, those who did engaged with it in ways that met their specific needs.

US Critics Watch *Little Mosque on the Prairie*

The Canadian television system is enmeshed with the US commercial system in two important ways. It is linked, first, through direct exchange. US producers, who benefit from enviable economies of scale, export their programs across the world, but especially to Canada, where US programs have always been among the most popular (Rutherford 1993). Canadian producers export their programs, too, but the relationship is asymmetrical and favours the United States. Some programs benefit from subsidies meant to encourage production and overcome the disadvantages of Canada's small domestic market, making them cheaper to produce and easier to export (Conway 2005). Others become objects of curiosity when they differ from US programming. Such was the case of *Little Mosque on the Prairie*, although viewer curiosity was not enough to give networks a reason to carry the show.

The second link is a function of programs' intertextual properties. Because US programs are ubiquitous on Canadian networks, viewers share with Americans a wide range of cultural touchpoints. As the previous two chapters showed, Norman Lear's *All in the Family* was a frequent touchpoint for *Little Mosque*'s writers and producers, for CBC executives, and for viewers and critics. These references evoked a range of reactions for viewers, and their experience of the show was the basis for the conversation they then had about Islam in North America.

When *Little Mosque* first entered production, its subject matter attracted the interest of many US journalists. Neil MacFarquhar, the religion reporter for the *New York Times*, profiled the show in 2006, a month before its premiere. "'Little Mosque on the Prairie,'" he wrote, "ventures into new and perhaps treacherous terrain: trying to explore the funny side of being a Muslim and adapting to life in post 9/11 North America. Its creators admit to uneasiness as to whether Canadians and Americans can laugh about the daily travails of those who many consider a looming menace" (MacFarquhar 2006). Like almost every other US journalist, he put the show in the context of the riots in Europe and elsewhere by Muslims protesting the cartoons of Muhammed published in the Danish newspaper *Jyllands-Posten* in 2005. He wondered: would Muslims react similarly to *Little Mosque*?

In contrast to critics in Canada, who wrote about *Little Mosque* as a sitcom and its role in the CBC's program line-up, US journalists framed their discussions almost exclusively in terms related to terrorism. In that respect they maintained a pattern observed elsewhere in contemporary US media, where Muslim identity is always defined in relation to terrorism – even when Muslim characters are not terrorists, writers emphasize this negative identity rather than a different, positive one (Alsultany 2012a, 2012b). Three days before *Little Mosque*'s premiere, for instance, CNN's Paula Zahn invited a panel of Muslim critics onto *Paula Zahn*

Now to discuss humour and Islam. The first two-thirds of the show were devoted to other controversies, including the swearing-in of the first Muslim congressman (Minnesota's Keith Ellison, who opted to place his hand on a copy of the Quran) and the opposition Muslims faced when they tried to build mosques in neighbourhoods in Texas and Florida. The choice of stories maintained an easy, non-reflexive association between Islam and terror, which was evidenced in Zahn's framing question, "And how is this for the title of a brand-new sitcom, 'Little Mosque on the Prairie'? Is that going too far, or will anyone watch?" (2007a). The panelists expressed enthusiasm for the show, but the next night Zahn read emails she had received about the *Little Mosque* segment: "But Ruth in Virginia says, 'I see no humor in "Little Mosque on the Prairie." I see a Muslim and I think 9/11. This country has been without mosques since it began, and yes I see the religion in a negative light. I feel threatened by mosques being built in our country'" (2007b).[5]

Other news outlets maintained this frame. When journalists wrote about *Little Mosque*, their points of reference were people such as the so-called Toronto 18, a group of eighteen men and youths in Ontario who were caught at a training camp inspired by al-Qaeda, and Maher Arar, the engineer with dual Canadian and Syrian citizenship who was detained by US intelligence agents on suspicion of belonging to al-Qaeda.

When Zarqa Nawaz, Mary Darling, and others spoke to US news outlets, they had to respond to questions on journalists' terms. Thus, they had to insist, as they did in an article in the *Chicago Tribune*, that "this is not a political show. This is not about the Iraq war; it's not about 9/11. It's entertainment" (Nawaz, quoted in Duff 2007, 4). Or: "It really is a show that focuses on relationships and families; it's not about terrorism ... [The] assumption in the media that Muslims are going to riot in the streets, freak out and get upset is ridiculous" (Darling, quoted in ibid.).

This frame persisted after *Little Mosque* premiered. Muslims in the United States liked the show, when they could find it (either through cable in border towns or through YouTube). They were enthusiastic about its use of humour, but they still felt obligated to discuss it in the context of 9/11. Naheed Ali (2007, B7), who commented that the characters spoke "with American accents," wrote, "While it's impossible to portray Muslims without referring to the post 9/11 climate, it is very possible to show the everyday lives and mishaps of Muslims living in the West without creating an undertone of anxiety." Similarly, Charles Alawan, one of the founders of the Islamic Center of Detroit, said, "People who have a dark image of my faith, especially since 9/11, may get a better understanding of who we are" (quoted in Duffy 2007). Bloggers made similar arguments. Robert Salaam, author of the now-defunct blog "The American Muslim" (http://theamericanmuslim.net), wrote in January 2007 that he wished *Little Mosque* would air in the United States to counter images of 9/11.

Other Muslim viewers responded to the dominant frame by contesting it. Cenk Uygur, host of *Young Turks* on the Air America Radio network and a panelist on Zahn's show, had this exchange with Zahn (2007a):

> ZAHN: How do you pierce through that sole stereotype that exists in this country, which is – among some Americans – Muslims are bad?
> UYGUR: I mean, we do it all the time on our radio show. And I – nobody makes more suicide bomber jokes than I do. And the reason is, once you make fun of something, people go, "Wait a minute, you're right. That's silly. You know, of course, not all Muslims are suicide bombers. And of course they're not all bad guys, I don't know why I thought that."
> And you know, everybody has to break those things. And, you know, in TV, they said a show about Jews in New York will never work until *Seinfeld*. They said a black woman can't ever be a talk show host until *Oprah*. So I mean, I'm going to sell *2½ Muslims* and *Everybody Loves Muhammed*.[6]

In these responses differences appeared between the interpretive lenses through which Americans and Canadians watched *Little Mosque*: Canadians saw more than just terror or its potential. These differences help explain the challenge WestWind faced in syndicating the show in the United States. Susan Alexander, one of the writers during *Little Mosque*'s first season, recounts a trip she took to a bed and breakfast in California, where she encountered people who seemed to her to represent "middle America." When she told these guests about the show, they responded by saying that America is a country of Christians, and they expressed frustrations about "these people [Muslims] coming into our country" (interview with author, 2011). The idea that "middle America" would reject the show weighed heavily on network executives' minds, and it translated into an economic concern, as Darling explains: "I think that in the economy as it is ... there is some concern from a [media] buyer's standpoint that people get axed so easily in the [United] States for making a bad or risky decision" (interview with author, 2012). In other words, *Little Mosque* appeared to be a risk because it might alienate viewers, get low ratings, and cost the person who de-cided to air it his or her job.

Canadian Critics Watch US Media

According to a number of Canadian critics, including John Doyle (2007a) at the *Globe and Mail*, Safiyyah Ally (2007) and Michael Murray (2007b) at the *Ottawa Citizen*, and Vinay Menon (2007a) at the *Toronto Star*, one factor that increased their interest in *Little Mosque* was the at-tention it received in the United States. They noted, as did US journal-ists, that it demonstrated a number of important differences between US and Canadian television. For instance, John Doyle (2007a, R1), re-sponding to Paula Zahn among others, wrote (with a hint of self-deprecating irony), "This is Canada and we pride ourselves on being more tolerant here. We roll our eyes at the paranoia and ignorance of Americans, and believe it's legitimate to strengthen our tolerance by poking gentle fun at those who are intolerant, and even by poking fun at Muslims. After all, they are kinda wacky, like the rest of us." Along with other Canadian critics, he was concerned with its quality as a sit-com: "It's notable that *Little Mosque on the Prairie*, while it's a sitcom, isn't derived from the U.S. network model. It has a British feel to it," more in line with shows like *Ballykissangel, Hamish Macbeth,* and *Doc Martin,* all shows about outsiders who come to small, remote towns to practise their profession. Kamal Al-Solaylee (2007, R4) went still fur-ther, writing, "While top-rated U.S. network drama *24* has set tongues wagging with its portrayal of Arabs and Muslims at home and abroad as bywords for anti-American terror, a number of Canadian filmmakers [and] TV producers" – including those responsible for *Little Mosque* – "are examining the lives of their under-attack communities with con-siderably more understanding and far less fear-mongering."[7]

But Canadians were paying attention to more than just US responses to *Little Mosque.* They were also watching popular US shows. Zarqa Nawaz noted, for instance, that two shows that premiered in 2009, *Parks and Recreation* and *Community,* had Muslim characters who were "side-kicks," although she also observed that, in contrast to *Little Mosque,* "the characters you see on American television are more secular Muslims and Islam is not necessarily a major part of their life" (public forum, University of North Dakota, 2011).

Of special interest was *Aliens in America,* which ran on The CW, a broadcast "netlet" that launched in 2006 when two older netlets – The

WB and UPN – merged. It was a single-camera sitcom that told a fish-out-of-water story about a Pakistani exchange student named Raja Musharraf in the fictional small town of Medora, Wisconsin. In the first episode, the parents of Raja's soon-to-be host family, the Tolchuks, ask for an exchange student so their desperately unpopular son Justin will have at least one friend. The Tolchuks envision a good-looking Scandinavian boy and are surprised when Raja introduces himself at the airport.

Aliens was created by David Guarascio and Moses Port. They were long-time collaborators who had worked together on the sitcoms *Just Shoot Me!*, for which they were writers and producers, and *Mad About You*, for which they were writers. They saw religion as a way to generate comedic situations that had the added benefit of being relevant to contemporary geopolitics. As Guarascio explains, their idea for *Aliens* came from a brainstorming session where "we were sharing our own sort of nightmarish high school experiences with each other, all these embarrassing stories, and wondering if there is a fresh take on a high school show about teenage life, a fresh, honest take that could be – because it's sort of one of those areas that you see tried quite a bit in TV and in film" (NPR 2007). Despite its similarity to *Little Mosque*, Guarascio claimed to have devised its premise independently: "When Moses and I wrote the script for *Aliens*, back in 2005, we saw a blurb about (*Little Mosque*) in *Variety*," but they knew nothing of *Little Mosque* other than that (quoted in Strachan 2007b, F6).

Nonetheless, when *Aliens* premiered in October 2007, about nine months after *Little Mosque*, Canadian viewers were quick to note the similarities. Critics liked its pilot better than *Little Mosque's*, and they used it as a way to criticize the CBC. Vinay Menon, who had found *Little Mosque* "placid" (2007a, D5), said, "*Aliens in America* doesn't feel forced or contrived ... [It's] so bracingly funny, tender and enjoyable, you just never think about its real world relevance or social messaging" (2007b, L7). Michael Murray, who had found *Little Mosque's* humour too forced (2007a), saw *Aliens* as "effortlessly funny" (2007b, K1). *Little Mosque* suffered, he thought, because "sometimes, it seems that the CBC is happier to be thought of well abroad, rather than at home ... The production team behind *Aliens in America* seems to understand there's an analogy to be made between adolescence and immigrant culture" (2007b, K1). But Canadian critics quickly soured on *Aliens*; Alex Strachan (2007c, B8), for instance, wrote, "*Aliens*, while promising in its series opener, heads south fast with a smarmy, off-putting second episode that will air next week."

What makes these responses interesting is the light they shed on how Canadian critics saw Canadian TV (and its attendant questions of identity) in relation to US TV. They framed their responses to *Aliens in America* by talking about its quality as a sitcom, rather than focusing on questions of Islam, as US critics had done when watching *Little Mosque*. They recognized that its premise had the potential to push the limits of what viewers were used to seeing, but that was not their only focus. Some US critics identified a similar difference between the two countries: Scott Collins (2007, C14), writing in *Newsday*, thought "the premise of 'Aliens' is audacious by the standards of American TV comedies, which usually avoid any material that could be construed as remotely political. (The same is not always true elsewhere; Canadian broadcaster CBC has attracted much attention for its sitcom 'Little Mosque on the Prairie.')"

Collins's idea that a show that portrayed Muslims sympathetically was too "audacious" for US television was borne out by the controversy that surrounded the reality show *All-American Muslim*, about five Lebanese-American Muslim families living outside Detroit, Michigan. It ran from 2011 to 2012 on the cable network TLC, and it complemented the network's other shows about other minority religious groups (Lowry 2012). Although some critics were optimistic about the show's potential to humanize Muslims for non-Muslim viewers (e.g., Poniewozik 2011), other viewers found it threatening. After the show's premiere in November 2011 a conservative Christian organization called the Florida Family Association (2011) sent out email alerts to its members warning them, "All-American Muslim is propaganda that riskily hides the Islamic agenda's clear and present danger to American liberties and traditional values." It also put pressure on advertisers to pull their ads from the show, and two major advertisers – the home improvement store Lowe's and the travel website Kayak.com – did pull their ads, even if they also tried to distance themselves from the Florida Family Association when doing so (Birge 2011).

The controversy surrounding *All-American Muslim* has been well covered elsewhere.[8] Its value here comes from the insight it provides into the dynamics of representation of Islam on US television and the question of saleable diversity as it relates to *Little Mosque on the Prairie*. Viewers in the United States (as well as Canada) watched a wide range of shows that were linked through their subject matter to *Little Mosque*, such as *Aliens in America*, *All-American Muslim*, as well as *24* and the nightly news. They were also familiar shows that were linked to *Little*

Mosque through their genre, such as *The Cosby Show* and *All in the Family*, and many saw in *Little Mosque* an attempt to expand the range of representations of Islam, much as *Cosby* had done for blacks. (And these links, of course, do not exhaust the types of intertextual connections individual viewers made.) In the United States critics concentrated on intertextual connections related to subject matter – Islam and terror in particular – while in Canada they concentrated on those related to other genres and to other shows on the CBC.

Not coincidentally, the approach of Canadian critics also served a strategic function: when they drew attention to US critics' focus on terrorism, they also demonstrated one aspect of cultural difference that distinguished them from Americans. If it was true that Canadians were more open than Americans to the diversity *Little Mosque* presented, it was also true that their openness had multiple sources – a genuine curiosity about Muslims but also a desire to solidify their sense of identity. US viewers, on the whole, did not share this interpretive framework. For this reason WestWind struggled to sell that diversity to US network executives.

Little Mosque and Convergent Distribution

When WestWind finally did succeed in finding a distributor for *Little Mosque* in the United States, it was not because the diversity it presented was suddenly more saleable but because the fundamental logic of distribution changed. As convergent media have made content available in more discrete, on-demand chunks, the audience in United States has fragmented even more than it had after the rise of cable in the 1980s and 1990s. Companies such as Hulu and Netflix have begun to deliver original programs in addition to the second-run syndicated shows they license. By 2012 Hulu had released *Battleground*, a political drama set in Wisconsin, and Netflix had released *House of Cards*, a political drama starring Kevin Spacey that was one of on-demand television's first bona fide hits. But more important for WestWind was Hulu's emphasis on imported series, such as *Line of Duty*, a British police drama, and *Prisoners of War*, an Israeli series that inspired the hit *Homeland* on the premium Showtime network (Werts 2012).

Thus it was that WestWind struck a deal with Hulu to carry *Little Mosque* (whose title in the United States no longer included "on the prairie"). It premiered on 28 June 2012. According to Mary Darling, the deal came about because of the personal connection that executives at Hulu made with the show. Much like Anton Leo, who was instrumental in green-lighting *Little Mosque* at the CBC, the Hulu executives just "got it": "They knew of the show, they screened some screeners in preparation for [our] meeting, and they just wanted it." More important, Hulu had had an unexpected success with Korean shows it had imported as it looked for content to license: "Hulu launched a whole lot of Korean content for Koreans and they thought it would be something they could do to service the Korean market, but because they went through the trouble of doing subtitles, suddenly they found themselves in a position where those shows were rating really well. The comedy was translating in these Korean shows, so I think they're able to test things that otherwise don't get tested" (interview with author, 2012). In this respect *Little Mosque* appeared quite attractive: it was a solid hit in Canada, it had been syndicated in more than ninety countries, and its complete run was ready to air.

Shortly after Hulu began carrying *Little Mosque*, WestWind struck a deal with a new cable network called Pivot, which launched on 1 August 2013 with an initial reach of about 40 million US homes. Pivot was created by Participant Pictures, which had produced films such as *An Inconvenient Truth* that had a liberal activist bent. It targeted viewers between the ages of fifteen and thirty-four. Its president, Evan Shapiro, explained at its launch: "The mandate of Pivot is entertainment that inspires social change and our target is millennials, but other than that we are a general entertainment network with all types of content: drama, comedy, talk and documentaries" (quoted in Moore 2013). Pivot's initial lineup included series such as *Friday Night Lights*, a drama that had failed to attract many viewers on NBC despite the critical acclaim it received for its character development and exploration of social issues. Pivot had a hybrid strategy for finding viewers: it would make content available through conventional bundled cable subscriptions as well as through streaming apps with stand-alone subscriptions for smart phones and other portable devices.

It remains to be seen what success *Little Mosque* will have in these new environments. It appears that on-demand distribution will allow Hulu and Pivot to target narrower audience segments, lowering the threshold of financial success to a point where a show like *Little Mosque* can be sustained. But if experiments in other countries are any indication, the question of whether *Little Mosque*'s specific depiction of diversity can be successfully translated is not straightforward. WestWind might be able to sell *Little Mosque* to other networks, but will they be able to sell the show to viewers?

Canal+ and *Little Mosque*: Programming and Localized Reception

One network to which WestWind licensed *Little Mosque* was Canal+, a premium service with about 5.3 million subscribers in France, where it aired in 2007 and 2008 as *La petite mosquée dans la prairie* (Canal+ 2008, 97). Although it aired on a major network, it received little critical attention, and it circulated in a contradictory space: it was a foreign program used to meet French mandates about diversity in television, and it addressed debates central to French notions of identity while having its most visible impact at the periphery of French society. The diversity it depicted did not resonate with French viewers, even if the show met a need for Canal+.

Two trends in French broadcasting shaped how Canal+ programmed *Little Mosque* and how viewers interpreted it. The first grew out of a decade-long conversation among activists, network executives, and policymakers in France's regulatory agency, the Conseil supérieur de l'audiovisuel (CSA), about representations of minorities on French television. The second grew out of the strategies Canal+ adopted in the mid-2000s for branding itself and attracting subscribers. These trends – one cultural, one industrial – influenced each other, even when they had opposite effects: the criteria network executives used to make programming decisions often worked against the creation of programming that policymakers, under pressure from activists, wanted to encourage.

Both trends were intertwined with France's troubled relationship with its immigrant communities, especially those from North Africa, who are largely Arabic-speaking and Muslim. One of the more difficult legacies of French colonialism in North Africa is the existence of poor districts – *les banlieues* – on the outskirts of cities such as Paris, Lyons, and Marseilles. Many of the residents come from Algeria and other former colonies, and they suffer discrimination in education, housing, and employment. When they seek redress, they are put in a double bind. Much of the discrimination they face comes from their identity as North Africans, but the French government's approach to minorities is one of an official "indifference to difference." The French census, for instance, does not ask questions about religion or ethnicity. But this indifference has an unintended consequence that sociologist Éric Macé (2007, para. 5) describes as an "indifference to discrimination when, in the name of equality before the law, it becomes impossible to take de facto discrimination into account."[9] The French republican ideal, which emphasizes collective values over those of pluralism and diversity, makes it hard to put a name on the discrimination they face.

North Africans are also poorly represented on French television. The CSA began to examine representations of minorities only in 1999, after the artistic collective Égalité ("Equality"), headed by novelist Calixte Belaya, staged a series of protests at the Cannes film festival to draw attention to questions of representation. The CSA undertook a series of studies that showed that French programs featured few minorities, if any, and when minorities did appear on French screens, it was usually on imported programs. But even before the CSA published its initial report (CSA 2000b), the research it contained prompted the CSA to incorporate a clause into the licence agreement of Canal+ that obligated the network to "take into consideration the representation of diversity of origin and culture of the national community" (CSA 2000a, art. 8).[10] A year later it incorporated similar clauses into the licence agreements of TF1 and M6 and finally the other networks it had licensed by 2004 (CSA 2005).

Thus, *Little Mosque* held a certain appeal for Canal+ in that it would help the network meet part of its obligations. By Mary Darling's account, "There had just been more bombings and fires of cars or riots," and the buyer from Canal+ told her that the network's executives "thought this might be a good thing to just try to create some normalization" (interview with author, 2012). But its real appeal lay elsewhere, namely, in the way it appeared to help Canal+ in its efforts to brand itself in a crowded market. In 2007, when WestWind Pictures was working to syndicate *Little Mosque* in France, the country's television industry was worth about €7.8 billion, or a little more than 13 per cent of the overall European market. All the biggest companies were multinational corporations, including the RTL Group (based in Luxembourg, owner of M6), Vivendi (owner of Canal+), and the Société Télévision Française (owner of TF1) (Datamonitor 2008, 14–19).

It was in this context that Canal+ decided to carry *Little Mosque on the Prairie*. Canal+ had used comedy in the past to build its audience, a trend that *Little Mosque* continued. It helped the network set itself apart from its competitors (and persuade viewers to subscribe), and it was a strategy to which it was returning. As CEO Rodolphe Belmer explained about the beginning of the 2008 season, "The timing is right. People need to laugh. Also, humour is in Canal+'s genes. Finally, we have a pool of young talent at the network – writers, comedians, etc. – whom we've helped become better known these last few years. So we have what it takes to bring humour back!" (quoted in Canal+ 2008, 15).[11] At the end of 2008, when the network dropped *Little Mosque*, it was because it had shifted strategies again: "They aired the first two seasons on Canal+ and then the channel stopped focusing on comedy and didn't proceed with the other episodes" (Mary Darling, personal communication, 12 April 2013).

How was *Little Mosque* received? It aired on Saturdays at 1:30 in the afternoon. It received very little attention in trade journals such as *Le Film français*, where it warranted only three sentences before it aired (("Canal+ Accueille" 2007). It received a positive review on the Pure Médias website: "Rather than a political series, whose purpose would be to convey a message, [the show] is first of all an entertainment series to be taken as such ... *Little Mosque on the Prairie* won't thrill those who make their lives easier by putting people in boxes" ("La petite mosquée" 2007).[12] Otherwise, it did not receive critical attention. In addition, its relatively quick cancellation, not to mention the absence of public discussion by viewers, suggests it did not have a wide viewership.

So, speaking of *Little Mosque*'s reception is a bit strange in that there is little to talk about. But one event – an example of very localized reception – demonstrates how the show circulated within the contradictory environment created by France's approach to Muslim immigrants and citizens. During the month of Ramadan in 2007 the Institut des cultures de l'Islam (ICI), located in the working class Goutte d'Or neighbourhood in the north part of Paris, organized a series of evening events called the Veillées du Ramadan, during which Muslims came together to break their fast. During these events the ICI showed episodes of *Little Mosque*. As the ICI's director, Véronique Rieffel, explained, in Egypt and elsewhere a tradition had developed of breaking the fast while watching soap operas created just for Ramadan. The ICI wanted to bring that tradition to France, and the program it chose was *Little Mosque* (Desmoulières 2008).

The Veillées du Ramadan, which also included concerts, art exhibits, and public readings, had the official imprimatur of Paris's city government, which promoted them as a form of outreach to Parisians of all backgrounds (Mairie de Paris 2007). The ICI even invited Mary Darling and Clark Donnelly to give a talk about the show in October 2007. It was one point where the conversation described in chapter 1 involved WestWind executives talking directly with viewers. Their visit, however, demonstrated the contradictions of Islam in France. What made the promotion necessary was precisely the way Muslims were marginalized. The neighbourhood was isolated geographically, while its inhabitants occupied a remote region of the French psyche. Darling recalls, "We were invited into Paris ... and we went and talked at the Islamic centre, which to me really demonstrated why they're having so many issues – because the taxi driver didn't know where it was. Taxis don't go into that part of the city. Such a marginalized [group – there are] multiple forms of marginalization" (interview with author, 2012). The experience left Clark Donnelly wondering about how Islam (and *Little Mosque*) fit into French culture: "I remember when we were coming back from that talk in Paris, at this little Islamic centre, and we're driving along and going over whatever bridge with its rearing horses and golden statues, and you're thinking, 'How does this culture fit into this? Because this culture has such a strong sense of itself'" (interview with author, 2012).

Thus, the programming and reception of *Little Mosque* were symptomatic of the contradictions and divisions shaping French society. Despite airing on one of France's biggest networks, its greatest impact was felt at the margins. It made French TV more diverse, but it was an import. In this way, Éric Macé's (2007, para. 19) assessment hits the mark: "We will no doubt still have to wait before we have French proposals for antistereotypical fiction such as can be found on English-language television ... as made evident by this line of dialogue from the English Canadian program *Little Mosque on the Prairie* ... 'Do you have to wear a hijab if the swimming instructor is gay?'"[13]

TV2 Zebra and *Little Mosque* in Norway

WestWind also licensed *Little Mosque* in Norway, which has a mixed public broadcasting system. Norway's first broadcaster was the Norsk Rikskringkasting (NRK), which followed a conventional non-commercial model. The NRK launched its television service in 1960 and since then has expanded to offer other networks. In addition to the NRK Norway has a commercial broadcaster called TV2, which was launched in 1992. Its revenue comes from advertising rather than direct parliamentary appropriations, but it has a public service mandate that is part of a quid pro quo: in exchange for the service TV2 provides, the Kulturdepartementet (Ministry of Culture) gave it a monopoly on over-the-air commercial television and a guarantee that cable companies would be required to carry it (Syvertsen and Karlsen 2000, 78). *Little Mosque* aired on TV2's Zebra network in 2008 and 2010.

Little Mosque was not a big hit in Norway, in part because TV2 Zebra had a limited reach. The NRK's networks had a collective audience share in 2008 of about 40 per cent, in contrast to the share of about 30 per cent enjoyed by TV2's networks (TV2 2008, 14). TV2 Zebra, which was launched in 2004, attracted only a small fraction of TV2's viewers (about 3 per cent of the viewing audience). Its target audience was young men, and it programmed mostly sports and shows about various forms of competition.[14]

Like Canal+ (and the CBC), Norway's public service networks have mandates to reflect the country's diversity. As of 1996 the NRK, for instance, was required to "support, create and develop Norwegian culture, art and entertainment" and to "broadcast programmes for ethnic and linguistic minorities" (quoted in Syvertsen and Karlsen 2000, 75).[15] The Kulturdepartementet gave TV2 a similar mandate when it launched in 1992. In 2001, when the network negotiated a new licence to cover 2003–9 (the years during which *Little Mosque* had its first run), the Kulturdepartementet included a set of clauses similar to the NRK's, two of which related to diversity: "Art. 3.3.6: TV2 will have its own programs that reflect the diversity of Norwegian and international culture … Art. 3.3.8: TV2 will have its own programs or program segments for ethnic minorities" (Norway 2001).[16]

Although TV2 had these mandates, its 2008 annual report suggests they did not factor into executives' decision to carry *Little Mosque*. In both cases TV2 focused on programs it produced itself. In the first case it highlighted *Sarahs fornemmelse av kultur* ("Sarah's Sense of Culture"), which presented Norwegian and foreign artists, such as Marcus Paus, a composer who was working to turn Roald Dahl's *The Witches* into an opera for children (TV2 2008, 48). In the case of the second mandate it presented examples such as *Velkommen til Norge* ("Welcome to Norway"), which told the story of a refugee family from the Congo through the eyes of an eight-year-old child, and *Gudene vet* ("God Knows"), which discussed religious beliefs of ethnic minorities in Norway. The report explained, "Several representatives of minority groups in Norway participated in the show [*Gudene vet*], such as Afshan Rafiq, Norway's first member of Parliament from an immigrant background. As a modern Norwegian Muslim with a political career and a family, she is a role model for many. What does she think about the position of women in traditional Norwegian and Pakistani culture?" (TV2 2008, 54)[17]

Rather than responding to the mandates in its licence, the annual report suggests that TV2, like Canal+, was following a specific, long-standing programming strategy: it was branding itself as a source for quality foreign programming. "High-profile and fresh series from abroad are part of TV2's identity," it explained. "We ... introduced Norwegian viewers to *X-Files*, *Friends*, *NYPD Blue*, *24*, and *Ally McBeal*. Buyers from the major television markets are envious when they hear how many of the big Hollywood productions have gone on TV2" (TV2 2008, 42).[18] In 2008 the big shows from the United States were *Grey's Anatomy*, *Desperate Housewives*, *Cane*, *Brothers and Sisters*, *Californication*, and *Criminal Minds*, although the most watched foreign show (a series called *Anna Pihl*, which had 636,000 viewers) came from Denmark (ibid., 42–3).

Little Mosque did not figure in TV2's annual report. From an economic standpoint, it was only a modest success, achieving audience shares between 0.9 and 2.4 per cent in 2008 (John Ranelagh, interview with author, 2012). John Ranelagh, a programmer for TV2 Zebra, explains that sitcoms on the network tend to receive lower ratings because they usually do not air in prime time; *Little Mosque*'s performance was "OK – nothing special" (interview with author, 2012). The show received limited critical attention when it aired, usually in articles that described its success in Canada and the aspirations its makers had for it (Eriksen 2008). It reminded critics of *Northern Exposure* (CBS, 1990–5), which aired in Norway as *Det gode liv i Alaska* ("The Good Life in Alaska"). Like *Little Mosque*, *Northern Exposure* told a fish-out-of-water story about a professional from the big city who moved to a small town for a job. In *Northern Exposure* the professional was a Jewish doctor from New York rather than an imam from Toronto, but his presence made possible a similar urban-rural tension that served as a source of conflict and plot.

Much as in the case of Canal+, it is difficult to speak of *Little Mosque*'s reception in Norway because it was not widely viewed. TV2 Zebra's relative newness and limited reach did not help, nor did the thematic mismatch between *Little Mosque* and the sports programming that dominates TV2 Zebra. But also as in the case of Canal+, Mary Darling and Clark Donnelly did reach a different audience by travelling to Norway, much as they had to France, to address a group of viewers directly. In this case they spoke to an elite group of media professionals at the Nordic Media Festival in Bergen in 2008. They even participated in a panel called "Islamists 1, Freedom of Expression 0?"[19] which the event's organizers described in the following terms in their report: "The Canadian series [*Little Mosque*] manages the difficult balancing act of laughing at religious and cultural differences. Can Norwegian editors find the same balance? Or will Norway sleep at the moment when freedom of expression is being put to the test? The Muhammed cartoons provoked some strong reactions. Are Norwegian editors giving in to the pressure from Islamic fundamentalists, or is it not journalistically relevant to print the controversial cartoons?" (Nordiske Mediedager 2008, 5)[20] At the same conference Donnelly said, "We have received some inquiries from conservative Christians who say that we normalize the Muslims too much. Then I think we've done something right" (quoted in ibid., 23).[21]

In contrast to the marginalized viewers in France, the localized audience Darling and Donnelly addressed in Norway comprised an elite, cosmopolitan class. They were there to sell *Little Mosque*, and they had to balance cultural issues with economic ones: "So, first of all, if you're a buyer, at the front of it, it has to be a comedy that they think will rate. It has to be a show that they think can go the long run, but what the conversation would – without a doubt – turn toward would be the issues that people are having with Islam in their countries" (Darling, interview with author, 2012). But the show's limited impact among TV2 Zebra's viewers suggests they got more traction among the elite group of people attending the Nordic Media Festival. The diversity *Little Mosque* presented was more saleable among network executives than among network viewers.

Conclusion: Saleable Diversity and International Audiences

The conditions in which *Little Mosque* circulated were paradoxical: international syndication was a necessary condition for its domestic production and circulation. This paradox is not unique to *Little Mosque*. In fact, Serra Tinic (2005) identifies a similar pattern among producers in Vancouver, who make up for cuts in domestically funded programs by turning to international joint ventures and then using the profits to fund their domestic projects. In their case the joint ventures frequently resulted in bland programming designed to sell anywhere, while the productions they made possible were distinctive. In the case of *Little Mosque* the opposite was true: it was a distinctive program, which created a different set of challenges in attracting viewers outside Canada. In this way these conditions reveal the contingent nature of saleability and diversity. What made *Little Mosque* saleable differed from one context to another, in part because the questions that network executives and viewers were asking about diversity were rooted in different social and cultural contexts.

Little Mosque circulated through different publics in Canada, the United States, France, and Norway. Members of those publics interpreted it through different frames and drew on different intertextual references. When Canadians watched the first two seasons, as chapter 3 showed, their frames related to genre, to the CBC, to national identity, and to terror. They related it to other CBC programs, other sitcoms (especially *All in the Family*), as well as to the news and to dramas such as *24*. Their interpretations ranged widely, from "hokey" to "threatening," but no single interpretation dominated. In the United States, in contrast, the dominant frame was terror, and the main intertextual touchpoints were *The Cosby Show* (as an example of the type of program that might help disassociate Islam from terror) and dramas such as *24*. Within this frame *Little Mosque* was either "audacious" in its depictions of Muslims, or it was threatening because it glossed over Islam's links to terror. In France and Norway the viewing communities that paid attention to *Little Mosque* were narrower, and the interpretations arrived at by members of those groups were closely related to their specific situations. Muslim viewers in Paris saw the show through the lens of the treatment they themselves had experienced, which made the show refreshing and different, especially in contrast to the images of Islam they saw on French television. Norwegian viewers at the Nordic Media Festival saw the show through the lens of the controversy about the publication of the Muhammed cartoons in Denmark, and it gave them an opportunity to discuss their own responsibilities as media professionals. It provided a point of contrast – a successful use of humour to talk about Islam – that cast their own decisions about the cartoons controversy in a new light.

Chapter 5

Religion as Culture versus Religion as Belief

If the preceding chapters have shown anything, it is that the paradox of saleable diversity imposes a limit on the project of cultural translation. The people who made *Little Mosque on the Prairie* wanted to explain Muslims by expanding the range of characters viewers saw, but they could not push too far because they had to appeal to viewers' sense of the universal, at the expense of the particular. They wanted to show Muslim characters experiencing the full range of human emotions, but they could attribute characters' anger or frustration only to personal shortcomings, not to structural factors such as institutionalized racism. They wanted to talk about Islam in other national contexts, but commercial imperatives overrode cultural ones, and international network executives took more interest in the show than international viewers.

But the paradox of saleable diversity is not absolute, nor is it unassailable. People acting as cultural translators are reflexive in their practice, constantly evaluating and re-evaluating their approach and the results it yields. They recognize when their approach fails, and they do not sit idly by. In the case of *Little Mosque*, the executive producers were concerned by the third season that Islam had become merely an ornament, a trait that functioned more as accident than essence. They thought *Little Mosque* had become little more than a conventional sitcom: it was an ethnic comedy whose structure would not be fundamentally changed if the trait that marked characters as different were something else. The show was saleable, but was it meaningfully diverse?

Little Mosque's executive producers negotiated with CBC executives to resolve this problem, and they decided to abandon each episode's conventional return to stasis and to adopt a serial structure. They wanted to do two seemingly contradictory things: depict Muslims in new ways and, in an act of televisual metacognition, suggest that television was inadequate in representing actual Muslims in North America. The serial structure allowed them to do both. They could show characters' evolution and mark what Mary Darling called a "measurable transformation" in a character (interview with author, 2011). They could also develop characters in ways that viewers accustomed to formulaic sitcoms might not expect. Writers and producers could challenge the essentialism of the first seasons by exploring how characters grew more complex over time. They could also suggest, at least implicitly, that characters could not simply stand in for actual people: if characters could evolve, then surely actual people could, too, and they might not do so in the same way. After all, once a series is finished, its form is fixed, but the people it purported to represent continue to change. The tools of representation as a form of image creation are inadequate because they cannot keep up with the dynamic nature of the people they depict.

In this chapter I ask how *Little Mosque*'s production team used this new structure to address the limits of saleable diversity. I place their choices in the context of the conversation about Islam in post-9/11 North America I described in earlier chapters, but I shift my focus because the participants in that conversation had changed. By the third season fewer viewers – and fewer critics – were talking about *Little Mosque* in broad-circulation publications (or similar public venues) because they had largely made up their minds about whether they liked the show or not. The initial controversy it sparked had died down: an idea that had once been surprising – that the CBC would produce a sitcom about Muslims – became routine and even comfortable, precisely because *Little Mosque* had been on the air for two seasons. Viewers who had not liked the show stopped watching. Only at the end of the its run did critics again publish responses, this time to assess whether *Little Mosque* had lived up to its initial hype.

My focus in this chapter, as a result, is on the top half of figure 1, presented in chapter 1. By the end of season 3 executives at the CBC and the producers at WestWind were sensitive to the perception that *Little Mosque* depicted an interfaith or ecumenical utopia that was no longer anchored in the conflicts in the world outside of television. The serial structure they adopted allowed them to reintroduce conflict, in part by replacing the avuncular Rev. Duncan Magee, Amaar's ally through the first three seasons, with the proud, hard-edged Rev. William Thorne (played by Brandon Firla). In this chapter I closely examine Thorne's development and evolution. His story is one of ambivalent redemption:

his pride causes him to alienate the townspeople of Mercy, and he must learn humility to regain their trust.

I also examine on the evolution of the character Sarah Hamoudi, who had converted to Islam to marry her husband, Yasir. The actor who played Yasir, Carlo Rota, was less available for taping after the fourth season, making only a handful of appearances in the fifth, and leaving the show entirely in the sixth. The writers explained his disappearance as the result of a divorce, which left Sarah with a choice about whether to return to Anglicanism. Her story arc during season 6 was about that choice, and it was the subject of negotiations between CBC and WestWind executives, who wanted very different outcomes. As such, it was the best example of the negotiation that characterizes cultural translation – Darling and Donnelly acted as intermediaries, explaining Muslims to non-Muslims, but they had to work within a set of constraints that limited the types of interpretation they could perform. CBC executives wanted Sarah to convert back to Christianity because they thought that was what viewers would expect. Darling and Donnelly wanted her choice to grow out of her experience, even if that meant surprising viewers. In other words, at the risk of being reductive, the CBC wanted saleability, while WestWind executives wanted diversity.

I focus on these two characters for three reasons: first, they allowed *Little Mosque*'s makers to ask new questions about Islam in North America; second, they were the subject of more negotiation among the production team than any other characters; and third, they evolved more than any other characters.[1] Their storylines also converge at the series' end when Sarah accidentally burns down the church and Amaar, who has built a new mosque, invites Thorne and his congregation to worship there.

These two characters are valuable in another way as well. Mary Darling and Clark Donnelly spoke with me at length about two different approaches to religion. Is it a matter of belief, they asked, or of culture? They wanted to talk about belief, but the CBC, as they saw it, wanted to talk about culture. Rev. William Thorne and Sarah Hamoudi came to represent the two sides of that debate: Thorne gave voice to the idea of religion as culture, while Sarah, in her doubt and reflection about her religious identity, gave voice to the concept of religion as belief. By tying their storylines together the producers staged a symbolic resolution to the conflict between these views, where belief won out.

As in past chapters my approach here is thematic and chronological. I begin by fleshing out the culture/belief dichotomy, as Darling and

Donnelly (and others) saw it. I then examine how their concern about belief led them to introduce a serial structure and how they used seriality as a tool, first at the end of season 2 and throughout season 3 (when they experimented by introducing a love interest for Rayyan, the town's doctor), then in seasons 4 and 5 (when they introduced Thorne) and season 6 (when Sarah explored her faith and Thorne found redemption). The show's seriality and the convergence of Sarah's and Thorne's storylines showed that the limits of the paradox of saleable diversity could be pushed, even if they could not be overcome entirely. I conclude by looking at critics' assessment of the series after it ended.

Religion as Culture versus Religion as Belief

In a critique of the show, religious scholar Lauren Osborne (2012) writes that in it religion is reduced to culture, and "the storylines in *Little Mosque* do not address the topic of religious belief, despite the fact that religion is ostensibly at the root of the series ... Can such a comedic television show depict or do justice to belief, or does the topic naturally resist comedy?" The distinction also played an important role for the CBC and *Little Mosque*'s producers. Darling and Donnelly agreed with Osborne, and Donnelly even called her piece "one of the most intelligent articles we've ever seen about the show" (interview with author, 2012).[2]

The concern to present Islam as a function of the beliefs Muslims shared (rather than merely a set of cultural practices) had shaped *Little Mosque* since its inception. As chapter 3 described, the first season was topic driven because writers were trying to discover who the characters were and what motivated them. But everyone – the originator, the executive producers, CBC executives, and critics and viewers – wanted the show to be character driven, in line with the conventions of the sitcom. By the second season actors had grown into their roles, and writers had found ways to craft the characters to suit the actors. Stories began to grow out of the relationships between characters more than the practice of Islam. *Little Mosque* continued to have its "pedagogical effect," as I wrote in chapter 2, but critics found it to be less stilted.

The executive producers, however, were frustrated by a change that took place between season 1, when writers could take time to explore the nuances of Islam, and season 2, when they had to adopt a "factory model" to keep up with the faster production pace the longer season required (Darling, interview with author, 2011). They thought questions of belief were no longer central: the characters could have been members of a different minority without changing the show substantially. The solution, as they saw it, was to do away with the return to stasis. Darling explains, "So by the time we hit season 3, we went and talked to the CBC and said ... we just thought with religion or spirituality ... to address transformational occurrences in a person's life, there's some measurable that goes with that, right? ... I was feeling very much like we're missing the heart now. We're missing the thing where ... a character can have memory ... I want there to be a memory of where we've been so that we can begin to measure where we want to go" (interview with author, 2011).

But that change did not address the more fundamental disagreement between WestWind and the CBC. Each understood character motivation differently. CBC executives saw religious motivations as predominantly cultural. In this they shared much in common with policy practitioners from across a range of federal domains, who tended to subsume "consideration of religious diversity in the design, implementation, and evaluation of public policies ... under the more general rubric of 'culture'" (Gaye and Kunz 2009, 44). In the CBC's specific case the Broadcasting Act framed its responsibilities to viewers in cultural (or regional) terms, as described in chapter 2. The category "culture" fit more neatly into network executives' conception of diversity than the category "religion."

Darling and Donnelly saw this mindset as reductive: "I think the prevailing viewpoint is that characters adhere to a religion for strictly cultural reasons, and if that's the case, then ... perhaps Yasir tended to be a bit that way, you know, whose religion is good for business." When they would assert, "it's a religious comedy," the CBC "kicked it back and said, 'No, no, it's a cultural comedy.'" Ultimately, "it's hard for people to understand that people with real belief – who actually believe something – that is their character, it becomes their character ..." (Donnelly, interview with author, 2012). They wanted characters who were motivated by an earnest, firmly held belief about the unseen and unprovable that might defy explanation (at least among those who saw religion as mere cultural ornament) but still motivated people to act. According to Darling:

> We were always able to get a better hearing [with the CBC] when we were like, "Hello! There's a mosque in a church! Hello! Our characters *believe* in something. The reason that they're not kissing in the back alley in secret is

that they're adhering to something that they believe." The reason that we don't have our characters touching is because [of their beliefs]. So people said, "No, we want to hear from characters." Well, we *are* hearing it from characters, but I mean talk about a fine line, a fine balance, because you have to still get a hearing from your broadcaster, you still have to get episodes approved, you still have to get – while there's still a misfire, a misunderstanding on what makes characters actually tick. (Interview with author, 2012)

These divergent views were made manifest in different ways through the course of *Little Mosque*'s run. In its early seasons religion as culture dominated, but by the end, as the next sections show, WestWind was able to persuade the CBC to incorporate elements of religion as belief.

Seasons 2 and 3: Strategies for Talking about Unspoken Norms

Before they could explore religion as belief, the producers first had to implement a serial structure. One of the first things they did was introduce a story arc involving Rayyan, Amaar, and a new character named J.J. (played by Stephen Lobo), who first appeared near the end of season 2. Up to that point there had been an understated romantic tension between Rayyan and Amaar. In many ways, such a tension is a conventional aspect of the sitcom, especially the workplace sitcom (Hartley 2001). However, in the case of *Little Mosque* there were limits to how that tension could play out, given Rayyan's and Amaar's observance of Muslim mores concerning relations between men and women. As such, the tension frequently served as a vehicle for conveying information about Muslim customs, for example, when writers would give Rayyan dialogue explaining why she refused to shake hands with a man to whom she was not related or why she insisted on wearing a hijab. When J.J. was introduced, he became Rayyan's love interest, although in a similar way, which allowed writers to provide information about Islam to viewers, for example, about the need for an unmarried man and woman to have a chaperone when out on a date. The Amaar-Rayyan-J.J. triangle provided another source of conflict and misunderstanding in line with sitcom conventions, while also showing the results of the producers' decision to abandon the return to stasis. Over the course of season 3 Rayyan and J.J. became engaged and planned a wedding (again, treated in a way that explained Muslim customs), but J.J. left Rayyan (and the show) in the season finale. The Amaar-Rayyan story arc continued during seasons 4 and 5, and the couple married at the end of season 5.

But the focus was still largely on culture rather than belief. In individual episodes writers contrived situations where characters talked about things they normally would not need to discuss explicitly because they belonged to the set of unspoken norms they shared with other Muslims, at least on the show.[3] One strategy they used was to give characters a task that related to the norm.[4] Consider the episode "Security Alert" (season 2, episode 18). The plot concerned Rayyan and J.J.'s efforts to find someone to chaperone their first date. Throughout the episode, characters discuss the need for a chaperone, but not the beliefs that ground that need, and the dialogue is filtered through the conventions of the sitcom. For instance, in a scene in the first act Rayyan is in Fatima's café and she is talking to Sarah, who says she can't chaperone Rayyan's date because she'll be watching *Magnum P.I.* with Yasir. Rayyan turns to Fatima.

RAYYAN: Hey Fatima, can you chaperone my date with J.J. tonight?
FATIMA: I have to work.
SARAH: That's okay. Rayyan and J.J. could just have dinner here.
RAYYAN: No, I don't want our first date to be at Fatima's. (Fatima scowls.) Sets the bar too high – the second date could only disappoint.
FATIMA: Nice try. What about Baber? (The women look at Baber as the camera pans to him.)
BABER (looks up): What? Do I have crumbs on my beard?
SARAH: Rayyan needs a chaperone for a date.
BABER: I see. What sort of date?
RAYYAN: J.J. and I want to go see a movie tonight, *Gabriel's Heart*.
BABER: No! None of the sinful night dating! If I am going to be chaperone, we will go on a proper outing in the daytime. I propose a nature hike!
RAYYAN: *Magnum P.I.* it is. (Gets up to leave.)
SARAH: Is night dating really sinful?
BABER: No, I just don't want to watch a movie called *Gabriel's Heart*.

Rayyan and J.J. never explain why they need a chaperone because the other characters take the need for granted, but they do make it an explicit object of discussion. The episode points to a challenge the writers faced. It achieves its pedagogical effect not by teaching, which producers feared would alienate viewers, but by bringing such assumptions into the foreground as part of the dialogue.

Another strategy was to embed discussions in familiar sitcom "scripts," such as a break-up scene where one party tries to let the other down softly. Sitcoms rely heavily on iterations of such scripts, where writers maintain the structure of the conversation but change the details of the content. Indeed, one of the pleasures of watching comes from the recognition of such scripts. Later in the same episode, for instance, Rayyan and J.J. finally agree to use Baber as their chaperone, and the date is a disaster. In the episode's resolution, Baber enters Fatima's diner, where Rayyan and J.J. are eating, and tells them that he will teach them to play bocce ball.

> RAYYAN: Actually, Baber, J.J. and I were thinking, we really had fun today, but it might be best if the three of us didn't go out any more.
> BABER: You're calling it quits? But you've only had one date.
> J.J.: No, what Rayyan means, I think, is it might be best if the two of us didn't go out with, well, *you*.
> BABER: You don't want to go out with me anymore? Is there somebody else, somebody younger?
> J.J.: No, no, we just don't want to get tied down to one chaperone right now.
> BABER: Don't give me that old line!
> RAYYAN: We just know that you're going to make some young couple a *wonderful* chaperone one day.
> BABER: Why don't you just leave!
> J.J.: Baber, listen –
> BABER: Just go! Go!

The final scene, a few days later, casts Baber as the "jilted" chaperone who must interact awkwardly with the new chaperone, Yasir.

These episodes made viewers aware of customs followed by many Muslims, but they lacked mention of the sources of the customs or, more to the point for *Little Mosque*'s producers, what would prompt characters to make choices that likely appeared strange to viewers. In the second and third seasons they also focused largely on issues internal to the world of Mercy, Saskatchewan, in contrast to the ongoing sectarian conflict in the outside world. It was those conflicts that prompted the CBC's Anton Leo and *Little Mosque*'s executive producers to alter the show once again, this time by replacing the well-loved Rev. Duncan Magee with his opposite, the hard-edged and bigoted Rev. William Thorne.

Season 4: Rev. William Thorne and Conflict in the World

As *Little Mosque* ended its third season, executives at both the CBC and WestWind felt it had drifted from the makers' original vision. It had become too comfortable, "a nirvana of [sorts] ... ecumenical perfection, where ... if the imam's [and reverend's] congregation would just ... do what [they think] they should do, the world would be a great place" (Darling, interview with author, 2011). The world, on the other hand, was not so rosy. The Taliban were resurgent in Afghanistan, where the United States was still waging part of its war on terror. Peace talks had stalled (again) between Israelis and Palestinians. In late 2009 Nidal Malik Hasan shot and killed thirteen soldiers at Fort Hood, Texas. Fear of Islamic extremism was rising, at least among Americans (Pew Research Center 2009). Anton Leo was especially concerned. News about Islam was cyclical, he noted: "There was a time where every front page of every newspaper during the beginnings of *Little Mosque* was about Muslims and terrorism, and then the bottom fell out of the economy around the world, and it became less of – that fear of outsiders became a fear of total and complete global economic collapse" (interview with author, 2011). The time had come, he thought, to bring attention back to the conflict in the world.[5]

It was in this context that Leo and Darling decided to introduce Rev. William Thorne. His introduction was controversial, both among *Little Mosque*'s makers and among viewers. As such, it was the subject of negotiations among Zarqa Nawaz, WestWind Pictures, and Anton Leo. What was at stake was not just the direction of the show but the more fundamental question of the meaning of Islam in post-9/11 North America. In a narrow sense, according to Nawaz, through season 3 *Little Mosque* provided an idealized outlet for Muslims who wanted to escape the conflict they experienced in their everyday lives. It provided what many found to be a persuasive argument about how Muslims could or should belong to North American society; Thorne reminded them of what they were escaping (interview with author, 2011).

In a broader sense Thorne's introduction provided another analytical point of entry into the contrast *Little Mosque*'s makers were making between religion as culture and religion as belief. He was, in Darling's words, "a man of the Church," while Magee was "a man of God" (interview with author, 2011). He was preoccupied with the trappings of the Church, and he was especially concerned with prestige, which for him meant having a large congregation in Toronto.

His presence contributed to the culture/belief divide in a second way, too. What the show lost when he arrived was a fictive ecumenism that characterized the relationship between Amaar and Magee. In retrospect, that ecumenism came to appear as a form of religion as belief. It grew out of the idea that Amaar and Magee related to each other on the basis of their underlying beliefs, which were fundamentally the same, even if they were expressed through different religious traditions. This notion of ecumenism reflected Darling's and Donnelly's beliefs as Bahá'ís: "If people really understood the foundations of their religion, the Jews and Christians and Muslims are all people of the book,[6] and they actually foretell one of the other and they agree and each recognizes the other and – meaning, the messengers anyway, they each refer to each other – what are we really disagreeing about here?" (Darling, interview with author, 2011).

The idea to create Thorne came first from Leo, who developed it with Darling. Leo felt that "the dramaturgy of the show required some more conflict" (interview with author, 2011). Darling agreed: conflict with Thorne would help with her desire to mark characters' evolution over time: "conflict moves story forward and causes character to grow" (interview with author, 2011). Thorne is proud, and he does not want to be in Mercy. When he arrives, he does not even know the church is sharing its space with the Muslims. His contempt for the townspeople, not to mention the Muslims in "his" church, is tangible throughout the season 4 premiere. It is encapsulated at the end of the episode, where he is standing in the pulpit on Sunday morning, after inviting Amaar to attend. A series of tighter and tighter close-ups frame Amaar and Thorne as Thorne says in grandiloquent tones, "My brothers and sisters, Jesus urged us to love our enemies, enemies who say that Jesus was a prophet, and not the messiah. Love them, enemies who pray in gibbering tongues, dressed in colourful, outlandish garb. Choke back your gorge and love them. Yes, my brothers and sisters, love your enemies, but never forget, *they are your enemies.*" Darling admits "we [brought] him in a little bit of a too heavy-handed way," but that first episode, "probably more than the rest of them, tried to show what we're going after, and that is a conversation which puts Amaar back on his heels a little bit and creates a world in Mercy which is more in sync with the world outside, and sees Amaar struggling to get his footing, all the while being constantly hit with – first of all, Rev. Thorne arrives – he doesn't know that Rev. Magee allowed the mosque to set up inside the church, he's surprised to find it, and you're not even sure – does he like brown people? You just don't know really who this guy is – that's the real world" (interview with author, 2011).

Not everyone liked Thorne. Nawaz, for instance, notes that many viewers were upset when Magee left because, she speculates, they wanted to see the ecumenism the show depicted. Muslim viewers were especially upset: "I thought that they would ... understand where that character was coming from. But in fact they were watching that show for sort of this fantasy of us all getting together, and it sort of disoriented them, so you know after that season, we tried to soften him. And he did become a more interesting character. But I did notice that it affected our ratings, and that people were angry whenever they would talk to me about how strongly they felt" (interview with author, 2011). Darling thought Thorne made *Little Mosque* feel "just like the rest of the real world" for Muslim viewers, where they faced discrimination and distrust; Magee's church was "a place where they could go that wasn't engaged in that conversation where they have to engage in every day" (interview with author, 2011).

Indeed, the story arc that carried through the fourth season involved Thorne's efforts to evict the Muslims from the church. In the early episodes he refuses to sign a formal lease with Amaar, after discovering that Amaar and Magee had only an informal agreement. In later episodes, Thorne manipulates Baber into ousting Amaar once he learns that Amaar can serve as imam only as long as he has the popular support of the members of the mosque. Thorne encourages Baber to institute a conservative dress code for women, which Amaar refuses to enforce. Baber in turn convinces a majority the mosque's board to fire Amaar. But when Baber takes over as imam, he goes too far and invites an ultra-conservative "reformer" from the outside to help reshape the mosque. The reformer alienates even Baber himself, and the changes he institutes (such as allowing a band of travelling Muslims to set up camp in the mosque, where they cook over an open flame and hang their laundry to dry) frighten Thorne's parishioners. Thorne uses his parishioners' concern as an excuse to kick the Muslims out of the church, since they do not have a formal lease. The season finale begins with an extended Broadway-style dance sequence where Thorne celebrates the success of the coup he has manufactured. But his celebration is cut short when he learns that the bishop is coming to visit, and he is eager to see the mosque, which he thinks is an exciting effort to encourage interfaith dialogue. Thorne, who realizes that impressing the bishop would be good for his career, has to scramble to convince Amaar to come back and reassemble his congregation. Amaar uses the opportunity to sign a formal lease with Thorne, and he resumes his role as imam.

Seasons 5 and 6: Thorne's Redemption

Turning Thorne's triumph into defeat allowed *Little Mosque*'s writers to set up a story arc over the course of the final two seasons where Thorne could redeem himself. In this section I consider this story arc as it intertwines with that of Sarah, the character who converted to Islam when she married Yasir. During season 5 the actor who played Yasir, Carlo Rota, was in high demand, with guest roles on shows such as *The Mentalist*, *Bones*, and *Breaking Bad*. As he got more Hollywood roles, he became hard to schedule in Toronto and Saskatchewan, where *Little Mosque* was shot. He left the show altogether after season 5. Yasir's absence was explained by his divorce from Sarah, who thus lost her original reason for converting. Over the course of season 6, she deals with the divorce and has to decide whether to remain Muslim. Her exploration of belief provides a thematic counterpoint to Thorne's efforts to redeem himself. She explores her own doubt, and he explores his own conviction. She finds strength as she asks what Islam means to her and how faith comes from family and personal history, and he finds humility as he opens to the possibility that people with different beliefs are not inherently wrong. Sarah's actions also bring about the conditions in which Thorne can demonstrate his humility: as she reflects on her choice, she visits the church and accidentally knocks over a lighted censer, and she burns down the church. In the series finale Amaar invites Thorne and his congregation to worship in Mercy's brand new mosque, and Thorne accepts his offer of hospitality.

Thorne's redemption begins in season 5. At the beginning of the season, townspeople are angry with him, and early in the first episode he asks a congregant why. She says, "You're a snake in the grass!" When Thorne asks what he did to her, she says, "First, you turned us against those nice Muslims. Then you kicked them out of their mosque. And then, this." She holds up her cell phone and shows him a video where he falls to the ground and cries, "It can't be! You can't leave me here in this one-horse town filled with morons and imbeciles!" She then informs Thorne that she has posted the video to "the YouTube" (season 5, episode 1).

To recover, Thorne has to learn humility, and he has to appeal to Amaar, his nemesis, for help. Amaar, in turn, has to find a way to trust and forgive Thorne. But at first Thorne struggles to earn Amaar's trust because he approaches Amaar cynically and tries to manipulate him into becoming his friend. In "Roomies" (season 5, episode 5), for instance, Amaar must find a place to stay when the roof of his loft begins to leak. Against his better judgment he agrees to stay with Thorne in the parsonage. When he tries to find a hotel for the second night, Thorne reserves all the rooms in town, forcing him to stay longer. But over the course of the season Thorne and Amaar have a number of tête-à-têtes where Thorne pleads with Amaar, with varying degrees of sincerity, to realize how much they have in common. Amaar finally acquiesces and continues to live in the parsonage, where Thorne does things like cook extravagant meals for him, and they develop a tenuous friendship. By the end of the season Thorne even helps throw a bachelor party for Amaar, who proposed to Rayyan in the season's premiere. Of course, he is not entirely reformed: at the bachelor party he tries to outdo Rev. Duncan Magee, who makes a guest appearance, by organizing a paint-ball party where Muslims face off against Christians.

The point, according to Mary Darling, was to soften Thorne's character and demonstrate the potential for change. She compares Thorne to *All In the Family*'s Archie Bunker and explains the production team humanized him "by giving him his ... Edith Bunker in a way. Because Archie could be racist until the cows come home, but Edith was the moderator that showed the audience that the writers knew it was wrong, right? And I think in [the fifth] season ... we give him some of that moderation both with Amaar" and with a love interest named Rose (interview with author, 2011). Indeed, by the end of season 5 Thorne recognizes he is beginning to feel at home. He befriends the women in the church's quilting circle, with whom he shares an affinity based on their sharp and cutting wit (season 5, episode 9). In a later episode he and Magee, who is visiting for Amaar's bachelor party, are having coffee at Fatima's, and Thorne comments that something's different – the coffee seems better somehow. Magee says it hasn't changed:

MAGEE: I think I know what's going on here.
THORNE: What?
MAGEE: You've got a bad case of the Mercys. You're beginning to fit in, my friend.
THORNE: You take that back!
MAGEE: It starts with the coffee, and before you know it, the town seems a little less stinky.

THORNE: But the town is less stinky. I mean, have you seen the new flower pots on Main Street? (Gasps.) By the band-aids of Lazarus, it's true! I've got the Mercys! How could this happen? (Season 5, episode 12)

Thorne even falls into a comfortable relationship with Baber, who became imam when Amaar and Rayyan left for their honeymoon. It is an oddly ecumenical relationship, like the photographic negative of Amaar and Magee through seasons 1 to 3. It is based on what on the surface looks like mutual contempt: the two religious leaders get along by constantly reminding each other that one is right and the other wrong. It is a comfortable mode of interaction for both Thorne and Baber, but one that ironically allows them to be friends. For instance, in "The Dating Game" (season 6, episode 4) Amaar has nominated Mercy for a multifaith award given by an organization in Toronto, and Thorne and Baber object. Amaar is sitting in Thorne's office, talking to Thorne and Baber, who are standing side by side. The shot/reverse-shot set-up emphasizes Thorne and Baber's similarity by putting them in the same frame, where they make similarly derisive comments. Despite the literal content of their dialogue, their comfortable interactions say they like each other and enjoy sharing a sense of superiority over Amaar:

THORNE: Now why would you nominate us for a multifaith award without even mentioning it first?

AMAAR: I did. I sat right here and I said I'm submitting us for the multifaith spirit award.

THORNE: Oh, see, I heard "multi-use table saw."

BABER: When did you do this? And by "when" I mean, what were you thinking?

AMAAR: Look, Mercy is a unique place. We're pioneers of multifaith, and we can inspire others to be the same.

BABER (reading a letter from the multifaith organization): "For your belief that no religion is superior to the others"? (Laughs with Thorne.) I understand the words, but the sentence makes no sense!

THORNE: Yeah, who in their right mind thinks that every religion is equal?

AMAAR: Me.

BABER: Yes, but you're not normal.

THORNE: No.

AMAAR: I mean look at you two. Look how well you guys get along.

BABER (wagging his finger): We do not get along well. We *disagree* well.

THORNE: Yes, the only thing we agree on is that one of us is wrong. (Points to Baber.)

Scenes such as this mark a real shift from the first and second seasons of *Little Mosque*. Much like those of the early seasons, there is an earnestness to the scene, and Amaar's lines convey the message that Zarqa Nawaz and WestWind Pictures wanted to communicate. The overtness of the message is clear later in the episode, when the multifaith organization gives Amaar the award after Thorne and Baber mock each other's faiths in front of the judge. But the ease in Thorne and Baber's relationship works to draw what they say into question, and the contrast between Thorne's character when he is introduced and his character after he has gained a sense of humility is enough to raise the question of whether he still means what he says. As season 6 progresses, the writers give him actions that contradict his words, and in the final episode Thorne is able to accept Amaar's offer of a space to worship in the new mosque he has built. The Thorne of season 4 would have been too proud to accept this hospitality; that the Thorne of season 6 is able to do so demonstrates the "measurable transformation" he has undergone. More important, this transformation works against the paradox of saleable diversity. It is not, of course, a repudiation of that logic – the writers still used Thorne's apparent bigotry to generate humour – but it does demonstrate that the need to limit the range of characters' emotional experience is not absolute.

Season 6: Sarah's Choice

Season 5 ends with Amaar and Rayyan's wedding, after which they leave for their honeymoon. The first scene of the season 6 premiere shows them returning and talking about Rayyan's parents' divorce. The announcement was a surprise to viewers; although Yasir had been absent much of season 5 (on the pretence of visiting his overbearing mother in Lebanon), there was no indication that a divorce was imminent, and the scripts in season 6 did not offer much of an explanation. In fact, many viewers were disappointed to lose one of the only representations of a middle-aged couple in a long-standing, loving relationship (Donnelly, interview with author, 2012).

The unavailability of the actor who played Yasir left WestWind with a series of decisions, which were the subject of more negotiation between WestWind and the CBC than perhaps any other in the show's six seasons. First, they had to account for Yasir's absence: would it be death or divorce? Second, they had to decide how they would deal with Sarah's reaction: would they force her to make a choice, or would they allow her story to remain open-ended? Finally, they had to decide what Sarah's choice would be: would she remain Muslim, or would she return to the Anglicanism of her youth? The CBC and WestWind disagreed on all three points. CBC executives thought that viewers would be more willing to accept a divorce than a death, that they wanted closure to Sarah's story, and that they expected her to return to Christianity. Darling and Donnelly wanted the opposite: they thought that death was a more plausible explanation than divorce, that Sarah's quest should remain open ended, and that, if she had to make a decision, she would choose Islam rather than Christianity. How did the negotiations over these points play out, and what implications did they have for *Little Mosque*'s depiction of religion as belief, rather than merely culture?

When it became clear that Rota was leaving the show, one of West-Wind executives' first ideas was to explain Yasir's absence through a funny accident: "we even talked about a scene, as one of the potential scenes to kick the [season] off, where there would be this little funeral in the little graveyard in Mercy, and you can see the grain elevator off in the distance, and there's the sign 'Mercy' but the Y was this long paint stain that goes from top to bottom. In other words, he had a contract to paint the sign and fell off the scaffolding, something silly. But then you would still be sad for her. You would feel good about the relationship, but we could not get that one through" (Donnelly, interview with author, 2012). Another idea was to start the timeline in season 6 a couple of years after that of season 5: "So you'd come back and Rayyan and Amaar have a couple little kids, and one of them is named Yasir ... [And characters would say] 'I wish your grandfather was here to see you,' you know, that kind of thing ... all the sadness is gone, it just is that life goes on now that Yasir's gone" (Darling, interview with author, 2012).

But CBC executives did not agree. Anton Leo, who had shared the originator's and executive producers' vision in the show's early seasons, had left the CBC (and gone to work for WestWind). The person who took his place "simply didn't get the show and was very afraid of anything to do with controversy ... there was a desire towards real political correctness" (ibid.). This avoidance of conflict took many forms. The evolving relationship between Thorne and Baber was one such example: when they exchanged barbs, their actions still indicated they liked each other, and confrontations, such as they were, took place when they played checkers or Parcheesi, where the focus of the conflict shifted to the games themselves. Another example was the concern about Yasir's departure: CBC executives did not think viewers would accept his death as an explanation. Divorce was more plausible, despite the fact that nothing in earlier seasons indicated trouble between Yasir and Sarah, other than her frustration with his doting attention to his mother, which was well within the bounds of sitcom conventions.

With the divorce Sarah lost her main reason for being Muslim. Since the beginning her observance of Islam's tenets had been irregular. She never wore a hijab other than in the mosque, she did not pray five times a day, and she struggled with vices that Muslims treat as taboo. In "The Convert" (season 1, episode 5), for instance, she tries – and fails – to perform the *salat* (the daily prayers), and in "Lucky Day" (season 2, episode 4) she buys lottery tickets, despite Islam's proscription of gambling. She also expresses nostalgia for the trappings of Christianity, such as Christmas parties and cards ("Eid's a Wonderful Life," season 2, episode 10, and "A Holiday Story," season 5, special episode). As chapter 2 described, she was the character who could ask naive questions the executive producers thought viewers might ask. With the divorce, her return to Christianity would not have appeared out of character.

WestWind, on the other hand, did not want to resolve her storyline. If *Little Mosque* was to be about belief, they reasoned, they wanted her to explore what genuine, deeply held belief meant – to continue to ask questions on viewers' behalf – and they thought such an exploration would be more meaningful if Sarah did not arrive at a conclusion (Darling, interview with author, 2012). But here again CBC executives disagreed. They wanted closure because they thought viewers wanted closure.

The one point where WestWind prevailed was in the question of whether Sarah would remain Muslim or become Christian again. It was not clear until the final two episodes what her choice would be, and she spent much of season 6 questioning her beliefs and motivations and flirting with the ways of her former life. Thorne and Baber realize her affiliation is up for grabs and spend the season trying to convince her to take their respective side, and their competition gives her more opportunities to weigh one set of beliefs against the other.

In the episodes about Sarah writers posed some of the most direct questions about belief. As chapter 3 shows, in the first season they contrived situations (such as the open house) that gave Muslim characters the chance to talk to each other (and indirectly to viewers) about Muslim customs and mores. By season 6 they contrived situations to address belief head-on, such as in "Mosque of Dreams" (episode 7). In the scene that sets up one of the plots Sarah is in her kitchen and Rayyan enters. Sarah is cooking what appears to be bacon.

RAYYAN: Hello.

SARAH: Hi.

RAYYAN (alarmed): Mom, is that bacon? That's bacon. What are you doing?

SARAH: I'm not eating it. Well, not yet anyway. Do you know I haven't had bacon for over thirty years?

RAYYAN: Because it goes against our beliefs?

SARAH: Well, I'm just not sure what our beliefs are any more.

RAYYAN: Mom, what do you mean? You're a Muslim!

SARAH: What if I'm a Muslim just because I was married to a Muslim?

RAYYAN: Well, how long have you been feeling this way?

SARAH: Well, I've been on a date, I've had wine, and something else Ann put in my drink, and now I'm thinking about trying bacon. (Lifts a piece to her mouth, which Rayyan slaps out of her hand.)

RAYYAN: No, don't do it!

SARAH: Hey! That's turkey bacon!

RAYYAN: Oh.

SARAH: I'm not going to jump in head-first, I'm going to dip my toes in a little. (Rayyan reaches for some turkey bacon, and Sarah slaps her hand.)

RAYYAN: Ow! Fine, I guess I had that coming.

In a later scene Sarah is talking to Amaar, who asks her for help in publicizing his plans to build a new mosque, and she says she cannot help because she cannot commit to something she is not sure she still believes in. Near the end of the episode she tries real bacon, which Rayyan also bites because she thinks it is turkey. At the end of the episode Sarah tells Amaar she has sold Yasir's business and wants to put the profits towards the new mosque. The episode demonstrates a certain flexibility in the sitcom's conventions. Like the scene between Amaar, Thorne, and Baber quoted above, the dialogue is unusually direct in the way it raises big questions, but the successive scenes still derive their humour from a series of misunderstandings (such as Rayyan's bite of what she thinks is turkey bacon – she spits it out and mistakenly takes a drink of what Sarah tells her is wine).

Asking these questions allowed WestWind to leave Sarah's choice a mystery until the final two episodes. The CBC thought returning to Christianity "might somehow represent something more relatable to our 'mainstream' sort of audience." Even the writers were surprised: "throughout the season in the room as we were talking about it, writers really – I think mostly because we have non-Muslim writers – really saw her going back to the Church" (Darling, interview with author, 2012). In "The Worst of Times," the second-to-last episode, it appears that Sarah has decided to revert to Christianity. She tries out for the church choir, and she approaches Thorne about Sunday school. But during the first choir practice, she stumbles when she sings "Amazing Grace." The choir sings the first three lines of the second verse: "'Twas grace that taught my heart to fear/And grace, my fears relieved!/How precious did that grace appear." Sarah sings the last line as a solo. She starts – "The hour I first ..." – but she cannot bring herself to say "believed." In a later scene she talks about her hesitation with Amaar and Rayyan. She says to Rayyan, "Don't ask me to explain, honey. I like being in church. It's the world that I know. I mean those traditions really stay with you." Near the end of the episode she is in the sanctuary talking with Thorne:

THORNE: Sarah, come on, what's the real reason you came back to the church?

SARAH: It's hard to say. It's complicated.

THORNE: No it's not! I mean, being Anglican, you simply need to believe in the thirty-nine articles, the sacraments – oh, and of course, the good old Nicene Creed.

SARAH: You know something, I don't know what to believe.

THORNE: Well, I'll make it easy for you. Believe in Jesus. Isn't that what brought you back?

SARAH: I don't think so. I came here because I – I miss something.

THORNE: Yes, well you clearly missed the point of the church.

SARAH: You're right.

THORNE: Yeah, I usually am. But about what specifically?

SARAH: Maybe I'm looking for the wrong thing in the wrong place. I don't want to be Christian again. I'm sorry.

THORNE: No, no, no, come on, don't be sorry. It's only your eternal soul. Kidding! Sort of. Eighty percent. (Rises.) It's your call. The church will always be here if you change your mind. Again.

SARAH: Well, the church has really changed since I was a little girl.

THORNE (with kindness): No, I think you've changed. But traditions have their pull.

SARAH: They sure do! I used to love that brassy thing with the incense in it.

THORNE: The censer?

SARAH: Yeah.

THORNE: I'll tell you what. (Picks up the censer.) If you decide to come back, I will light it up in your honour. Now, if you'll excuse me, I have some real Christians to tend to.

SARAH: I'm just going to stay here for a minute and say my last good-bye.

THORNE: Of course.[7]

When Thorne leaves, she walks nostalgically through the sanctuary and swings the lighted censer. It hits the altar, and she leaves in a panic without noticing the ashes on the altar cloths. Two scenes later the altar, framed in the centre of the screen, goes up in flames.

The dialogue with Thorne makes the culture/belief divide explicit. Sarah recognizes that what drew her back was the censer, which becomes a metaphor for the cultural traditions that used to provide her with a sense of belonging. But what she no longer accepts is the Nicene Creed, a metaphor for belief.[8] What prompted Sarah to make her choice? Darling explains that her son-in-law is an imam and her daughter is devout, and "she's been a Muslim now for thirty years. Through osmosis or whatever else, she's learned a number of things ... It wasn't meant to be any really big statement, just sort of a nice soft little – you know people make choices you might not expect" (interview with author, 2012). The last idea – that people make unexpected choices – is the strongest case *Little Mosque* presents against the essentialism to which many viewers, especially Muslims, objected during the show's first seasons. It is the point at which *Little Mosque*'s diversity was the least saleable, at least according to the CBC's assessment. In this way Sarah's choice realized some of the potential Darling and Donnelly saw when they convinced the CBC to abandon the return to stasis. Sarah's "measurable transformation" was internal, rather than external. It was not, as some expected, her return to Christianity, to the culture whose outward expression filled her with nostalgia. Instead, it was her act of coming to understand – or better yet, to actively claim – her own beliefs, rather than acquiesce to those around her and go along with what they prescribed. A return to Christianity would have been tantamount to a rejection of the thirty years she had spent as a Muslim; the choice she faced brought into focus the unnoticed ways she had incorporated Islam into her identity. But even here the limits of saleable diversity are apparent: in the dialogue with Thorne, it becomes clear that her choice is motivated by her beliefs, but the substance of her beliefs – what motivates them – goes unmentioned.

Thus, over the course of the season 6, Sarah ceased to be the naive convert and began to engage with what Darling and Donnelly saw as the ineffable mystery of belief, rather than simply go through the motions of culture attached to Islam. Where she used to wrestle with the cultural side of Islam (the recitation of prayers, the donning of a hijab), she now wrestled with the beliefs it represented. She found her counterpoint in Thorne, who underwent a transformation that appeared to be the inverse of hers – he backed down from his absolute certainty and opened up to the idea that others might experience faith in different ways. In fact, his transformation, too, was one from culture to belief: he began to empathize with people whose beliefs differed from his own. Through his engagement with alterity he began to explore the nature of belief itself. If he had not, he would have been incapable of accepting Amaar's offer of hospitality, and the show's symmetry – the mosque moved into the church in the premiere, and the church into the mosque in the finale – would have been lost.

Critics Watch *Little Mosque*'s Final Season

There were not as many responses to the *Little Mosque*'s finale as to its premiere. When the show premiered, critics were responding to the hype that surrounded it, and they were excited about the potential it might realize. When it ended, there was less urgency because there was less hype. The show had run its course and, if anything, those who wrote about it were responding to their memory of the hype.

Their responses addressed themes similar to those in their first reviews – its quality as a sitcom and its ability to counter stereotypes about Muslims – but they also marked a slight shift in the discussion of the show and the meaning of Islam in post-9/11 North America. With respect to the first theme, by the end of its run even those critics who had liked *Little Mosque* in the beginning thought it had lost its frisson and had become predictable and staid: "With all due respect to the show's ability to diminish anti-Muslim suspicions and conjure gentle comedy from Muslims and Christians closely co-existing, it was never quite funny enough, or even memorably entertaining, to matter. It was a very old-school Canadian show. A great idea at the beginning. Then, over the seasons, a nice idea. Pity it all got a bit dreary. Pity it was not the CBC's *Corner Gas*" (Doyle 2012, R1). The evolution of their opinion was reflected, for instance, in the way they attributed different meanings to "hokey." When John Doyle (2007a, R1) described the show's premiere as "hokey as hell," he also described it as "terrifically good-natured." Daphne Bramham (2007), writing at the same time, thought "hokey" implied "rural": "Critics of *Little Mosque* – most of whom are based in big cities – say it's too hokey." In a review two months later Doyle (2007b, R3) again called the show "hokey," by which he meant "ludicrous" and "lightweight," although he now saw the show as "not nearly lightweight enough." But by 2012 he had revised what he meant by "hokey" again, now seeing it as a limit to *Little Mosque*'s humour: "It was always too broad, repetitive and bogged down in the most hokey kind of comedy ... Too often the humour had a 'hey look at us, we're wisecracking Muslims' quality" (Doyle 2012, R1). Over time "hokey" took on increasingly negative connotations as critics grew more disappointed about what they saw as *Little Mosque*'s failure to live up to its potential as a successful Canadian sitcom.

With respect to the second theme, Tarek Fatah of the Muslim Canadian Congress, who wrote a scathing review of *Little Mosque*'s premiere, maintained his opinion over the course of the show's run. After it had finished, he said, "I think it was a terrible comedy. And I think it survived purely because of what I call 'white man's guilt.' If this were any other group of people, it would have been shut down in a month. Most people watched it with the fear that if they didn't laugh, they'd be considered racist. It was a massive fraud" (quoted in Menon 2012, E1). At the same time some non-Muslims continued to express the fear that "as the media get more and more saturated with such self-acclaimed 'funny and heart-warming' offerings, the media (hopefully unintentionally) aid in building ... citadels for dangerous, Islamic covenant theology," as one blogger wrote (Greenberg 2012).[9]

But others offered more hopeful accounts. Waleed Ahmed (2012), writing for the website MuslimMatters.org, said that despite its shortcomings, *Little Mosque* "was the most accurate depiction of Muslims to date ... It represented all the characters we find in our mosques: the uncles, the converts, the feminists and the rebellious teenagers. It captured the conflicts between the young and the old, the tension between the liberals and conservatives." Vinay Menon (2012) explored the idea that *Little Mosque* was for Muslims what *The Cosby Show* had been for blacks in the United States (and elsewhere) in the 1980s. Many journalists, of course, had drawn parallels between the two shows, most notably CBS's Katie Couric in 2010. Menon interviewed scholars such as Ozlem Sensoy, who said, "*The Cosby Show* ... did two things. It made white folks much more comfortable with a certain kind of black family. But it did so without addressing the very structural conditions that made that show necessary. I think *Little Mosque on the Prairie* has a similar place. It also grew out of a particular social moment, 9/11, and had these pedagogical goals – teaching white folks about a different kind of Muslim person in the context in which Muslim men had become the new brute, the new group to be feared" (quoted in ibid., E1). Minelle Mahtani agreed: "The show has gone a long way in helping Western audiences see beyond the tired stereotype of Muslims as barbaric, exotic, dangerous and primitive" (quoted in ibid., E1).

In other words, for Muslim critics the question of authenticity – itself a contested notion – remained paramount. The shift in emphasis was more apparent among non-Muslim critics. They showed more interest in *Little Mosque*'s ability to humanize Muslims, but the question of the show's quality as a sitcom took precedence over that of the role of the CBC in Canadian society, which had received more attention after the show's premiere. Menon and most of the academics he quoted saw the work to humanize Muslims as positive for society, on the whole. But that work came at a price: Doyle and critics like him found *Little Mosque* too staid because of the work it performed. *Little Mosque* increased the range of depictions of Muslims, but at the cost of comedy with wide appeal.

Conclusion: The Limits of Saleable Diversity

In other words, although WestWind pushed against the limits of saleability by expanding the range of representation (as described in earlier chapters) and the mode of representation (as described in this chapter), the limits continued to push back. *Little Mosque*'s makers did not succeed in overcoming the paradox of saleable diversity, but they did succeed in changing the terms on which producers could engage it. They created *Little Mosque* in response to the stereotypes about Islam circulating in North American media, and they adjusted their approach as needed. To counter stereotypes, they widened the range of characters depicted, and they found ways to help viewers know more about Islam. To counter the essentialism of those characters, they found ways to make them evolve. To counter the idea that Islam was merely a collection of cultural practices, they had characters ask questions about faith, all in support of the executive producers' ideas about the role of belief in people's everyday lives. In the end, they painted a picture of ecumenism – of people of different faiths coming together to discover and share what they had in common. The gentle humour they employed followed from and shaped this sense of ecumenism.

In the concluding chapter I will examine this idea of oneness and its relation to humour. Other notions of ecumenism, especially those that allowed more space for conflict, might have engendered different types of humour, and it is a valuable exercise to ask how they might have made it possible to push even harder against the limits of saleable diversity.

Identity and Difference
in North American Sitcoms

Little Mosque on the Prairie ends in a tidy fashion: Amaar has invited Rev. William Thorne into the mosque, and Thorne has accepted. The final words in the series belong to Fred Tupper. He is speaking to his listeners, and his brief soliloquy begins as a voice-over as the final scene of interfaith harmony – Amaar and Thorne are standing together – remains on screen. "Well, folks," he says, "it is an upside-down world here in Mercy. First we had a mosque in a church, now we got a church in a mosque. I guess nothing that happens in this little town should surprise any of us anymore. Anyhoo, I think I hear the old fat lady singing. Time for Freddy Tupper to sign off. Over and out, my friendlies. And, uh, listen – thanks for dropping by." The music swells. The song is David Wilcox's "To Love," which has played over the credits during season 6, and the lyrics reiterate the theme of the show: "A commandment of one god to love, everybody fighting over one god to love."

This tidiness obscures something more interesting. My analysis in the last chapter left some important loose ends. The final season, especially the finale, relies on a specific conception of ecumenism, one that makes such a tidy ending possible. In effect, "ecumenism" became a sign under which the makers of *Little Mosque*, especially its executive producers, strategically gathered specific meanings that allowed them to account for two shifts in the North American public imaginary. First, many Muslims have adopted a new orientation in their experience of North America. They have come to see it not as a place of transit, from which they will return to the Muslim world, but as their home, a place that *belongs* to the Muslim world (Bilici 2012, 114–19). Second, many non-Muslims, through their engagement with television shows or works of fiction about Muslims, have broadened the scope of their imagination. In a general sense, as Kwame Appiah (2006, 85) writes, "Conversations across boundaries of identity – whether national, religious, or something else – begin with the sort of imaginative engagement you get when you read a novel or watch a movie or attend to a work of art that speaks from some place other than your own ... [This engagement] doesn't have to lead to consensus about anything, especially not values; it's enough that it helps people get used to one another." To encourage that engagement was one of the goals of *Little Mosque*. In other words, at the same time as North America is becoming Muslim (in addition to Christian, Jewish, atheist, and so on), Muslims are becoming North American, not just in juridical terms (it is more than a question of citizenship), but also in phenomenological terms.

These shifts are not without contradictions, of course. Not all Muslims feel North America offers Islam a home, and many people are openly hostile to the idea of North America becoming Muslim. They fear that the category "Muslim" excludes others in a pluralist society, and they worry that "becoming Muslim" means imposing Sharia law or curtailing non-Muslims' rights to religious practice. The processes Bilici and Appiah describe are marked by ongoing engagement, not by their realization.

The sign of ecumenism, as *Little Mosque*'s makers deployed it, allowed them to resolve these contradictions, at least in Mercy, Saskatchewan. Clark Donnelly describes how ecumenism functioned in a metaphor, that of the bench where Amaar and Rev. Duncan Magee would sit to talk about their congregations in early seasons: "you had this young imam and this older priest ... who sat together and weren't quite sure how it worked, but they know it's true, they both believe in a god, they both believe that that's real and true and they're both trying to figure it out, and that was kind of a metaphor for the show. And whenever things were blowing up, they could sort of sit down there, and they didn't usually even have much advice that would help each other, but there was that coming together" (interview with author, 2012).

But this idea of ecumenism did not change the world outside Mercy. Canadians continued to view Islam unfavourably, more so than any other religion.[1] In fact, over the years *Little Mosque* aired, suspicion of Muslims increased. In 2009, 46 per cent of Canadians outside Quebec held an adverse view of Islam; in 2013, 54 per cent held such views.[2] Similarly, 32 per cent of people outside Quebec said they would object if a family member wanted to marry a Muslim, up from 24 per cent in 2009 (Angus Reed Global 2013; Geddes 2013). And violence in many places in the majority-Muslim world continued apace: as *Little Mosque* ended, sectarian conflict was increasing in Syria, and the Muslim Brotherhood was gaining influence in Egypt, in ways that would lead to a violent crackdown months later.

In this concluding chapter, I examine *Little Mosque* in the context of these contradictions. I ask how representations of Muslims have changed in North American media since 2007, and I consider *Little Mosque*'s role in that change. Producers of other shows about Muslims (such as *Aliens in America* and especially the cable reality show *All-American Muslim*) made similar efforts to counter stereotypes. *Little Mosque* did not cause these changes; instead, it participated in the conversation about Islam I describe in the first chapters in this book, a conversation that preceded it and continued after it ended. It was the conversation itself, rather than the individual programs, that brought about changes in representation. *Little Mosque*'s impact, such as it was, came from the way it added one more layer. Viewers had another set of references at their disposal when talking about Islam, and even those who rejected the show's depictions of Muslims still referred and responded to them.

This is a subtle change. Examining *Little Mosque* in the context of this conversation makes it possible to acknowledge the contradictions of the world without giving up on the hope for transformation shared by the show's originator, producers, and writers. It also allows for the possibility that *Little Mosque*'s influence will not be felt for a much longer time: the eddy it created might be overwhelmed by the conversation's stronger current, or it might bring about a series of small changes that in the end change the river's course.[3] Finally, it raises the question with which I conclude this book: what might *Little Mosque*'s makers have done to have a greater impact on the conversation about Islam in post-9/11 North America? The notion of ecumenism that underpinned it and the sitcom conventions its makers adopted were linked in a relationship of mutual influence. The idea of religious unity – the bench shared by two religious leaders – encouraged the development of a gentle form of humour, which the producers and writers used to promote the idea of religious unity. What if the show had been based on a different notion of ecumenism, one that did not assume that the Abrahamic religions were essentially the same? Or what if it had employed a different type of humour? How might such changes have shaped the show and, in turn, the broader conversation about Islam in post-9/11 North America?

To answer those questions I consider other media texts, including sitcoms and other forms of comedy, in relation to *Little Mosque*. In contrast to the preceding chapters, where my purpose was to explain, my purpose here is also to provoke: I do not provide an exhaustive account of these texts (an impossible task) but use them instead to ask how shows like *Little Mosque* might approach representation differently.[4] I consider other modes of humour by asking how they challenge (or do not challenge) viewers' ideas about identity and difference. I conclude by observing that the people responsible for *Little Mosque* might have made more challenging choices, but they would have risked limiting the program's reach. The compromise they struck allowed them to bring about the conditions of possibility for incremental change, whose value should not be underestimated.

The Double Bind of Ecumenism in *Little Mosque*

The ideal of unity that underpins the notion of ecumenism in *Little Mosque* accords well with the executive producers' Bahá'í faith, which emphasizes the oneness of humanity. As chapter 5 demonstrates, Mary Darling and Clark Donnelly approach faith as the expression of a foundational relationship between people and God, even if the expression differs between religious traditions. They believe people encounter the mysteries of faith in a variety of ways, but the mysteries themselves are the same for everyone. What differs is the way people express the beliefs that grow out of their personal encounter with the unseen and unprovable.

But with *Little Mosque* they were caught in a double bind. Discussion of belief, more than anything else, demonstrated how Muslims were different from non-Muslims, and they were concerned that viewers would not see past the surface difference to the more profound sameness. Thus, the very ideas they wanted to explore were out of bounds, or, at the very least, they could not be broached without the considerable work it took to shift the emphasis from religion as culture to religion as belief in the final seasons.

For that reason they had to find other means to translate this ecumenical ideal. In the early seasons, they relied on other measures of equivalence, as chapter 1 described: they emphasized traits that characters had in common, such as their personal political views, and deemphasized their differences. That is, in the name of diversity they erased the very differences – those that came from the expression of belief – that mattered most. This approach, as chapters 2 and 3 showed, flattened out Muslim characters' beliefs. It also resulted in the gentle humour that characterized the show: what made it gentle was its emphasis on similarities. The choice to develop the humour in this way was deliberate and, to a person, everyone involved in the show – Zarqa Nawaz, Mary Darling, Clark Donnelly, and even actors such as Zaib Shaikh – said its value lay in the promise it held to overcome many non-Muslims' sense that Islam posed a threat.

In this way gentle humour was an expression of that notion of ecumenism. It gave *Little Mosque*'s makers a set of discursive tools to overcome the contradictions between religious traditions by arguing that the differences were only superficial. But a wide range of viewers, as chapter 3 showed, found this resolution unsatisfying. Many Muslims thought it artificially bounded the range of "acceptable" Canadian Muslim identities (Fatah and Hassan 2007; Greifenhagen 2011). And although on the show *Little Mosque*'s makers could resolve contradictions, they remained in the world viewers experienced outside Mercy. Viewers were not persuaded by the idea that religions such as Christianity and Islam were fundamentally the same.

It is worth asking, then, whether a different notion of ecumenism, one that did *not* presuppose the fundamental sameness of all religions, might have encouraged a different type of humour. How might *Little Mosque* have looked if its producers had endorsed an ecumenism that did not need people to agree on substantive matters in order to coexist?

Overcoming Ideas of Difference as Threat

In fact, *Little Mosque*'s approach to ecumenism is a symptom of a broader phenomenon. We tend to think of difference in one of two ways. On the one hand, difference prompts so much fear (and fear prompts so much discrimination, violence, and injustice) that we frequently treat it as inherently negative – to draw attention to difference is to exclude (or to provide the tools or motivation to exclude). But this reflex misses the point: difference matters, especially in the specifics that define people's identity. To deny difference is to deny people their full sense of themselves.

On the other hand, we also repeat slogans like "celebrate difference," although such celebrations risk reducing deep cultural difference to surface manifestations, such as dance or food or dress. How do we speak of difference in ways that do not reduce it merely to a source of division or something we "celebrate" from a safe distance? What we need is a way to acknowledge and affirm difference without making it a source of fear. This is a more delicate and difficult act than accepting (or failing to question) the blanket assertion that difference leads to fear and injustice, and it is a more subtle act than eating different food while watching people dance in traditional costumes.

This is where an examination of *Little Mosque* within the broader programming ecology is useful. In chapter 4 I described points where *Little Mosque*'s makers and Canadian viewers engaged actively with other programs such as *Aliens in America*. Here, I describe points of passive engagement. *Little Mosque* circulated in the presence of other shows with Muslim characters, and it is likely that the people who made it (and watched it) watched those shows, too, even if they did not talk about them in interviews with journalists or with me. They interpreted *Little Mosque* in light of those shows, which took different approaches to representing Islam. I am interested in those approaches for two reasons. First, I am interested in the potential effect their divergent approaches had on non-Muslim viewers' understanding of Muslims. Second, I am interested in what they suggest about the potential other approaches present for overcoming the paradox of saleable diversity.

To that end I adapt an observation made by the nineteenth-century German theologian Friedrich Schleiermacher, who saw two approaches to translation. In 1813 he wrote that translators have a choice either to "[leave] the reader in peace, as much as possible, and [move] the author toward him" or to "[leave] the author in peace, as much as possible, and [move] the reader toward him" (1992, 149). Translation studies scholars now describe these approaches as domesticating or acculturating, in the first case, or foreignizing, in the second. If we use this lens to examine cultural translation and television, we might ask how shows leave viewers undisturbed or how they challenge them. Specifically, do they allow viewers to hold on to their stereotypes about Muslims, or do they prompt viewers to question them?

We can consider three sites of intervention, in increasing levels of abstraction. The first is that of identity: do programs obscure or highlight characters' identity? The second is that of difference, or the space between identities: when programs highlight identity, do they then emphasize similarities or differences between characters? The third is the deployment of identity and difference in the show itself: is it parodic (concerned with formal qualities) or satirical (concerned with cultural critique)? In other words, how do media-makers work within humour's formal and affective dimensions to encourage viewers to question stereotypes (or not)?

The value of these categories is heuristic, and programs might challenge viewers in some ways (*Little Mosque* highlighted identity in a way that challenged stereotypes) but not others (it downplayed difference and favoured parody over satire). Of course, the textual devices that mark these sites present a potential encoded in programs that goes unrealized until viewers decode it, and nothing guarantees that viewers will decode it as producers intended. In fact, the mode of polysemy I describe in chapter 1 makes it hard to discern one single intended meaning: irony functions by presenting two or more competing interpretations. Thus, these sites are useful for identifying points where other approaches are possible and for asking how else media-makers might approach the project of cultural translation, but they represent only part of an uncompleted circuit.

Identity

The first question is how media-makers treat categories of identity. Do they obscure it or highlight it? By what means and to what effect? Other shows with Muslim characters suggest at least two ways to obscure identity and two to highlight it, each of which holds the potential to leave viewers undisturbed or to challenge them. In Table 2, I present a matrix that pairs approaches to identity with effects on viewers, and I expand on the results below.

Obscuring Identity

One way to obscure religious identity is by focusing instead on other traits. Zarqa Nawaz talked about this approach in a public forum at the University of North Dakota in 2011. She remarked that other sitcoms had Muslim characters, whom she described as "sidekicks," people whose religious beliefs were not an important part of their character. One is Tom Haverford, played by Aziz Ansari on the ensemble comedy *Parks and Recreation* (NBC, 2009–15). Tom works in the Parks and Recreation department of the city government of the fictional town of Pawnee, Indiana. Early in the second season, when asked about his name, he explains, "My birth name is Darwish Zubair Ismail Gani. Then I changed it to Tom Haverford, because you know, brown guys with funny-sounding Muslim names don't make it far into politics."[5]

Table 2. Identity as site of intervention

		Effect on viewers	
		Leave viewers undisturbed	Challenge viewers
Obscure identity	by highlighting other traits	Deny Muslim characters a potentially important part of their identity	Suggest Muslims are defined by more traits than religion
		Examples: *Parks and Recreation, Community*	Examples: *Parks and Recreation, Community*
	by substituting similar categories (e.g., South Asians)	Invoke stereotypes by suggesting "Muslimness"	
		Example: *That '70s Show*	
Highlight identity	by explaining Muslims' customs and beliefs	Use explanations to ridicule	Show stereotypes to be wrong
		Example: Conservative talk radio (as parodied in *Little Mosque*)	Examples: *Little Mosque on the Prairie, Aliens in America, All-American Muslim*
	by exaggerating stereotypes	Rely on stereotypes for humour	Draw stereotypes into question
		Example: Vaudeville-style ethnic humour	Example: *Whoopi*

Beyond that admission, however, his identity as a Muslim plays no role in his character. Instead, he is a schemer and a self-styled ladies' man, especially in the first seasons.

Nawaz also mentioned Abed Nadir (played by Danny Pudi) in *Community* (NBC, 2009–15), a sitcom about some misfit friends who form a study group at a community college in Colorado. Abed is Palestinian American, and in the episode "Comparative Religion" (season 1, episode 12) he tells the group he is Muslim. But it is one of the only points where religion matters, in part because the episode is premised on another character's discomfort with the fact her friends are not Christian. Otherwise, Abed, a film major, is known for his inability to relate to other people except through references to movies and other popular culture.

Other shows obscure religious identity through another means: they avoid mentioning it altogether, although they might suggest it by giving characters proxy traits. For instance, many feature South Asians, who are marked by skin colour, accent, and profession as "other," as "a good stand-in for Arab and Muslim characters in this post-9/11 reality of fear" (Thakore 2014, 149). By focusing on their geographic origins producers can imply "Muslimness" without drawing attention to characters' religious affiliation. In fact, Evelyn Alsultany (2012a) describes similar strategies that contribute to the "simplified complexity" of recent shows featuring Muslim (or Arab) characters. Media-makers have a lot more latitude to evoke stereotypes about Muslims if they let viewers do the work of connecting characters to Islam. In sitcoms this approach is evident in programs like *That '70s Show* (Fox, 1998–2006), where the character Fez (played by Wilmer Valderrama) has dark skin and a suggestive but unplaceable accent. He is an exchange student, but his country of origin is never revealed, and he responds to a long line of nicknames such as "Ali Baba," "Ahmed," and "Desi" that suggest he is from an Arabic country or from the Indian subcontinent. (He also responds to "Pelé," the name of the famous Brazilian soccer player, thus further obscuring his origins.)

Of these two approaches the first holds more potential to challenge viewers to question stereotypes. On the one hand, highlighting traits other than religion denies Muslim characters a potentially important part of their identity. On the other, it signals that Muslims are characterized by more than religion and, in fact, some might grow up Muslim or come from places where Muslims are a majority but still consider themselves secular. Take both *Parks and Recreation* and *Community*: only viewers paying close attention will catch characters' references to Islam (because they make those references only once or twice in the series), so there is little chance to explore that aspect of their character. But why would a Muslim not be a lackadaisical bureaucrat or an awkward film buff? As for the second approach, that of substituting categories, it is difficult to imagine any way in which it would not reinforce stereotypes. Viewers who are prompted to question stereotypes would be those who read such shows oppositionally.

Highlighting Identity

In contrast, other shows highlight identity. This was the case, of course, for *Little Mosque*, along with *Aliens in America* and the reality show

All-American Muslim, all of which made Islam the core of their characters' or stars' identities. As the preceding chapters show, they sought to explain Islam and demonstrate that Muslims were "just like" non-Muslims, at least in the ways producers thought mattered. Of course, Muslims are too diverse simply to be "explained," as viewers' debates about the authenticity of *Little Mosque*'s characters demonstrated.

Such an explanation was thus an imperfect attempt to encourage viewers to overcome stereotypes. But this is not the only type of explanation possible, and explanation can also be used to perpetuate stereotypes. Notably, Fred Tupper, Mercy's local radio shock jock, frequently "explained" the town's Muslims in order to ridicule them. His explanations distorted how Muslims would describe themselves. In "Can I Get a Witness?" (season 3, episode 20), for example, Fred attends Rayyan and J.J.'s wedding and delivers a heartfelt speech after J.J. leaves her. When Fred leaves the reception to prepare his show for the next day, Amaar asks him what the topic will be, and he says, "Crazy Muslim weddings" (Cwynar 2013, 57). The parody works by evoking other media with which viewers would be familiar – Fred's show is modelled after Sean Hannity's (and others), which airs in Canada on Fox News.

But there are other ways to highlight identity, such as through the exaggeration of stereotypes. Ethnic dialect comedies, for instance, were a staple of the nineteenth-century vaudeville circuit, and they made the transition to radio in shows such as *The Goldbergs*, about Jewish immigrants in the Bronx, and *Amos 'n' Andy*, the "blackface" comedy (where white actors adopted accents and speech patterns considered "black"), which was the most popular program in the history of US radio. For their humour they relied on their characters' accents and the stereotypes they evoked. In fact, when *Amos 'n' Andy* made the transition to television in the 1950s, civil rights organizations objected to its reliance on stereotypes and mounted a protest that led eventually to its cancellation (Marc 2005).

Of course, such humour is less acceptable now. Contemporary sitcoms that exaggerate stereotypes tend to do so in order to draw them into question. The short-lived sitcom *Whoopi* fell into this category. It ran on NBC from 2003 to 2004 and starred Whoopi Goldberg as an opinionated hotelier named Mavis Rae. It featured an Iranian-American character named Nasim (played by Omid Djalili), and the writers played up (and played on) stereotypes about Muslim immigrants. In fact, the show played with stereotypes about all of its characters. It exaggerated them in an attempt to show their absurdity, although its "message" as such was unstable because of the inherent contradictions in irony's mode of polysemy. For instance, in "The Vast Right Wing Conspiracy" (episode 6), President Bush has to interrupt a motorcade by stopping at Mavis's hotel to use the restroom. Nasim tells Mavis that the president is there, and Mavis, a vocal critic of the president, tells Nasim to tell him to leave. In front of the press, which has gathered to ask about the president's visit, Nasim responds, "Oh, yeah, right, an Iranian immigrant telling the president to go. Why don't I just run around the airport and yell, 'yeah, Jihad! Holy War! Holy War!'" Stacy Takacs (2011, 430) reads this scene as a reversal of stereotypes: "Nasim assumes Americans cannot distinguish between an Arab and a Persian, a brown man and a terrorist ... The joke works not by countering the stereotypical associations between Arabs and terrorism, or Middle Easterners and Arabs, but by turning the process of stereotyping around so that the normative majority population gets a taste of what it is like to be stereotyped." She is half right, but we cannot assume that viewers will take the joke's ironic meaning as the intended one; the joke works because of the tension between the literal and ironic levels of meaning. Without that tension, there is no joke.

Thus, both obscuring and highlighting identity hold the potential to leave viewers undisturbed or to challenge their preconceptions about Muslims. *Little Mosque* emphasized identity in an effort to show where stereotypes went wrong, but it neglected secular Muslims, as some critics wrote. *Parks and Recreation* and *Community* obscured identity, which suggested that Muslims can integrate into North American society without their religious identity being a focal point, but also that religious identity does not matter.

Difference

This discussion of the category of identity raises a related question. If we set aside shows in which media-makers obscure identity and instead examine the ones where they highlight it, what do we find? Do they emphasize similarities or differences between groups?

Emphasis on Similarities

As the preceding chapters have shown, *Little Mosque* talked about religious difference and emphasized similarities between groups. The idea that Muslims and non-Muslims shared more in common than not underpinned its treatment of ecumenism: each character had his or her counterpart among the other group because, at their core, their beliefs led back to the same god.

We can find a similar emphasis in other places, such as the Muslim stand-up comedy that has grown in popularity in the last decade. Performers include Bryant "Preacher" Moss and Azhar Usman of the group Allah Made Me Funny and Ahmed Ahmed, Maz Jobrani, Aron Kader, and Dean Obeidallah of the group Axis of Evil. Obeidallah explains, "Our hope is that like other ethnic groups and races before us, we can use comedy to foster understanding about who we are and redefine ourselves in an accurate, positive way" (quoted in Amarasingam 2010, 463). They do not shy away from religion but try instead to use jokes that are relevant to Muslims' lives while inviting non-Muslims to see the world as they do. For instance, in one of his opening bits, Usman begins by greeting the audience: "Salaam alaikum. (*The audience responds 'wa alaikum salaam.'*) I notice we have some non-Muslim friends and family in the crowd, so I'll explain what that means. (*Pause.*) It means we're going to kill you! (*The audience laughs.*) I'm just kidding! (*He imitates an audience member.*) He goes, 'What? I always wondered what they're talking about. Salami and bacon?' (*Audience laughs.*) Let me explain: 'salaam alaikum' is a beautiful greeting. It's the greeting of peace. It's the greeting of the angels in heaven. And it means 'peace be with you.'"[6]

By making non-Muslims' anxiety the punch-line of his opening joke he makes it appear strange. The purpose of the explanation that follows is to demystify the greeting they do not understand. In his routine Usman repeats the phrase by doing impressions of Muslims of different races greeting each other, drawing on stereotypes about blacks, Arabs, Hispanics, and whites, and transposing those stereotypes into a Muslim setting. His approach is like that of other comedians who rely on observational humour – he could just as well be talking about how people of different races drive cars or interact on the street. Greeting others in Arabic becomes just one more thing people of different races do differently. It ceases to be threatening, at least in the context of his routine.[7]

Emphasis on Difference

This emphasis on similarities stands in contrast to media that emphasize difference to perpetuate stereotypes either passively (by repeating them uncritically) or actively (by using difference as a source of derision). Such emphasis on difference is clear, as I alluded to above, in conservative talk radio, of which Fred Tupper was a parody. It is even clearer in polemics against Islam like that of British video blogger Pat Condell, whose YouTube channel features entries such as "The Religion of Fear" that "[use] humor based on incongruence to differentiate 'us,' Europeans, from Islam, which is 'othered' as a violent threat that 'wants' to 'take over the world'" (Hirzalla, van Zoonen, and Müller 2013, 51). In one bit, for example, he says, "Islam without *violence* is a like an egg-free omelette. The religion is predicated on *violence* and the threat of *violence*. It's a religion of peace in the same way North Korea is a people's democratic republic. But we're not allowed to say that, because when we do, we'll be threatened with *violence*" (quoted in ibid., 52; emphasis added).

Clearly, Condell and Fred Tupper-style talk show hosts use derision to perpetuate stereotypes, but their polemics are not the only approach to difference. Usman's routine, to give one example, hints at ways it might be possible to emphasize difference without perpetuating stereotypes: he brings difference into sharp focus but holds it in suspension, and he is aggressive in his use of irony to cut stereotypes down to size.[8] How might a sitcom do similar work? What would happen if a sitcom focused on differences between Muslims and non-Muslims but rejected the idea that "different" meant "bad"?

Irony

The third site of intervention is that of irony and the mode of its deployment. Here the question is what exactly specific instances of irony draw into question. Does irony take the form of parody, which engages with formal imitation, or of satire, which engages with cultural critique?[9] And what do those categories reveal about ways television comedy might emphasize difference without perpetuating stereotypes?

Parody

Parody does not have as sharp an edge as satire. Instead, parodies "legitimate their original texts ... because their transgressions are always authorized by the norms they seek to subvert" (Cwynar 2013, 52). But this does not mean they cannot challenge stereotypes. Consider the YouTube video called "I Am a Muslim!" sponsored by the New Jersey Chapter of the Muslim American Society. The video is a spoof of the popular (and widely imitated) "I Am Canadian!" ad campaign by Molson Brewery in the early 2000s. It follows the same structure of the best known of these ads, known as "The Rant." Both begin with a young man who walks onto a stage, stands in front of a plain curtain, and then timidly lists all the things he is not (a lumberjack in the case of the Molson ad, a terrorist in the case of the Muslim YouTube video). The man then responds to an implied question about whether he knows another Canadian or Muslim (Jimmy, Sally, or Susie in one case, Ahmed in the other) by saying he does not. As he gains confidence, he corrects people's pronunciations ("about" not "aboot," "Islam" with a non-vocalized "s" not a vocalized "s") before finally declaring that "Canada is the best part of North America" or that the Quran is "the greatest book ever." The purpose of both videos is to address stereotypes head-on – Americans' stereotypes about Canadians in one case, non-Muslims' about Muslims in the other.

The parodic nature of "I Am a Muslim!" is both a strength and a weakness. On the one hand, its speaker takes advantage of the pleasure people find in parody: being in on a joke can create a sense of solidarity among those who have the cultural capital to recognize a shared set of references. But both videos operate in a paradoxical way: their speakers define themselves on someone else's terms, those of the people who hold the stereotypes they are responding to. Because "I Am a Muslim!" is a parody, its speaker is even further removed from describing his identity on his own terms, since even the structure of his speech is not his own.

Satire

What happens when irony draws into question more than other texts with which a program shares formal qualities? Here an examination of satire is useful. Satire has received a lot of attention as the popularity of *The Daily Show*, *The Colbert Report*, and other comedy news shows has risen. These shows use irony to critique politicians, for instance, by juxtaposing "real footage of a politician's statements on several different occasions to demonstrate his/her duplicity" (Day 2011, 8). They challenge the rationality and even-handedness on which the genre of news is premised and, consequently, they challenge the genre itself.

Space limitations will not allow me to explore satirical news in anything more than a superficial way, but the topic has been well covered elsewhere.[10] My point, as I write above, remains to provoke, not just explain – I want to use the idea of satire to identify other choices the people responsible for *Little Mosque* might have made. In that respect *The Daily Show* offers a relevant example in a skit that Aasif Mandvi created in response to Katie Couric's suggestion that the United States needed a "Muslim *Cosby Show*." The skit – a five-minute "pilot" for *The Qu'osby Show* – turned the sitcom against itself, much as *The Daily Show* turned the genre of news against itself. It raised questions about whether *The Cosby Show* really did – or whether a Muslim equivalent really would – change people's attitudes. It aired in February 2011, and it was both parodic and satirical, a meta-commentary about the role of the sitcom in addressing racial or religious stereotypes.

The skit opens with a sequence drawn directly from *Cosby*: Mandvi and the other members of the cast dance to the music of *The Cosby Show*'s opening credits. They mimic the style of the original show's cast members, and the sequence ends with what appears to be Mandvi dancing with Keshia Knight Pulliam (Rudy from the original) – her image from *Cosby*'s second season opening credits has been superimposed over Mandvi's. The story that follows looks a lot like *The Cosby Show*: Mandvi's son is doing poorly in school, his daughter wants a certain boy to ask her out, and Mandvi solves both problems by applying just the right amount of fatherly cleverness. It even includes some of Bill Cosby's signature conventions. He was known for using his show to deliver lessons about black history and contributions blacks had made to art and culture. In *The Qu'osby Show*, Mandvi and his wife deliver a lesson about the invention of algebra by Muslims.

The satire in *The Qu'osby Show* is apparent in the way Mandvi's character feels compelled to deny his Muslim identity. He begins by bringing snacks to his family, and they are all pork. He even offers his children "pork juice" in a two-litre pop bottle. About a minute into the clip, he asks his son to turn up his music, which happens to be Toby Keith, and the family gets up and dances the two-step. When they lean forward as part of the dance, their neighbour enters and says, "Hi neighbours! Oh sorry – I didn't realize you guys were praying." Mandvi replies, "Praying? Not us! Unless you mean praying to the god of Oklahoma country music!" Later, the clip makes even clearer the challenge of representing Muslims. Mandvi says to his son, "You got a D in algebra! Now why would you do that?" His wife chastises him, "Oh don't blow up at him again!" He replies, "Why would you say that? 'Blow up'? I would never do anything like that! That's just a very strange way to put things." He turns to his neighbour and asks, "Am I right?" In a later scene, he reacts similarly to a metaphor about bullets. His overreaction to weapon imagery calls attention to itself, to the imagery, and to his efforts to dissociate Islam from terrorism (and himself from Islam).

The Qu'osby Show passes from parody to satire when it uses elements of *The Cosby Show* to question Couric's idea that sitcoms can end racism. But because it is ironic, its critique, heavy-handed as it is, operates in constant tension with its denoted meaning. To emphasize the ironic level of meaning *The Daily Show* also aired a faux-news sequence called "Allah in the Family" where Mandvi, now in the role of a reporter, describes his efforts to create a Muslim *Cosby Show*. It opens with a clip of Couric's statement, followed by Mandvi's description of what it would take to do as she suggests. He seeks out experts to help him and explains, "No one knows better how to create a Muslim *Cosby Show* than Alvin Poussaint, the Harvard psychologist who served as a consultant on the original *Cosby Show*, which cured racism against black people." The *Daily Show* audience laughs at the naivety and incongruity of the last line: racism against blacks in the United States has not disappeared. To drive the point home, Mandvi assembles a test audience "of the kind of people we'd have to win over: average Americans." He shows them watching the pilot, and they shake their heads. At the end, he asks them whether they would watch such a show, and everyone says no. One even says, "You gotta have that closet terrorist or something. And they gotta keep him hidden 'cause they don't want the rest of the neighbourhood to know ... You can have, like, an uncle, Uncle Rahib or something, who came over, and he's a Bedouin, and he lives in the basement in a sandbox with a goat." In a voice-over Mandvi concludes, "So apparently the best way for a show to combat Muslim stereotypes is to confirm Muslim stereotypes."

These two clips use juxtaposition to suggest a deep scepticism about the sitcom's ability to cure the ills of society. In contrast, *Little Mosque*'s makers maintained their faith in the genre's ability to influence people for the better. In this way even this limited examination of satire helps us ask: what if the producers of a Muslim-themed sitcom pushed the genre to its breaking points?

Pushing the Sitcom Further

The Daily Show's satire goes only so far. It suggests that sitcoms are inadequate to the task Couric (and others) saw for them, but it gives no sense of what might take their place. It questions the sitcom's tidiness by suggesting there are no tidy endings outside of TV, but it gives no sense of what a *messy* sitcom might look like.

The preceding sections help us imagine a messy sitcom. Its messiness would come from its treatment of identity and difference as equivocal categories, not necessarily good or bad but instead contingent on specific circumstances. It would show identity where it mattered but acknowledge that not all aspects of identity matter at all times. It would admit of difference but acknowledge that difference need not be threatening, although it can be. The ecumenical vision encapsulated by *Little Mosque*'s last scene, where Muslims and Christians come together in harmony, is lovely, but it rings hollow in a world where militants and terrorists use Islam to justify their acts of violence. Many non-Muslims find Islam threatening because the Muslims they see most frequently, in the news and other media, utter threats directed at them and their way of life. It will be necessary to recognize this fact before finding a way to move beyond it and show non-Muslims that their Muslim neighbours are not likely to be extremists.

Little Mosque's ecumenism helped make the diversity it described saleable. What I am suggesting here would trouble the world of harmony it depicted. A messy sitcom would negotiate an uneasy, ambivalent terrain where people with conflicting ideas – about Islam, but about other value systems, too – confront each other. Truces in such a world are rare, fragile, and hard won. The goal would be something like *convivencia*,[11] a term Franz Greifenhagen (2010, 9) uses to mean "a living together that extends the circle of trust beyond family and friends; the sharing of activities and daily life across religious and cultural boundaries such that differences are accepted and become positive and productive sources of cross-fertilization and creativity." But it would be a goal, not a state already achieved, and it would require characters to commit to an ongoing way of living together, regardless of the fact that some differences between religions can be irreconcilable. Such a commitment need not be dependent on shared beliefs: "We can live together without agreeing on what the values are that make it good to live together; we can agree about what to do in most cases, without agreeing about why it is right" (Appiah 2006, 71).

This version of ecumenism is incipient in *Little Mosque* in the relationship between Baber and Thorne in the sixth season. They disagree with each other but are forced by circumstance to share the same space. They do not come to share the same beliefs in the end, but they do agree to continue sharing a space when Amaar invites Thorne and his congregation to worship in the new mosque. Thus, rather than the bench Amaar and Magee share in the first seasons, a better metaphor for the show's ecumenical impulse might be the large desk Baber and Thorne fight over for their respective offices, the one in front of which they stand together when they tell Amaar, "We do not get along well. We *disagree* well" (season 6, episode 4).

This agonistic ecumenism faced its limit in *Little Mosque*'s tidy ending. Pursuing it further would mean challenging viewers' expectations of the sitcom genre, where humour depends on broad characterizations and ambivalence is rare. This is where the value of *The Daily Show*'s satire is apparent: it is self-conscious and reflexive, and even if it does not propose a way to address the sitcom's limitations, it is effective in pointing them out. One limitation is the sitcom's reliance on broad characterizations. Another is the assumption that sitcoms, because they depict minorities as being "just like us," are their ticket into mainstream culture. If this book has shown anything, it is that the idea that Muslims are "just another wacky and lovable family living amidst us," to return to an early review cited in the introduction (Murray 2007a), is *not* simple. It performs a form of ideological labour that works against depictions of meaningful difference when it might appear threatening.

What type of humour would an agonistic notion of ecumenism have engendered? Probably something with a harder edge, along the lines of Thorne's confrontational style when he was first introduced. Thorne was not shy about his contempt for Muslims, and his contempt was closer to what people heard in other media, especially conservative sources . The gentle humour of the first seasons failed to acknowledge the perspective he brought, and the absence was conspicuous enough to make viewers doubt the rest of what they saw. Giving voice to his contempt brought that missing discourse into the world of Mercy. Making it the subject of satire troubled the logic that shaped it. But even then, satire cut both ways: many viewers shared Thorne's contempt, and although they might recognize the ironic meaning and the effort to make his contempt look silly, satire's polysemic structure gave them the ability to reject the ironic meaning in favour of the literal one.

What effect would an agonistic ecumenism have had on *Little Mosque*'s saleability? It would likely have made viewers uncomfortable, and it would have represented a risk for *Little Mosque*'s makers. The show's audience included people who liked its gentle humour, and in season 4 Darling, Donnelly, and Nawaz heard from fans that they did not like Rev. William Thorne. An agonistic ecumenism would be a hard sell, and the messiness I am suggesting would have made it harder for fans of the show to watch it as a form of escapism. More to the point, a more radical critique of existing social structures would likely cause viewers to dig in their heels if they felt their way of life (and unacknowledged privilege) was threatened. Messiness might push the limits of the sitcom in ways that trouble its simplistic presentation of identity and difference, but it would put producers and networks in a bind if it cost them viewers.

Where does this leave the question of cultural translation?

Conclusion: Cultural Translation and Television

The makers of *Little Mosque* wanted to translate Muslims for non-Muslims. They wanted to transform stereotypes into images of diversity and move Muslims from the realm of the foreign to that of the familiar. They chose the sitcom because it activated a productive type of polysemy: jokes said two things simultaneously, and their ironic meaning could draw their literal meaning into question. What is more, laughter (or discomfort) disposed viewers to engage with these contradictions. But they could go only so far. They needed viewers to watch, so they had to make the diversity they depicted saleable. The theme of ecumenism – the idea that the Abrahamic religions, at their most fundamental level, are the same – allowed them to contain the contradictions of their program and suggest ways Muslims and non-Muslims were coming to see Muslims as North American. Some members of the viewing public agreed with the show's depiction of diversity, but others thought it was tendentious. *Little Mosque*'s makers responded by engaging with their critics (and the events taking place in the world outside Mercy, Saskatchewan). They adjusted their approach as the seasons progressed and *Little Mosque* evolved.

Little Mosque's value lies only partially in this translation. Although its makers were conscientious, their acts of explanation flattened out characters' beliefs. There was value to what *Little Mosque* taught viewers about Islam, but the show's real value lay in the way it worked to make some non-Muslims feel more familiar and comfortable with Muslims. That comfort held the potential to give receptive viewers the ability to explore difference without feeling threatened. (Time will tell what effect familiarity will have on viewers who were hostile to the show.) Such comfort is valuable in so far as it disposes people to commit to working to live together, not necessarily to get along but to "disagree well" – to disagree without letting difference become divisive.

Notes

Introduction

1 The title of the show is a play on *Little House on the Prairie* (1974–83), the beloved US family drama based on the works of Laura Ingalls Wilder. Executive producer Mary Darling says the title was in part an homage to her home state of Minnesota (interview with author, 2011), although writers from the show provide a different account. The similarities between the two shows do not extend much beyond the title and rural setting, however. They were different genres (the first a drama, the second a sitcom), were about different time periods (the first historical, the second contemporary), and were produced under very different industry circumstances. Scholars and critics tend to focus instead on the 1970s Norman Lear sitcom *All In the Family* when seeking comparisons to *Little Mosque*.

2 I am speaking here of English-language television scholarship. I have written extensively about French-language television elsewhere (e.g., Conway 2011), but its history is different.

3 Controversies similar to the one surrounding the use of Sharia law were also taking place in French-speaking Canada. Many in Quebec, for instance, thought that religious minorities were abusing the province's provisions for reasonable accommodations. Historically, such accommodations were intended to make it possible for people with physical disabilities to perform their jobs, but by 2006 there was a growing perception that a number of Muslims, Hasidic Jews, and Sikhs were requesting accommodations on religious grounds, bringing into question the secular nature of the province's public institutions. See Bouchard and Taylor (2008).

4 News about religion, however, accounted for less than 1 per cent of all mainstream news in 2011, down from 2 per cent in 2010 (Pew Research Center 2012, 2).

5 Elsewhere I have examined cultural translation in television news
(Conway 2011), where a series of contradictions is manifest. In particular,
although journalists might want to expand the range of people they profile, the constraints imposed by the need to tell stories efficiently forces
them to be reductive in the details they include. But news differs from sitcoms, not only in its generic constraints, but also in its mode of address,
which usually avoids humour and irony.

6 The interviewees are listed in the acknowledgments and the references.
I conducted most interviews in person or by telephone, and they lasted
between thirty and ninety minutes. I conducted one interview by email
when the interviewee had limited availability. I structured interviews
around the following questions: What relationships (e.g., between
Muslims and non-Muslims) did the interviewee want to influence? What
issues did the interviewee see as salient in the context of those relationships? How did they shape the interviewee's actions in producing *Little
Mosque*? Per institutional review board guidelines, I cite by name only
those interviewees who gave me explicit permission to do so.

7 For a complete list of episodes see the CBC's website for *Little Mosque*,
which is available at www.cbc.ca/littlemosque/.

8 Historically, "ecumenism" has referred to efforts to bring Christians of
different denominations together. Over time the term has come to mean
"interfaith understanding or reconciliation" more broadly. In this book
I use the terms "ecumenical" and "interfaith" interchangeably.

1 Sitcoms, Cultural Translation, and Saleable Diversity

1 In fact, it was the first North American sitcom about Muslims, although a
small cadre of Muslim stand-up comedians had been touring North America
in an effort to reach "mainstream" non-Muslim audiences in the long after-
math of the 9/11 attacks. See Amarasingam (2010) and Michael (2013).

2 This is not to say that everyone takes this equivalence at face value.
Much of the field of translation studies since the cultural turn in the 1990s
has been concerned with questioning this appearance of equivalence.
See Bassnett and Lefevere (1990) and Marinetti (2011).

3 For a sense of the term's history see Conway (2013). For a sense of its
range of uses across the fields of anthropology, comparative literature,
cultural studies, and translation studies see Conway (2012a).

4 If we carry through with this analogy, Muslims in North America, or at
least a subset of the community, were the analogue of the source text.
Or, in Lienhardt's (1954) anachronistic terminology, they were the

analogue of the "remote tribe" anthropologists sought to explain to readers, and *Little Mosque* was the analogue of the anthropologist's monograph.

5 Polysemy, of course, is not unique to sitcoms. As nearly four decades of audience research in cultural studies have demonstrated, all TV is open to multiple interpretations: "To be popular, the television text has to be read and enjoyed by a diversity of social groups, so its meanings must be capable of being inflected in a number of different ways" (Fiske 1987, 66). What makes the sitcom different is its mode of activating that polysemy.

6 Couric made the suggestion, of course, before Cosby was accused of rape.

7 This is the very definition of irony, according to Kenneth Burke (1941, 438), who describes it as what happens when "what goes forth as A returns as non-A."

8 Although the makers of *Little Mosque* went out of their way to emphasize similarities between Muslims and non-Muslims, humour can emphasize differences between groups, too. Divisive humour – in essence, laughing *at* rather than laughing *with* – can enforce barriers when one group applies it to another. This potential resides in irony as well (see Meyer 2000).

9 The label "gays and lesbians" is reductive and carries with it certain prescriptive, exclusionary notions of sexuality. As the analysis of "gay sitcoms" on US television demonstrates, however, its reductiveness is consistent with the depictions in question.

10 My description of this circuit derives from the circuit models of culture proposed by scholars such as Stuart Hall (1980) and Julie D'Acci (2004). See Conway (2012b) for an application specific to cultural translation. Note that I describe interventions by different people as if they were discrete moments, but they were not. This description is valuable heuristically, but it is a bit misleading. Because people were always reacting to as well as predicting their interlocutors' responses, the structure of exchanges was more fluid than my description suggests.

2 Representation between the Particular and the Universal

1 The real culprits in the film are a group of environmentalists who are frustrated that they cannot generate the publicity they desire. See Nawaz (2014, 113–29).

2 From "The Bahá'í Faith: The International Website of the Bahá'ís of the World." info.bahai.org, retrieved 31 January 2012.

3 As I write in chapter 5, one result of this concentration on issues was a focus on the cultural trappings of Islam, at least as it was practised on the show, at the expense of questions of belief.

4 This paradox has been well explored in literature. Jorge Luis Borges's story "The Congress" (1977) is probably the best in the genre.

5 Transcribed from the video at "Canada's 'Little Mosque on the Prairie,'" CBSNews.com, 18 January 2011, www.cbsnews.com/videos/canadas-little-mosque-on-the-prairie/

3 The Paradoxes of "Humanizing Muslims"

1 The Canadian publications I examined were the *Toronto Star*, the *Globe and Mail*, the *Ottawa Citizen*, the *Montreal Gazette*, the *National Post*, the *Vancouver Sun*, the *Toronto Sun*, *Maclean's*, and Canada NewsWire. US newspapers included the *New York Times*, the *International Herald Tribune*, the *Chicago Tribune*, the *Los Angeles Times*, the *Seattle Times*, the *Washington Post*, the *Boston Globe*, the *Christian Science Monitor*, the *Atlanta Journal-Constitution*, the *Detroit Free Press*, and the McLatchy news service. UK newspapers included the *Guardian*, the *Times*, and the *Observer*. In this chapter I focus on the Canadian newspapers, which ranged from conservative to liberal but remained "mainstream" enough to attract sufficient numbers of readers.

2 All the writers described in this section identified themselves as Muslim in their articles or letters to the editor or on their professional web pages.

3 Taken from littlemosqueontheprairie.wordpress.com/2007/01/10/episode-1-title/#comments. In this and other quotations from non-professional media I have made slight formatting changes, but I have maintained authors' original spelling and syntax.

4 Taken from the Muslim Canadian Congress, mission statement, www.muslimcanadiancongress.org/mission.html.

5 Nawaz's observation is consistent with the findings of more formal studies of second-generation Muslims in North America. Rubina Ramji (2008, 108), for instance, finds that second-generation Canadian Muslims "did not, on the whole, feel disempowered or disadvantaged; nor did they seem fearful of their futures." Mucahit Bilici (2012, 114–18) also observes a similar generational difference in Muslims in the United States. Second- and third-generation Muslims are likely to view the United States as home and view with suspicion the majority-Muslim countries from which their parents emigrated. In contrast, first-generation Muslims are more likely to be suspicious of the United States and see their homelands as the point of reference for evaluating what is Islamic and what is not.

6 In point of fact, the mandate is to "provide radio and television services incorporating a wide range of programming that informs, enlightens and entertains" (Broadcasting Act, 1991, sec. 3.1.l).

7 Interestingly, some Muslim viewers were also offended on behalf of Christians in response to the Protestant/prostitute joke. Zarqa Nawaz tells a story about "one Muslim guy [who] was so offended on behalf of Protestants that he picketed the CBC ... on Christmas Day" (public forum, University of North Dakota, 2011). She relates that sensitivity back to the "traumatizing" experience of being the subject of jokes for Muslims who were new to that experience. This reaction demonstrates the break *Little Mosque* made with shows that came before it: it marked one of the first times that jokes about Islam were meant to cause people to laugh *with* Muslims, rather than *at* them.

8 In her memoir Nawaz (2014, 183–4) writes that Wente was "one of my favourite columnists at the *Globe and Mail*." She was eager to read her column, and she was "a little shocked that Margaret didn't believe that among the billion Muslims on earth there might not be a few good-looking imams."

9 This logic resembles the one Evelyn Alsultany (2012a) identifies in recent dramas with Muslim characters. One recurring device writers use to avoid stereotypes is to create characters who are wrongly accused of terrorism. To prove their patriotism they must accept the injustice of the racism they face. To criticize it would be to call into question the justness of US foreign and domestic policy since the rise of al-Qaeda, but especially since the attacks of 9/11.

10 That suspicion stemmed from faulty intelligence from the Royal Canadian Mounted Police. He was deported to Syria, where he was tortured. When he was returned to Canada, a Canadian commission of inquiry cleared him of all charges (Canada 2006). The controversy surrounding Arar's "extraordinary rendition" and return to Canada was well covered by the CBC.

11 Fox News has been available in Canada since 2004. Cwynar (2013, 57) asserts that Fred stands in for conservative US radio: "Fred represents ignorance, hypocrisy, and crass commercialism – values that have long been associated with the United States in Canadian national discourse." As such, he argues, Fred serves as a point of negative identification for Canadians.

12 This comment refers to a plot point made earlier: Yasir signed a lease to rent the church basement for his business, but the lease does not mention the mosque.

4 Saleable Diversity and International Audiences

1 Transcribed from the video at "Katie Couric Speaks Against Anti-Muslim Bigotry, Suggests Muslim 'Cosby Show,'" published by the *Huffington Post*,

1 January 2011, www.huffingtonpost.com/2011/01/01/katie-couric-muslim-bigotry-cosby-show_n_803208.html.

2 Transcribed from the video at "Canada's 'Little Mosque on the Prairie,'" CBSNews.com, 18 January 2011, www.cbsnews.com/videos/canadas-little-mosque-on-the-prairie/.

3 Why Fox did not carry through with its plans is unclear. Zarqa Nawaz proposes, "We [in Canada] didn't have 9/11, and we have a public broadcaster. 9/11 affected the American psyche in a major way, and you have to be sensitive to that" (quoted in Adair 2011, E2). Others are more blunt. Evan Shapiro, president of the cable network Pivot, which licensed *Little Mosque* in 2013, says, "It has never been seen in the United States because the word 'mosque' is in the title" (quoted in Moore 2013).

4 I focus here on non-Muslim-majority countries because I want to understand the way *Little Mosque* translated Muslims for non-Muslims. It aired in Muslim-majority countries, too, and although the show's reception there would provide insight into how Muslims and non-Muslims talk across cultural lines, it is not my focus here.

5 Zahn (2007b) was quick to correct the email author's misperception: "For the record, research shows Muslims have been living and worshipping right here in the U.S. for at least 180 years."

6 CNN's online transcript of this exchange contains inaccuracies, which I have corrected.

7 Even the US State Department noted these differences, although it saw them in a different light, as a diplomatic cable published by WikiLeaks reveals: "The Canadian Broadcasting Corporation (CBC) has long gone to great pains to highlight the distinction between Americans and Canadians in its programming, generally at our expense ... A December 2007 episode [of *Little Mosque*] portrayed a Muslim economics professor trying to remove his name from the No-Fly-List at a US consulate. The show depicts a rude and eccentric US consular officer stereotypically attempting to find any excuse to avoid being helpful. Another episode depicted how an innocent trip across the border became a jumble of frayed nerves as Grandpa was scurried into secondary by US border officials because his name matched something on the watch list" (United States 2008). There is no evidence to suggest that the State Department's concern had any effect on WestWind's ability to syndicate *Little Mosque* in the United States, but it does reveal a great deal about television's perceived power to shape national identity, as Serra Tinic (2013, 37) writes: "To equate 'distinctions between Americans and Canadians' with 'anti-Americanism' marks a lack of understanding of the sense of negative identity that long dominated

Canadian cultural discourses. Namely, that the American cultural other permeates the broader Canadian cultural imagination and that domestic broadcasting policy has long stressed that a televisual border of difference needed to be fostered if Canadians were to see themselves as a unique imagined community. Ironically, the state department's alarm is evidence that, in recent years, the CBC has fulfilled its mandate [to promote Canadian identity]."

8 See, for instance, the special section in the 2012 volume of the *Journal of Mass Media Ethics* (Alsultany 2012b; Bronstein 2012; Ivancin 2012; Sisco 2012; Whitehouse 2012), where contributors debate the implications of the decision by Lowe's to pull its advertisements.

9 Original: "l'indifférence aux discriminations dès lors que c'est au nom de l'égalité en droit qu'on s'interdit de prendre en compte les discriminations de fait." Unless otherwise noted, all translations in this chapter are my own.

10 Original: "prendre en compte dans la représentation à l'antenne, la diversité des origines et des cultures de la communauté nationale."

11 Original: "La conjoncture s'y prête bien. Les gens ont besoin de rire. De plus, l'humour fait partie des gènes de CANAL+. Enfin, nous avons au sein de la chaîne un vivier de jeunes talents – auteurs, humoristes, etc. – que nous avons contribué à faire émerger ces dernières années. Donc nous disposons de tous les atouts pour renouveler l'humour!"

12 Original: "Avant d'être une série politique, où ses propos seraient porteurs d'un message, elle est avant tout une série de divertissement et à prendre comme telle ... *La Petite Mosquée dans la prairie* ne ravira pas ceux qui se facilitent la vie en mettant les individus dans des boîtes."

13 Original: "Il faudra sans doute encore attendre avant d'avoir des propositions françaises de fictions antistéréotypée tel que les proposent les télévisions anglo-saxonnes ... et comme en témoigne cette phrase de dialogue tiré de la série canadienne anglophone *La petite mosquée dans la prairie* ... 'peut-on ne pas porter le foulard islamique pendant les cours d'aquagym si le prof est gay?'" The plot referred to in the line of dialogue comes from the season 1 episode "Swimming Upstream," but the line as such is not in the episode. Macé's assessment of *Little Mosque* as "antistereotypical" represents a rather superficial reading of the program. It might be antistereotypical in the French context, but it still suffered from reductive logic of synecdochic representation described in chapter 2.

14 As a point of comparison with France, Canada, and the United States, in 2007, when WestWind was working to syndicate the show in Norway, the television advertising industry in that country was worth about NOK3.1 billion, or about US$611 million, based on an exchange rate

of US$1 = NOK5.075 (Smith 2008, 20). This amount did not account for the NRK, whose three networks did not accept advertising.

15 Original: "Støtte, skape og utvikle norsk kultur, kunst og underholdning" and "Sende programmer for etniske og språklige minoriteter." The translations come from the NRK.

16 Original: "TV2 skal ha egne programmer som gjenspeiler mangfoldet i norsk og internasjonalt kulturliv" (art. 3.3.6) and "TV2 skal ha egne programmer eller programinnslag for etniske minoriteter" (art. 3.3.8).

17 Original: "Flere representanter for minoritetsgrupper i Norge deltok i programmene, blant annet fikk vi møte Afshan Rafiq, Norges første stortingsrepresentant med innvandrerbakgrunn. Som moderne norsk muslim med politisk karriere, mann og barn, er hun et forbilde for mange. Hva tenker hun om kvinnerollen i tradisjonell norsk og pakistansk kultur?"

18 Original: "Høyprofilerte og friske serier fra utlandet ble tidlig en del av TV2s identitet. Vi ... introduserte norske tvseere for 'X-files,' 'Venner for livet,' 'NYPD Blue,' '24' og 'Ally McBeal.' Innkjøpssjefer fra de store tv-markedene får gjerne vann i munnen og tårer i øynene når de hører hvor mange av de store Hollywoodproduksjonene som har gått på TV2."

19 Original: "Islamistene vs. Ytringsfriheten 1-0?"

20 Original: "Den kanadiske serien klarer den vanskelige balansegangen med å lage humor av religiøse og kulturelle forskjeller. Klarer norske redaktører å balansere like godt? Eller sover Norge i timen når ytringsfriheten blir satt på prøve? Karikaturtegningene av Muhammed har ført til sterke reaksjoner. Gir norske redaktører etter for presset fra de islamske fundamentalistene, eller er det ikke journalistisk relevant å trykke de kontroversielle tegningene?"

21 Original: "Vi har fått enkelte henvendelser fra konservative kristne som sier at vi normaliserer muslimer for mye. Da tenker jeg at vi har gjort noe riktig." Donnelly's original statement was no doubt in English, but it was published only in Norwegian.

5 Religion as Culture versus Religion as Belief

1 Other characters evolved, too, but not to the same degree. In the early seasons, for instance, Fred Tupper, the local radio shock-jock, showed his more sensitive side when he tempered his rhetoric about Muslims out of respect for his intern Layla Siddiqui (season 2, episode 17). Similarly, Baber Siddiqui showed occasional signs of moderating his conservative outlook, especially in season 2, when he developed a bond with Fatima, the owner of the local diner. But in both cases the producers maintained the

characters largely as they were because they helped generate conflict by
serving as foils for more moderate characters.

2 Many religious studies scholars see the distinction between culture and
belief as a false dichotomy, one whose roots lie (among other places) in the
Cartesian split between body and mind (Woodhead 2011; Vásquez 2011;
Stausberg 2012; Phelps 2015). They argue that the distinction, reworked
here as external manifestations of culture and internal forms of belief, does
not hold: the physical movement of ritual acts, for instance, can strengthen
believers' convictions. What matters here, however, is the influence it had
on *Little Mosque*'s makers.

3 These norms were not universal, as a number of critics pointed out, and
would vary depending on whether people were Shia or Sunni, or even
whether they were conservative or liberal (Fatah and Hassan 2007; Hirji
2011).

4 A number of viewers and critics picked up on this technique, especially
in the early seasons. See, for example, Sherazi (2007).

5 By the fourth season the need the writers felt to make assumptions explicit
was waning. Sadiya Durrani worked as an intern during seasons 3 and 4
and as a writer for seasons 5 and 6. She was the only Muslim writer other
than Nawaz. By the time she began writing, she says, much of the work
to familiarize viewers with Muslim conventions already had been done:
"We didn't have to explain so much – there were certain terms and cultural references that were established already, so some of them we'd have to
remind the audience, but not every single sort of odd thing that happens ...
There's a lot of things established, like the saying of [the greeting] 'salaam
alaikum' [peace be upon you] and [the response] 'wa alaikum salaam'
[and upon you be peace] that we didn't have to [explain]. And the chaper-
oning and stuff, we didn't always have to put a finger on it" (interview
with author, 2011).

6 The phrase "people of the book" refers to the idea that Jews, Christians,
and Muslims all trace their lineage back to Abraham. Appeals to the
Abrahamic tradition have increased among people encouraging interfaith
exchange since the 9/11 attacks, especially in the United States (Bilici 2012,
145–70). Nonetheless, we must not overlook the fact that, although such
appeals are grounded in a sense of shared history, they are also inherently
rhetorical and, as such, they are not as simple as Darling asserts here. Jews
and Christians, for instance, trace their lineage back to Abraham's son
Isaac and Muslims to his son Ishmael. They also understand differently
one of the central tenets of Christianity: the idea of the Holy Trinity,
or God as Father, Son, and Holy Spirit. Consequently, different Christian

denominations disagree about how much exactly they share with Muslims (see Volf 2012; Qureshi 2015). Nor are such appeals necessarily the only approach to interfaith relations in *Little Mosque*. Franz Volker Greifenhagen (2010), for instance, argues that *Little Mosque* demonstrates the virtues of *convivencia*, where groups decide to live together and maintain an ongoing conversation about their differences. The point of the conversation is not to demonstrate that two groups are the same, but to recognize that the will to coexist is fragile and in need of constant, deliberate effort.

7 This exchange reveals a dimension of faith and the distinction between culture and belief that remain unexplored in *Little Mosque on the Prairie*. Sarah's emotional attachment to Christian ritual suggests a deep connection to her childhood faith, one that is qualitatively different from her attachment to Islam, which until this scene appeared to be one of convenience. Her conversion was pragmatic – it let her marry Yasir. But the depth of her emotional connection suggests that ritual – which appears to fall under the category of religion as culture – is something greater. It suggests that ritual is an embodied form of knowing, one that is outside the bounds of the rational, Cartesian self. In other words, this scene raises an interesting but unanswered question. In what way does tradition become an outward expression of belief? And what effect does this crossing-over have on our understanding of the culture/belief distinction?

8 The Nicene Creed is, in fact, more than a metaphor – it is a doctrinal statement, an expression of orthodoxy, that forms the core of the Anglican Church (and many other Christian churches).

9 Notably, this blogger cited Asrat (2008), whose critique I mentioned in chapter 3.

Conclusion

1 Sikhs came second: 39 per cent of Canadians outside Quebec viewed them unfavourably in 2013. Fewer than 30 per cent of Canadians held adverse views on any other religion (Angus Reid Global 2013).

2 Rates were higher in Quebec (69 per cent in 2013), where the Parti Québécois proposed a Charter of Values, which would have banned public servants from wearing "conspicuous" religious clothing, including veils worn by Muslim women (Angus Reid Global 2013).

3 Indeed, Sohad Murrar, a graduate student at the University of Wisconsin – Madison, conducted an experiment that demonstrated that, in contrast to people who watched a sitcom without Muslim characters, people who

watched *Little Mosque* "had more positive attitudes toward Muslims both immediately after the viewing and four to six weeks later" (Haq 2016).

4 My list of other texts is far from complete and does not account for all possible iterations of ironic humour about Muslims. In the future it will be important, for instance, to examine the co-option of the Twitter hashtag #MuslimRage. In that instance *Newsweek* asked Muslims to post about what made them angry, after many had protested against the anti-Islam film *Innocence of Muslims*. Instead, they sent tweets such as "I'm having such a good hair day. No one even knows. #MuslimRage" (Chappell 2012). But such a project is distinct from what I have undertaken here.

5 From "The Stakeout" (season 2, episode 2), according to the Internet Movie Database (www.imdb.com/character/ch0140327/quotes).

6 Transcribed from the video "Allah Made Me Funny – Azhar Usman 1/2," posted to YouTube, https://www.youtube.com/watch?v=sQ3owg0jcxo.

7 However, as Jaclyn Michael (2013) explains, not all jokes are created equal, and rather than translating Muslims for non-Muslims, some have a disciplining effect for members of the Muslim community. For instance, she describes a joke made by Preacher Moss of "Allah Made Me Funny." In an effort to encourage Muslims to be confident despite the suspicion they face, he repeats, "Let me tell you something. If you didn't do anything, *act* like you didn't do it!" He follows this line with a prescription for how US Muslims *should* act, describing as weak those who are too fearful to greet other Muslims with "salaam alaikum." Michael cites this line as evidence that humour "can serve two related but seemingly contradictory functions: [it can be] a device of group solidarity and ... an enforcer of group boundaries" (2013, 144–5).

8 Of course, nothing guarantees that audience members will take his ironic critique as the intended meaning. His jokes rely on polysemy, and thus they offer a literal meaning that could be construed as perpetuating stereotypes.

9 This distinction between parody and satire is not my own, and I am borrowing here, as in chapter 3, from Christopher Cwynar (2013), who borrows from Jonathan Gray, Katarzyna Rukszto, Zoë Druick, and most of all Linda Hutcheon.

10 The work of Jeffrey Jones (2010 and Gray, Jones, and Thompson 2009) is exemplary here, as is that of Amber Day (2011). Day's account is especially relevant because she considers how satirists use irony to advance earnest political goals and speak to specific interpretive communities to privilege satire's ironic meaning over its literal meaning.

References

Interviews

Alexander, Susan (*Little Mosque* producer/writer, season 1). 2011. Interview, Toronto, ON, 21 July.

Darling, Mary (WestWind Pictures/*Little Mosque* co-executive producer). 2011. Interview, Toronto, ON, 20 July.

Darling, Mary, and Clark Donnelly (WestWind Pictures/*Little Mosque* co-executive producer). 2012. Interview, Dundas, ON, 30 May.

Darling, Mary. 2014. Telephone interview, Grand Forks, ND, and Toronto, ON, 4 March.

Durrani, Sadiya (*Little Mosque* intern, seasons 3 and 4; writer, seasons 5 and 6). 2011. Telephone interview, Grand Forks, ND, and Toronto, ON, 11 August.

Kennedy, Michael (*Little Mosque* director). 2011. Email interview, Grand Forks, ND, and Toronto, ON, 9 September.

Leo, Anton (former creative head of CBC television comedy). 2011. Telephone interview, Grand Forks, ND, and Montreal, QC, 9 July.

Nawaz, Zarqa (*Little Mosque* creator and writer). 2011. Interview, Grand Forks, ND, 8 April.

Nawaz, Zarqa. 2011. Public forum, University of North Dakota, Grand Forks, 8 April.

Rae, Al (*Little Mosque* writer, seasons 1, 2, and 6). 2011. Interview, Winnipeg, MB, 19 July.

Ranelagh, John (media buyer, TV2, Norway). 2012. Email interview, August-September.

Schechter, Rebecca (*Little Mosque* writer, seasons 1, 2, and 6). 2011. Telephone interview, Grand Forks, ND, and Toronto, ON, 12 August.

Publications

Adair, Marcia. 2011. "Cultural Exchange: The Globe Takes to Canada's Television." *Los Angeles Times*, 10 April, E2.

Adams, Michael. 2009. "Muslims in Canada: Findings from the 2007 Environics Survey." *Horizons* 10 (2): 19–26.

Ahmed, Waleed S. 2012. "'Little Mosque on the Prairie' Ends: The First Muslim Sitcom in Review." *muslimmatters.org*, 1 May. http://muslimmatters .org/2012/05/01/little-mosque-on-the-prairie-ends-impact-of-the-first-muslim-sitcom/.

Ali, Naheed. 2007. "Muslim ... and Funny, Too." Santa Rosa, CA, *Press Democrat* 1 February, B7.

Ally, Safiyyah. 2007. "Little Mosque, Lotta Hype." *Ottawa Citizen*, 14 January, B8.

Al-Solaylee, Kamal. 2007. "Like Jack Bauer, but with an Open Mind." *Globe and Mail*, 22 February, R4.

Alsultany, Evelyn. 2012a. *Arabs and Muslims in the Media: Race and Representation after 9/11*. New York: New York University Press.

Alsultany, Evelyn. 2012b. "Protesting Muslim Americans as Patriotic Americans: The *All-American Muslim* Controversy." *Journal of Mass Media Ethics* 27 (2): 145–8. http://dx.doi.org/10.1080/08900523.2012.684588.

Amarasingam, Amarnath. 2010. "Laughter the Best Medicine: Muslim Comedians and Social Criticism in Post-9/11 America." *Journal of Muslim Minority Affairs* 30 (4): 463–77. http://dx.doi.org/10.1080/13602004.2010.533444.

Ang, Ien. 1991. *Desperately Seeking the Audience*. New York: Routledge. http://dx.doi.org/10.4324/9780203321454.

Angus Reid Global. 2013. "Canadians View Non-Christian Religions with Uncertainty, Dislike." Press release, 2 October. http://www.angusreid global.com/wp-content/uploads/2013/10/Canadians-view-non-Christian-religions-with-uncertainty-dislike.pdf.

Angus Reid Public Opinion. 2010. "Four-in-Five Canadians Approve of Quebec's Face Veil Legislation." Press release, 17 March. https://www .visioncritical.com/wp-content/uploads/2010/03/2010.03.27_Veil_CAN.pdf.

Appadurai, Arjun. 1990. "Disjuncture and Difference in the Global Cultural Economy." *Theory, Culture & Society* 7 (2): 295–310. http://dx.doi.org/ 10.1177/026327690007002017.

Appiah, Kwame Anthony. 2006. *Cosmopolitanism: Ethics in a World of Strangers*. New York: Norton.

Asrat, Kidist Paulos. 2008. "How Canada's Little Mosque on the Prairie Is Aiming for Our Souls." American Thinker blog, 13 December. http://www .americanthinker.com/2008/12/how_canadas_little_mosque_on_t.html.

Bakhtin, M.M. 1986. "The Problem of Speech Genres." In *Speech Genres and Other Late Essays*, ed. Caryl Emerson and Michael Holquis, trans. Vern W. McGee, 60–102. Austin: University of Texas Press.

Barclay, Harold. 1971. "A Lebanese Community in Lac La Biche, Alberta." In *Immigrant Groups*, ed. Jean Leonard Elliott, 66–83. Scarborough, ON: Prentice-Hall.

Bassnett, Susan, and André Lefevere, eds. 1990. *Translation, History and Culture*. New York: Pinter.

Becker, Ron. 2006. *Gay TV and Straight America*. New Brunswick, NJ: Rutgers University Press.

Bhabha, Homi. 1994. *The Location of Culture*. New York: Routledge.

Bilici, Mucahit. 2010. "Muslim Ethnic Comedy: Inversions of Islamophobia." In *Islamophobia/Islamophilia: Beyond the Politics of Enemy and Friend*, ed. Andrew Shryock, 195–208. Bloomington: Indiana University Press.

Bilici, Mucahit. 2012. *Finding Mecca in America: How Islam Is Becoming an American Religion*. Chicago: University of Chicago Press. http://dx.doi.org/10.7208/chicago/9780226922874.001.0001.

Bissoondath, Neil. 1994. *Selling Illusions: The Cult of Multiculturalism in Canada*. Toronto: Penguin.

Birge, Robert. 2011. "We Handled This Poorly." Kayak blog, 14 December. https://www.kayak.com/news/we-handled-this-poorly-updated-dec-15/.

Borges, Jorge Luis. 1977. "The Congress." In *The Book of Sand*, trans. Norman Thomas di Giovanni, 27–49. New York: E.P. Dutton.

Bouchard, Gérard, and Charles Taylor. 2008. *Building the Future: A Time for Reconciliation (Abridged Report)*. Quebec City: Commission de consultation sur les pratiques d'accommodement reliées aux différences culturelles.

boyd, danah. 2006. "A Blogger's Blog: Exploring the Definition of a Medium." *Reconstructions* 6, no. 4. http://www.danah.org/papers/ABloggersBlog.pdf.

Bramham, Daphne. 2007. "Real Canada Is the Land Beyond the Big Cities." *Vancouver Sun*, 13 January, C5.

Bredin, Marian, Scott Henderson, and Sarah A. Matheson, eds. 2012. *Canadian Television: Text and Context*. Waterloo, ON: Wilfrid Laurier University Press.

Broadcasting Act (S.C. 1991, c. 11). http://laws-lois.justice.gc.ca/eng/acts/b-9.01/.

Bronstein, Carolyn. 2012. "Advertising and the Corporate Conscience." *Journal of Mass Media Ethics* 27 (2): 152–4. http://dx.doi.org/10.1080/08900523.2012.684597.

Buden, Boris, and Stefan Nowotny. 2009. "Cultural Translation: An Introduction to the Problem." *Translation Studies* 2 (2): 196–208. http://dx.doi.org/10.1080/14781700902937730.

Burke, Kenneth. 1941. "Four Master Tropes." *Kenyon Review* 3 (4): 421–38.

Buzelin, Hélène. 2011. "Agents of Translation." In *Handbook of Translation Studies*, Vol. 2, ed. Yves Gambier and Luc van Doorslaer, 6–12. Amsterdam: John Benjamins. http://dx.doi.org/10.1075/hts.2.age1.

Caldwell, John Thornton. 2008. *Production Culture: Industrial Reflexivity and Critical Practice in Film and Television*. Durham, NC: Duke University Press. http://dx.doi.org/10.1215/9780822388968.

Canada. 1967. Department of the Secretary of State, Canadian Citizenship Branch. *The Canadian Family Tree: Centennial Edition, 1867–1967*. Ottawa: Queen's Printer.

Canada. 2005. Statistics Canada. "Population by Religion, by Province and Territory (2001 Census)." http://www.statcan.gc.ca/tables-tableaux/sum-som/l01/cst01/demo30a-eng.htm.

Canada. 2006. Commission of Inquiry Into the Actions of Canadian Officials in Relation to Maher Arar. *Report of the Events Relating to Maher Arar: Analysis and Recommendations*. Ottawa: Minister of Public Works and Government Services. www.sirc-csars.gc.ca/pdfs/cm_arar_rec-eng.pdf.

"Canada's 'Little Mosque on the Prairie.'" 2011. CBSNews.com, 18 January. www.cbsnews.com/videos/canadas-little-mosque-on-the-prairie/.

"Canal+ accueille une petite mosquée." 2007. *Le Film français*, 9 May. www.lefilmfrancais.com/92265/canal-accueille-une-petite-mosquee.

Canal+. 2008. *Rapport Annuel*. Paris: Canal+. http://www.larp.fr/dossiers/wp-content/uploads/2010/10/CANAL+-Bilan-financier-2008.pdf.

Cañas, Sandra. 2008. "The Little Mosque on the Prairie: Examining (Multi) Cultural Spaces of Nation and Religion." *Cultural Dynamics* 20 (3): 195–211. http://dx.doi.org/10.1177/0921374008096309.

CBC/Radio-Canada. 2007. *Public Broadcasting in Canada: Time for a New Approach*. Ottawa: CBC/Radio-Canada. www.cbc.radio-canada.ca/_files/cbcrc/documents/parliamentary/2007/mandate.pdf.

Chappell, Bill. 2012. "'Muslim Rage' Explodes on Twitter, but in a Funny Way (Yes, Really)." The Two-Way blog, 17 September. http://www.npr.org/sections/thetwo-way/2012/09/17/161315765/muslim-rage-explodes-on-twitter-but-in-a-funny-way-yes-really.

Cohen, Andrew. 2007. *The Unfinished Canadian: The People We Are*. Toronto: McClelland & Stewart.

Collins, Scott. 2007. "A Foreign Concept." *Newsday*, 30 September, C14.

Conway, Kyle. 2005. "Heading South to Make It Big: The American Success of Canada's *You Can't Do That on Television*." *American Review of Canadian Studies* 35 (1): 45–65. http://dx.doi.org/10.1080/02722010509481249.

Conway, Kyle. 2010a. "Cultural Diversity and the Expansion of Political Imagination: A Response to Margaret Ogrodnick." *North Dakota Quarterly* 77 (1): 51–8.

Conway, Kyle. 2010b. "News Translation and Cultural Resistance." *Journal of International and Intercultural Communication* 3 (3): 187–205. http://dx.doi .org/10.1080/17513057.2010.487219.

Conway, Kyle. 2011. *Everyone Says No: Public Service Broadcasting and the Failure of Translation.* Montreal: McGill-Queen's University Press.

Conway, Kyle. 2012a. "A Conceptual and Empirical Approach to Cultural Translation." *Translation Studies* 5 (3): 264–79. http://dx.doi.org/10.1080/ 14781700.2012.701938.

Conway, Kyle. 2012b. "Cultural Translation, Global Television Studies, and the Circulation of Telenovelas in the United States." *International Journal of Cultural Studies* 15 (6): 583–98. http://dx.doi.org/10.1177/ 1367877911422291.

Conway, Kyle. 2012c. "Cultural Translation, Long-form Journalism, and Readers' Responses to the Muslim Veil." *Meta* 57 (4): 997–1012. http://dx.doi .org/10.7202/1021229ar.

Conway, Kyle. 2012d. "Quebec's Bill 94: What's 'Reasonable'? What's 'Accommodation'? And What's the Meaning of the Muslim Veil?" *American Review of Canadian Studies* 42 (2): 195–209. http://dx.doi.org/10.1080/02722011 .2012.679150.

Conway, Kyle. 2013. "Cultural Translation: Two Modes." *TTR: Traduction, Terminologie, Rédaction* 26 (1): 15–36.

Coren, Michael. 2007. "Show Is Visual Drudgery." *Toronto Sun*, 13 January, 17.

CSA (Conseil supérieur de l'audiovisuel). 2000a. "La Convention de Canal Plus." www.csa.fr/var/ezflow_site/storage/csa/rapport2001/liste_ annexes/3_tele_conv_cplus.htm.

CSA (Conseil supérieur de l'audiovisuel). 2000b. "Présence et représentation des minorités visibles à la télévision française: une étude du CSA." *La Lettre du CSA* 129. calixthe.beyala.free.fr/etudeCSA.htm.

CSA (Conseil supérieur de l'audiovisuel). 2005. "La représentation de la diversité des origines à la télévision." *La Lettre du CSA* 190. www.csa.fr/ Etudes-et-publications/Les-dossiers-d-actualite/La-representation-de-la- diversite-des-origines-a-la-television.

Culler, Jonathan. 1997. *Literary Theory: A Very Short Introduction.* New York: Oxford University Press.

Cwynar, Christopher. 2013. "The Canadian Sitcom and the Fantasy of National Difference: *Little Mosque on the Prairie* and English-Canadian Identity." In *Beyond the Border: Tensions across the Forty-ninth Parallel in the Great Plains and Prairies*, ed. Kyle Conway and Timothy Pasch, 39–70. Montreal: McGill-Queen's University Press.

Czach, Liz. 2010. "The 'Turn' In Canadian Television Studies." *Journal of Canadian Studies. Revue d'Etudes Canadiennes* 44 (3): 174–80.

D'Acci, Julie. 2004. "Cultural Studies, Television Studies, and the Crisis in the Humanities." In *Television after TV: Essays on a Medium in Transition*, ed. Lynn Spigel and Jan Olsson, 418–45. Durham, NC: Duke University Press. http://dx.doi.org/10.1215/9780822386278-021.

Datamonitor. 2008. *Broadcasting & Cable TV in France: Industry Profile*. Reference Code 0164–2016. EBSCOhost.

Day, Amber. 2011. *Satire and Dissent: Interventions in Contemporary Political Debate*. Bloomington: Indiana University Press.

Desmoulières, Raphaëlle Besse. 2008. "'Les Veillées du ramadan' pour 'étendre les cultures de l'Islam.'" *Le Monde*, 19 September. www.lemonde.fr/societe/article/2008/09/19/etendre-les-cultures-de-l-islam_1097032_3224.html.

Dib, Kamal. 2006. "Now That Religious Diversity Is upon Us." *Canadian Diversity* 5 (2): 39–43.

Dole, Janice A., and Gale M. Sinatra. 1998. "Reconceptualizing Change in the Cognitive Construction of Knowledge." *Educational Psychologist* 33 (2–3): 109–28. http://dx.doi.org/10.1080/00461520.1998.9653294.

Doyle, John. 2007a. "Little Mosque is Gloriously Canadian." *Globe and Mail*, 9 January, R1.

Doyle, John. 2007b. "Love and Marriage (and Breast Implants)." *Globe and Mail*, 7 March, R3.

Doyle, John. 2007c. "Little Mosque Is Back and It's a Lot Funnier." *Globe and Mail*, 3 October, R3.

Doyle, John. 2012. "Goodbye, Little Mosque: Nice Idea, Not So Funny." *Globe and Mail*, 2 April, R1.

Duff, Beth. 2007. "Canadian Sitcom Places Muslims in the Spotlight." *Chicago Tribune*, 2 January, 4.

Duffy, Mike. 2007. "Hit Sitcom Shows Muslims Can Take a Joke." McLatchy-Tribune Business News, 5 February.

Eid, Mahmoud, and Sarah Khan. 2011. "A New-Look for Muslim Women in the Canadian Media: CBC's *Little Mosque on the Prairie*." *Middle East Journal of Culture and Communication* 4 (2): 184–202. http://dx.doi.org/10.1163/187398611X571355.

Eriksen, Elise Nyborg. 2008. "Vil utrydde hat med latter." *ABC Nyheter*, 8 May. http://www.abcnyheter.no/nyheter/kultur/2008/05/08/66264/vil-utrydde-hat-med-latter.

Ertmann, Birte. 2007. "Oh Ye of Little Faith." *Ottawa Citizen*, 17 January, A11.

Fatah, Tarek, and Farzana Hassan. 2007. "CBC TV's Mosque Sitcom: Little Masquerade on the Prairie." *Toronto Sun*, 12 February. http://muslimcanadiancongress.info/wp-content/uploads/2013/08/CBC-TVs-Mosque-Sitcom-Little-masquerade-on-the-prairie-Februaury-12-20071.pdf.

Feuer, Jane. 2001. "Situation Comedy, Part 2." In *The Television Genre Book*, ed. Glen Creeber, 67–70. London: BFI.

Fiske, John. 1987. *Television Culture*. New York: Methuen.

Florida Family Association. 2011. "Lowe's Will Not Advertise Again on All-American Muslim." http://floridafamily.org/full_article.php?article_no =117.

Galewski, Elizabeth. 2006. "Counter/publicity: Conceiving the Means of Effective Representation." In *Engaging Argument*, ed. Patricia Riley, 250–6. Washington, DC: National Communication Association.

Gallie, W.B. 1962. "Essentially Contested Concepts." In *The Importance of Language*, ed. Max Black, 121–46. Englewood Cliffs, NJ: Prentice Hall.

Gardee, Ihsaan. 2007. "A TV Show That Allows Muslims to Laugh at Themselves." *Toronto Star*, 11 January, A23.

Gaye, Nicola, and Jean Kunz. 2009. "Reflecting Religious Diversity in Canadian Public Policy: Perspectives from Federal Policy Practitioners." *Horizons* 10 (2): 44–9.

Geddes, John. 2013. "Canadian Anti-Muslim Sentiment is Rising, Disturbing New Poll Reveals." *Maclean's*, 3 October. http://www.macleans.ca/ politics/land-of-intolerance/.

Gellner, Ernest. 1970. "Concepts and Society." In *Rationality*, ed. Bryan R. Wilson, 18–49. New York: Harper & Row.

Gitlin, Todd. 1979. "Prime-Time Ideology: The Hegemonic Processes in Television Entertainment." *Social Problems* 26 (3): 251–66. http://dx.doi.org/ 10.2307/800451.

Gray, Jonathan, Jeffrey P. Jones, and Ethan Thompson, eds. 2009. *Satire TV: Politics and Comedy in the Post-Network Era*. New York: NYU Press.

Greenberg, K.J. Hannah. 2012. "'Little Mosque on the Prairie': An Unfortunate Media Spin." *Jerusalem Post* Middle Eastern Musings blog, 13 February. http://www.jpost.com/Blogs/Middle-Eastern-Musings/Little-Mosque-on-the-Prairie-An-unfortunate-media-spin-366108.

Greifenhagen, Franz Volker. 2010. *On the Way to Muslim-Christian Understanding*. Camrose, AB: Chester Ronning Centre for the Study of Religion and Public Life.

Greifenhagen, Franz Volker. 2011. "La série télévisée *Little Mosque on the Prairie* de Zarqa Nawaz et le discours de l'authenticité musulmane." *Théologiques* 19 (2): 151–72. http://dx.doi.org/10.7202/1024732ar.

Hall, Stuart. 1980. "Encoding/Decoding." In *Culture, Media, Language*, ed. Stuart Hall, et al., 128–38. London: Hutchinson.

Hartley, John. 2001. "Situation Comedy, Part 1." In *The Television Genre Book*, ed. Glen Creeber, 65–7. London: BFI.

Haq, Husna. 2016. "Can a TV Sitcom Reduce Anti-Muslim Bigotry?" *Christian Science Monitor*, 30 January. www.csmonitor.com/Science/2016/0130/Can-a-TV-sitcom-reduce-anti-Muslim-bigotry.

Hingorani, Asha. 2007. "CBC Is Brilliant for Showing Little Mosque." *Ottawa Citizen*, 17 January, A11.

Hirji, Faiza. 2011. "Through the Looking Glass: Muslim Women on Television – An Analysis of *24*, *Lost*, and *Little Mosque on the Prairie*." *Global Media Journal – Canadian Edition* 4 (2): 33–47.

Hirzalla, Fadi, Liesbet van Zoonen, and Floris Müller. 2013. "How Funny Can Islam Controversies Be? Comedians Defending Their Faiths on YouTube." *Television & New Media* 14 (1): 46–61. http://dx.doi.org/10.1177/1527476412453948.

Ivancin, Mari. 2012. "Business Ethics and the Return on Reputation." *Journal of Mass Media Ethics* 27 (2): 150–2. http://dx.doi.org/10.1080/08900523.2012.684593.

Jaleel, Anjum. 2007. "'Little Mosque' Shows Muslims' Humanity." *Ottawa Citizen*, 14 January, A11.

Jalees, Sabrina. 2007. "How Comedy Struggles with Being Race-y." *Toronto Star*, 23 January, D4.

Jhally, Sut, and Justin Lewis. 1992. *Enlightened Racism: The Cosby Show, Audiences, and the Myth of the American Dream*. Boulder, CO: Westview Press.

Jones, Jeffrey P. 2010. *Entertaining Politics: Satiric Television and Political Engagement*. 2nd ed. Lanham, MD: Rowman & Littlefield.

Jordan, Shirley Ann. 2002. "Ethnographic Encounters: The Processes of Cultural Translation." *Language and Intercultural Communication* 2 (2): 96–110. http://dx.doi.org/10.1080/14708470208668079.

Kalbach, Warren E. 1970. *The Impact of Immigration on Canada's Population*. Ottawa: Dominion Bureau of Statistics.

Karim, Karim H. 2003. *Islamic Peril: Media and Global Violence*. 2nd ed. Montreal: Black Rose Books.

Karim, Nur Kareelawati Abd., Norazirawati Ahmad, Ainurliza Mat Rahim, Muhammed Yusuf Khalid, and Roslizawad Mohd Ramli. 2011. "*Little Mosque on the Prairie*: Interfaith TV through Malaysian Eyes." In *The London Film and Media Reader 1 (Essays from Film and Media 2011: The First London Film and Media Conference)*, ed. Phillip Drummond, 173–82. London: London Symposium.

"Katie Couric Speaks against Anti-Muslim Bigotry, Suggests Muslim 'Cosby Show.'" 2011. *Huffington Post*, 1 January. www.huffingtonpost.com/2011/01/01/katie-couric-muslim-bigotry-cosby-show_n_803208.html.

Kay, Barbara. 2007. "The Joke's on Us." *National Post*, 11 January, A19.

Kay, Barbara. 2009. "Truth and Survival." *National Post*, 16 September, A24.

Kelly, Brendan. 2007a. "Canuck TV Finds Funny Bone." *Variety*, 5–11 November, 30.

Kelly, Brendan. 2007b. "Muslim Sitcom 'Mosque' Answers Ratings Prayers." *Variety*, 22–8 January, 20–1.

Khan, Sheema. 2007. "There Really Is a Canadian Way." *Globe and Mail*, 6 February, A19.

Kohanik, Eric. 2007. "Little Mosque a Wry and Witty Offering on CBC." *Ottawa Citizen*, 9 January, C12.

Lembo, Ron. 2000. *Thinking through Television*. New York: Cambridge University Press. http://dx.doi.org/10.1017/CBO9780511489488.

Lienhardt, Godfrey. 1954. "Modes of Thought." In *The Institutions of Primitive Society: A Series of Broadcast Talks*, by E.E. Evans-Pritchard et al., 95–107. Oxford: Basil Blackwell.

Longinovic, Tomislav. 2002. "Fearful Asymmetries: A Manifesto of Cultural Translation." *Journal of the Midwest Modern Language Association* 35 (2): 5–12. http://dx.doi.org/10.2307/1315162.

Lowry, Brian. 2012. "Niche Nets Have Faith." *Variety*, 20–6 August: 2, 9.

Lunau, Kate. 2009. "Youth Survey: Teens Lose Faith in Droves." *Maclean's* 7 April. www.macleans.ca/news/canada/teens-lose-faith-in-droves/.

MacDonald, Gayle. 2012. "Little Mosque Leaves the Prairie." *Globe and Mail*, 9 January, R1.

Macé, Éric. 2007. "Des 'minorités visibles' aux néostéréotypes: Les enjeux des régimes de monstration télévisuelle des différences ethnoraciales." *Journal des anthropologues*. Hors-série: Identités nationales d'État. jda.revues.org/2967.

MacFarquhar, Neil. 2006. "Sitcom's Precarious Premise: Being Muslim over Here." *New York Times*, 7 December. www.nytimes.com/2006/12/07/arts/television/07mosq.html.

Mairie de Paris. 2007. "Les veillées du Ramadan: Concerts, expositions, conférences, rencontres, lectures." www.paris.fr/portail/viewmultimedia document?multimediadocument-id=32582.

Marc, David. 2005. "Origins of the Genre: In Search of the Radio Sitcom." In *The Sitcom Reader: America Viewed and Skewed*, ed. Mary M. Dalton and Laura R. Linder, 15–24. Albany: State University of New York Press.

Marinetti, Cristina. 2011. "Cultural Approaches." In *Handbook of Translation Studies*, Vol. 2, ed. Yves Gambier and Luc van Doorslaer, 26–30. Amsterdam: John Benjamins. http://dx.doi.org/10.1075/hts.2.cul1.

Matheson, Sarah A. 2012. "Television, Nation, and Situation Comedy in Canada: Cultural Diversity and *Little Mosque on the Prairie*." In *Canadian*

Television: Text and Context, ed. Marian Bredin, Scott Henderson, and Sarah A. Matheson, 153–72. Waterloo, ON: Wilfred Laurier University Press.

Mayberry, Jessica. 2010. "The Need for Cultural Translation with Community Media." PBS Idea Lab, 26 July. http://mediashift.org/idealab/2010/07/the-need-for-cultural-translation-with-community-media207/.

McAndrew, Marie. 2010. "The Muslim Community and Education in Quebec: Controversies and Mutual Adaptation." *Journal of International Migration and Integration* 11 (1): 41–58. http://dx.doi.org/10.1007/s12134-009-0124-x.

McKenzie, Rob. 2007a. "Allah Be Praised!" *National Post*, 9 January, AL1.

McKenzie, Rob. 2007b. "Mosque Is on the Right Track As It Sparks Seinfeld-like Moments and Measured Discussions." *National Post*, 17 February, TO38.

Menon, Vinay. 2007a. "Little Mirth on the Prairie." *Toronto Star*, 9 January, D5.

Menon , Vinay. 2007b. "Big-hearted Satire a Winner." *Toronto Star*, 1 October, L7.

Menon, Vinay. 2012. "Little Show, Big Concept Nears End." *Toronto Star*, 25 March, E1.

Meyer, John C. 2000. "Humor as a Double-Edged Sword: Four Functions of Humor in Communication." *Communication Theory* 10 (3): 310–31. http://dx.doi.org/10.1111/j.1468-2885.2000.tb00194.x.

Michael, Jaclyn. 2013. "American Muslims Stand Up and Speak Out: Trajectories of Humor in Muslim American Stand-up Comedy." *Contemporary Islam* 7 (2): 129–53. http://dx.doi.org/10.1007/s11562-011-0183-6.

Miller, Mary Jane. 1993. "Inflecting the Formula: The First Seasons of *Street Legal* and *LA Law*." In *The Beaver Bites Back? American Popular Culture in Canada*, ed. David H. Flaherty and Frank Manning, 104–22. Montreal: McGill-Queen's University Press.

Moore, Frazier. 2013. "The Big Story: Pivot, Network for Millennials, Tries to Change TV." Associated Press, 27 March. http://www.sandiegouniontribune.com/news/2013/mar/27/pivot-network-for-millennials-tries-to-change-tv/.

Murray, Michael. 2007a. "Little Mirth on the Prairie." *Ottawa Citizen*, 20 January, K1.

Murray, Michael. 2007b. "For Mercy's Sake." *Ottawa Citizen*, 24 November, K1.

Nawaz, Zarqa. 2014. *Laughing All the Way to the Mosque*. Toronto: HarperCollins.

Newcomb, Horace M., and Paul M. Hirsch. 1983. "Television as a Cultural Forum: Implications for Research." *Quarterly Review of Film Studies* 8 (3): 45–55. http://dx.doi.org/10.1080/10509208309361170.

Nordiske Mediedager. 2008. *Rapport 2008*. www.nordiskemediedager.no/assets/Uploads/2008rsrapportNordiske-Mediedager.pdf.

Norway. 2001. "Konsesjonsvilkår for TV 2 AS i perioden 1. januar 2003 til 31. desember 2009." Oslo: Kulturdepartementet. https://www.regjeringen.no/ no/dokumenter/konsesjonsvilkar-for-tv-2-as-i-perioden-/id98962/.

NPR (National Public Radio). 2007. "Sitcom Takes Lighthearted Approach to 'Aliens.'" *Fresh Air*, 7 November. http://www.npr.org/templates/story/ story.php?storyId=16005234.

Osborne, Lauren E. 2012. "Believing, Belonging, and Laughing in *Little Mosque on the Prairie*." Martin Marty Center for the Advanced Study of Religion, 15 March. divinity.uchicago.edu/sightings/believing-belonging-and-laughing-little-mosque-prairie-lauren-e-osborne.

Pellerin, Brigitte. 2007. "Equal-Opportunity Humour." *Ottawa Citizen*, 9 January, A10.

Peterson, Valerie V. 2005. "*Ellen*: Coming Out and Disappearing." In *The Sitcom Reader: America Viewed and Skewed*, ed. Mary M. Dalton and Laura R. Linder, 165–76. Albany: State University of New York Press.

"La petite mosquée dans la Prairie." 2007. *Pure Médias*, 16 July. http://www.ozap.com/.

Pew Research Center. 2009. "Modest Rise in Concern about Islamic Extremism." Pew Research Religion and Public Life Project, 18 November. www.pewforum.org/2009/11/18/modest-rise-in-concern-about-islamic-extremism/.

Pew Research Center. 2011. *Muslim Americans: No Signs of Growth in Alienation or Support for Extremism*. August. www.people-press.org/files/legacy-pdf/ Muslim-American-Report.pdf.

Pew Research Center. 2012. *Religion in the News: Islam and Politics Dominate Religion Coverage in 2011*. 23 February. http://www.pewforum.org/files/ 2012/02/Religionandthenews2011.pdf.

Phelps, Hollis. 2015. "It *Is* about the Hijab: Wheaton College and the Narrowing Criteria for Evangelical Belonging." *Religious Dispatches*, 17 December. http://religiondispatches.org/it-is-about-the-hijab-wheaton-college-and-the-narrowing-criteria-for-evangelical-belonging/

Poniewozik, James. 2011. "Mideast Meets Midwest." *Time*, 14 November. http://content.time.com/time/magazine/article/0,9171,2098567,00.html.

Posner, George J., Kenneth A. Strike, Peter W. Hewson, and William A. Gertzog. 1982. "Accommodation of a Scientific Conception: Toward a Theory of Conceptual Change." *Science Education* 66 (2): 211–27. http://dx.doi.org/ 10.1002/sce.3730660207.

Provencher, Denis M. 2005. "Sealed with a Kiss: Heteronormative Narrative Strategies in NBC's *Will & Grace*." In *The Sitcom Reader: America Viewed and*

Skewed, ed. Mary M. Dalton and Laura R. Linder, 177–90. Albany: State University of New York Press.

Pym, Anthony. 2010. "On Empiricism and Bad Philosophy in Translation Studies." http://usuaris.tinet.cat/apym/on-line/research_methods/2009_lille.pdf.

Qureshi, Nabeel. 2015. "Do Muslims and Christians Worship the Same God?" *Ravi Zacharias International Ministries*, 22 December. http://rzim.org/global-blog/do-muslims-and-christians-worship-the-same-god.

Ramji, Rubina. 2005. "From *Navy Seals* to *The Siege*: Getting to Know the Muslim Terrorist, Hollywood Style." *Journal of Religion and Film* 9 (2). http://avalon.unomaha.edu/jrf/Vol9No2/RamjiIslam.htm.

Ramji, Rubina. 2008. "Creating a Genuine Islam: Second Generation Muslims Growing Up in Canada." *Canadian Diversity* 6 (2): 104–8.

Reta, Naseem A. 2007. "TV Show Refreshing, Funny View of Muslims." *Ottawa Citizen*, 12 January, A15.

Ribeiro, António Sousa. 2004. "The Reason for Borders or a Border Reason? Translation as a Metaphor for Our Times." *Eurozine*, 8 January. www.eurozine.com/pdf/2004-01-08-ribeiro-en.pdf.

Rutherford, Paul. 1993. "Made in America: The Problem of Mass Culture in Canada." In *The Beaver Bites Back? American Popular Culture in Canada*, ed. David H. Flaherty and Frank E. Manning, 260–80. Montreal: McGill-Queen's University Press.

Ryan, Phil. 2010. *Multicultiphobia*. Toronto: University of Toronto Press.

Said, Edward. 1997. *Covering Islam: How the Media and the Experts Determine How We See the Rest of the World*. Rev. ed. New York: Vintage.

Schleiermacher, Friedrich. 1992. "Extracts from 'Über die verschiedenen Methoden des Übersetzens.'" In *Translation/History/Culture: A Sourcebook*, ed. and trans. André Lefevere, 141–66. New York: Routledge.

Schwartz, Mattathias. 2008. "The Trolls Among Us." *New York Times Magazine*, 3 August. www.nytimes.com/2008/08/03/magazine/03trolls-t.html.

Shaheen, Jack G. 2001. *Reel Bad Arabs: How Hollywood Vilifies a People*. New York: Olive Branch.

Sherazi, Aisha. 2007. "'Little Mosque' Hits Home." *Ottawa Citizen*, 11 January, A15.

Sisco, Hilary Fussell. 2012. "When Lightning Strikes." *Journal of Mass Media Ethics* 27 (2): 148–50. http://dx.doi.org/10.1080/08900523.2012.684591.

Smith, Adam. 2008. "The EMEA Media Map." *Campaign*, 17 October: 4–24.

Steiner, George. 1975. *After Babel: Aspects of Language and Translation*. London: Oxford University Press.

Steyn, Mark. 2007. "The Little Mosque that Couldn't." *Maclean's*, 5 February. http://www.macleans.ca/culture/entertainment/article.jsp?content= 20070205_140131_140131.

Strachan, Alex. 2007a. "Small-town Life Shines through in Two Very Different Shows." *Ottawa Citizen*, 17 January, E8.

Strachan, Alex. 2007b. "Aliens in America Picks Up Where Little Mosque Leaves Off." *Ottawa Citizen*, 25 July, F6.

Strachan, Alex. 2007c. "With a Wink and a Nod, Little Mosque Spreads Its Wings." *Ottawa Citizen*, 3 October, B8.

Strachan, Alex. 2007d. "Witty and Wise, Little Mosque Is Enjoying a Fine Second Season." *Ottawa Citizen*, 24 October, F6.

Strachan, Alex. 2008. "Gentle and Disarmingly Funny, Little Mosque Has Come of Age." *Ottawa Citizen*, 5 March, C12.

Stausberg, Michael. 2012. "A New Theory of Religion? Introducing the Review Symposium on Manuel A. Vásquez: *More Than Belief* (2011)." *Religion* 42 (4): 597–608. http://dx.doi.org/10.1080/0048721X.2012.705480.

Stroumboulopoulos, George. 2011. "GST S1: Episode 88 – Zaib Shaikh." *George Stroumboulopoulos Tonight*, 27 January. www.cbc.ca/strombo/videos/gst-s1-episode-88-zaib-shaikh.

Syvertsen, Trine, and Gro Maren Mogstad Karlsen. 2000. "The Norwegian Television Market in the 1990s: Legal Framework, Market Situation, Financial Information and Programming of Public and Private Television." *Nordicom Review* 21 (1): 71–100.

Takacs, Stacy. 2011. "Burning Bush: Sitcom Treatments of the Bush Presidency." *Journal of Popular Culture* 44 (2): 417–35. http://dx.doi.org/10.1111/j.1540-5931.2011.00840.x.

Tinic, Serra. 2005. *On Location: Canada's Television Industry in a Global Market.* Toronto: University of Toronto Press.

Tinic, Serra. 2013. "The Borders of Cultural Difference: Canadian Television and Cultural Identity." In *Beyond the Border: Tensions across the Forty-ninth Parallel*, ed. Kyle Conway and Timothy Pasch, 29–38. Montreal: McGill-Queen's University Press.

Thakore, Bhoomi K. 2014. "Must-See TV: South Asian Characterizations in American Popular Media." *Sociology Compass* 8 (2): 149–56. http://dx.doi .org/10.1111/soc4.12125.

Thorne, Jennee-Lee. 2007. "Double Standard." *Ottawa Citizen*, 19 January, A11.

TV2. 2008. *Allmennkringkasterregnskap 2008.* Bergen: TV2. pub.cdn.tv2.no/ multimedia/TV2/archive/00710/TV_2_-_allmennkring_710419a.pdf.

United States. 2008. Department of State, U.S. Embassy in Ottawa. "Subject: Primetime Images of US-Canada Border Paint U.S. in Increasingly Negative Light." 25 January. Published by WikiLeaks, 1 December 2010. www .wikileaks.ch/cable/2008/01/08OTTAWA136.html.

Vásquez, Manuel A. 2011. *More Than Belief: A Materialist Theory of Religion*. New York: Oxford University Press.

Veilleux, Gérard. 1993. *Repositioning/Le repositionnement*. Toronto: CBC Research Centre.

Volf, Miroslav, ed. 2012. *Do We Worship the Same God? Jews, Christians, and Muslims in Dialogue*. Grand Rapids, MI: William B. Eerdmans.

Wente, Margaret. 2007. "Little Mosque: Way Too Cute." *Globe and Mail*, 9 January, A15.

Werts, Diane. 2012. "Online TV Clicks with New Series." *Newsday*, 28 August, B24.

Whitehouse, Ginny. 2012. "Lowe's Ethical Choices: Not Taking a Stand Means Taking a Stand." *Journal of Mass Media Ethics* 27 (2): 142–5. http://dx.doi.org/ 10.1080/08900523.2012.684584.

Woodhead, Linda. 2011. "Five Concepts of Religion." *International Review of Sociology* 21 (1): 121–43. http://dx.doi.org/10.1080/03906701.2011.544192.

Young, Jill. 2007. "Give It a Chance." *Ottawa Citizen*, 16 January, A11.

Zahn, Paula. 2007a. "Barriers Broken in Congress; Muslims in America." *Paula Zahn Now*, 4 January. transcripts.cnn.com/TRANSCRIPTS/0701/04/ pzn.01.html.

Zahn, Paula. 2007b. "Breaking Barriers in American Politics; Death Penalty Not Sought in Florida Homeless Attack; China Tightens Foreign Adoption Regulations." *Paula Zahn Now*, 5 January. transcripts.cnn.com/ TRANSCRIPTS/0701/05/pzn.01.html.

Zakrevsky, Sonia. 2007. "'Little Mosque' Shows Disrespect for Other Faiths." *Ottawa Citizen*, 15 January, A9.

Index

24 (television show), 86–8, 96–8

Abrahamic religions. *See* people of
   the book
Alexander, Susan, 47, 57, 85
Aliens in America (television show), 3,
   15, 82, 86–8, 125, 128–32
All-American Muslim (television
   show), 87–9, 125, 130–2
All in the Family (television show), 43,
   47, 83, 89, 98, 111, 143n1
Allah Made Me Funny (comedy
   troupe), 134
Alsultany, Evelyn, 6, 17, 30–1, 83, 131,
   147n9
Ansari, Aziz, 129–30
Appadurai, Arjun, 11
Appiah, Kwame, 124
Aristotle, 26
audience research, 23–4, 29, 48, 59–62;
   and focus groups, 48, 61
Axis of Evil (comedy troupe), 134

Bahá'í religion, 5, 38–9, 108, 126
Bakhtin, Mikhail, 24, 59
Banks, Boyd. *See* Peterson, Joe
   (character)

Bhabha, Homi, 22
Bilici, Mucahit, 6, 16, 26
Broadcasting Act (1991), 40, 73, 103,
   146n6
Buden, Boris, 22
Byers, Michele, 6

Canada Media Fund. *See* Canadian
   Television Fund
Canadian Broadcasting Corporation
   (CBC), 3–5, 12, 36, 39, 43, 54, 83,
   98; and audience research, 48, 67;
   and budget cuts, 41; and cultural
   translation, 14–15, 22, 55, 99–104,
   107, 113–18; and mandates, 14, 35,
   40–2, 68, 73, 146n6, 148n7; perceptions of, 24, 29–30, 67–73, 87–9, 100,
   121; and programming strategies,
   41–2, 55; and sitcom conventions,
   67–70, 73, 103, 118. *See also* Leo,
   Anton; religion as belief; religion
   as culture
Canadian Television Fund, 39, 42
Canadian television scholarship,
   6, 10
Canal+. *See* France
Cañas, Sandra, 47

Christians, 7–8, 16, 49–51, 57, 63, 85, 88, 97, 108, 130; in *Little Mosque on the Prairie*, 70, 101, 111, 114–19, 139; Protestants, 65, 70, 147n7. *See also* ecumenism; Magee, Rev. Duncan (character); people of the book; Thorne, Rev. William (character)

CNN, 54, 83–5

Collins, Scott, 88

commercial television, 4–5, 18, 27–30, 36, 41–3, 82–3, 94–5, 99

Community (television show), 86, 130

Condell, Pat, 135

convivencia, 139, 151n6, 154n11

Corner Gas (television show), 5, 42–3, 119

Cosby Show (television show), 25, 80, 89, 98, 120–1, 137–8. *See also* Mandvi, Aasif

Couric, Katie, 25, 51, 80, 120, 137–8, 145n6

critical production studies, 11

critical reception. *See* Doyle, John; Kay, Barbara; McKenzie, Rob; Menon, Vinay; Murray, Michael; Steyn, Mark; Strachan, Alex; Wente, Margaret

Crone, Neil. *See* Tupper, Fred (character)

cultural studies, 11–12; and circuit models of culture, 29, 73, 129, 145n10

cultural translation: definition, 4–5, 11–18, 21–4; and ecumenism, 16; evaluation of, 128–9; and humour, 10; limits of, 16–19, 52; as negotiation, 21–4, 59–61, 66, 78, 101; and saleable diversity, 30, 99; utopian horizon of, 141. *See also* humour

Cwynar, Chris, 28, 43, 75, 147n11, 153n9

Danish cartoons, 68, 83, 97–8

Darling, Mary, 5, 17, 22, 35–42, 101, 127, 140, 143n1, 151n6; and Bahá'í faith, 5, 14–15, 39, 108; and ecumenism, 126; and funding, 39, 42, 81; and global geopolitics, 47–8; and humour, 25–6, 70; and international audiences, 82–4, 92–7; and international syndication, 40–1, 81, 85, 89–90; and programming strategies, 18, 51–2, 55, 69, 85; and religion, 101–4, 107; and Rev. William Thorne (character), 107–10; Sarah Hamoudi (character), 113–15, 118–19; and sitcom conventions, 100, 103

DeGeneres, Ellen. *See Ellen* (television show)

difference: as category of identity, 133–5; as threat, 127–9

Dinssa, Fatima (character), 45–6, 57, 105–6, 111, 150n1

Donnelly, Clark, 5, 22, 35, 38–42, 101, 127, 140, 150n21; and Bahá'í faith, 5, 14–15, 108; and ecumenism, 124–6; and funding, 39–42; and international audiences, 82, 93–7; and programming strategies, 55; and religion, 101–4; and Sarah Hamoudi (character) 113–14, 118–19

Doyle, John, 68–9, 86, 119–21

drama (genre), 6–7, 31, 41, 89–90, 98, 147n9

Duncan, Arlene. *See* Dinssa, Fatima (character)
Durrani, Sadiya, 50, 151n5

Ellen (television show), 27
ecumenism, 16, 21, 38, 100, 107–9, 112, 122–7, 134; and agonism, 138–41
essentially contested concepts, 21

Fatah, Tarek, 50, 65–6, 120, 127
Firla, Brandon. *See* Thorne, Rev. William (character)
Florida Family Association, 88
France: Canal+, 91–4; and colonialism, 91–2; and Conseil supérieur de l'audiovisuel (broadcast regulator), 91–2

Gallie, W.B., 21
Gellner, Ernest, 20
Gitlin, Todd, 27
Goldberg, Whoopi, 132
Greifenhagen, Franz, 139, 151n6
Guarascio, David, 87

Hamoudi, Rayyan (character), 45–7, 58, 61, 77, 102–6, 111–17, 132
Hamoudi, Sarah (character), 15, 45–7, 65, 105; and character development, 101–2, 110, 113–19, 152n7; and Rev. William Thorne, 114–19; as stand-in for viewers, 49, 115. *See also* religion as belief
Hamoudi, Yasir (character), 15, 33, 42, 45–7, 58, 75–6, 103–6; departure from *Little Mosque on the Prairie*, 101, 110, 113–16
Hassan, Farzana, 50, 65–6, 127

Hewitt, Sitara. *See* Hamoudi, Rayyan (character)
Hirji, Faiza, 50
Hollywood, 10, 96, 110
Hulu, 89–90
humour, 37, 113, 116; affective dimensions, 19, 25–6, 128–9; agonistic forms of, 16, 126, 140; formal dimensions, 19, 24–5, 128–9; gentle forms of, 16, 122, 125–7, 140; and "hokeyness," 55, 68, 72–3, 98, 119–20; and minorities, 3, 10; and Muslims, 17, 25, 44, 63, 84; and polysemy, 4, 17–18, 26, 29, 74–6; and programming strategies, 92–3; theories of, 24–6; and transformative potential, 10, 13, 16, 24, 27–31, 52–3, 64, 130. *See also Aliens in America*; cultural translation; jokes; sitcoms; stand-up comedy; stereotypes

"I am Canadian" (advertisement), 135–6
international distribution, 40–1, 81, 85, 89–90. *See also* France; Norway; United States
Islam, 7, 17; American attitudes toward, 10; beliefs, 31–2, 35, 44, 48, 52–3, 56–7, 65–6, 99, 102–4; in Canada, 7–9, 38; Canadian attitudes toward, 9, 49, 56, 61, 66, 124–5; and diversity, 4, 33, 44, 86; and geopolitics, 35, 65; holidays, 47–8; and news coverage, 10, 54, 107; in North America, 30, 35–6, 59, 62, 70–3, 79, 100–1, 119, 124; pronunciation of, 136; in the United States, 9–10, 83–4, 88–9; and "the West," 4,

14. *See also* ecumenism; Hamoudi, Sarah (character); France; Muslims; Norway; people of the book

irony, 135–8. *See also* humour

Jaffer, J.J. (character), 104–6, 132
Jhally, Sut, 74
jokes, 4, 17–19, 24–6, 30, 49–50, 53, 56, 65–70, 133–6, 141, 153n7. *See also* humour
Jordan, Shirley Ann, 21
Jyllands-Posten. See Danish cartoons

Karim, Karim, 10
Kay, Barbara, 71–2, 76
Kayak.com, 88
Kennedy, Michael, 42–3

Lembo, Ron, 59
Leo, Anton, 22, 35, 51, 114; and the CBC, 36, 40–3, 89; and Rev. William Thorne, 106–8; and sitcom conventions, 47
Lewis, Justin, 74
Lienhardt, Godfrey, 20
Lobo, Stephen. *See* Jaffer, J.J. (character)
Longinovic, Tomislav, 22
Lowe's, 88

MacFarquhar, Neil, 5, 83
Maclean's (magazine), 7
Magee, Rev. Duncan (character), 46–8, 76, 100; departure from *Little Mosque on the Prairie*, 106–12; and ecumenism, 124, 140
Mandvi, Aasif, 136–8
Mary Tyler Moore (television show), 27

Matheson, Sarah, 6
McCarthy, Sheila. *See* Hamoudi, Sarah (character)
McGrath, Debra. *See* Popowicz, Ann (character)
McKenzie, Rob, 72
Menon, Vinay, 86–7, 120–1
multiculturalism, 35, 40–4, 52, 71–2, 79–81
Murray, Michael, 3, 69, 73, 86–7
Muslims: and Arabs, 6, 10, 17, 33, 62, 79, 86, 131–4; and "authenticity," 66–7, 70, 121, 132; and conservatism, 20, 25, 33–5, 38, 43–6, 50–1, 64, 109, 120; and France, 92–3; and "humanizing," 4, 15–22, 28–30, 35–7, 54–79, 88, 121; and racial profiling, 77–8; and responses to *Little Mosque on the Prairie*, 62–7; and sitcoms, 4; stereotypes of, 6, 10, 15–19, 25–30, 44, 48, 63–4, 73, 80, 85, 119–21, 125, 128–38, 141; as villains, 7, 17. *See also* Islam; Nawaz, Zarqa

Nawaz, Zarqa, 17, 22, 35, 146n5; biography of, 5, 37; and character development, 58, 68, 86, 129–30; and critics, 69, 147n8; and ecumenism, 113; and feminism, 4–5, 14, 37–8, 47; films of, 5, 25, 37–8, 49; and genesis of *Little Mosque on the Prairie*, 36–46; and humour, 25–6, 38, 127; and international distribution, 84, 148n3; and Islam, 18, 25, 37–8, 41–51, 55–6, 66–7, 86, 147n7; and programming strategies, 18, 44–6; and Rev. Willian Thorne, 107–9, 140

New York Times, 5, 54–5, 60, 83
news (genre), 6–7, 25–6, 31, 107; and
    satire, 136–9
Norway: Kulturdepartementet
    (Ministry of Culture), 94; TV2, 95–7
Nowotny, Stefan, 22

Obeidallah, Dean, 134
Oklahoma City bombing, 37
Osborne, Lauren, 102
Ottawa Citizen, 3, 63, 86

Parks and Recreation (television
    show), 86, 129–33
parody, 74–6, 129, 132, 135–8, 153n9
Parti Québécois, 9, 152n2
pedagogical effect, 18, 44, 59, 102,
    105
people of the book, 16, 108, 151n6
Peterson, Joe (character), 46
Peterson, Valerie, 27–8
Pivot (cable network), 90
political correctness. *See* multicul-
    turalism
polysemy. *See* humour
Popowicz, Ann (character), 45–7, 78
Port, Moses, 87
Pudi, Danny, 130
Pym, Anthony, 13

Quebec, 8–9, 57, 143n3, 152n2
Qu'osby Show. See Mandvi, Aasif

Rae, Al, 47–9, 53, 57
Ranelagh, John, 96
Rashid, Amaar (character), 45–8,
    74–8, 100–1, 104, 108–14, 116–19,
    123–4, 132; and ecumenism, 139–40
Regina, Saskatchewan, 5, 36–41

religion as belief, 15, 101–4, 107,
    113–19, 151n2. *See also* Hamoudi,
    Sarah (character)
religion as culture, 15, 101–10, 151n2;
    and public policy, 103. *See also*
    Thorne, Rev. William (character)
religious diversity, 7–8
representation. *See* saleable di-
    versity; strategic essentialism;
    synecdoche
Rota, Carlo, 33, 45; departure from
    Little Mosque on the Prairie, 101,
    110, 114. *See also* Hamoudi, Yasir
    (character)

Said, Edward, 10
saleable diversity: and cultural
    specificity, 32, 79–82, 88–9, 97–8;
    and cultural translation, 16, 30, 99;
    definition, 5, 11–14; and potential
    for change, 32, 99–102, 113, 121–2,
    128; and representation, 28–32, 35,
    48–55, 73–4, 118, 139–41
Saskatchewan, 3–5, 34, 39–40, 43, 71,
    110. *See also* Regina, Saskatchewan
satire, 47, 74–5, 129, 135–40, 153n9
Schechter, Rebecca, 43, 52, 58
Schleiermacher, Friedrich, 128
Shaheen, Jack, 10
Shaikh, Zaib, 51, 58–9, 80–1, 127.
    See also Rashid, Amaar (character)
Siddiqui, Baber (character), 25, 33,
    45–7, 51, 57–8, 78, 105–6, 109, 112;
    and ecumenism, 113–16, 139–40,
    150n1
Siddiqui, Layla (character), 46–7, 57,
    150n1
simplified complex representations.
    See Alsultany, Evelyn

sitcoms, 5; and character development, 101, 110–13; and conservatism, 4–5, 27–31; and genre
conventions, 4, 42–4, 55–9, 67–70,
73–8, 99–100, 104–6; and identity,
129–33; and minorities, 3–4; and
programming strategies, 96; and
serial structure, 99–100; and transformative potential, 4, 31, 100,
138–41. See also humour
Sood, Manoj. See Sidiqqui, Baber
(character)
stand-up comedy, 134, 144n1. See
also Allah Made Me Funny (comedy troupe); Axis of Evil (comedy
troupe)
Steiner, George, 19
stereotypes, 4, 19, 26, 130, 145n8. See
also Muslims
Steyn, Mark, 71–2, 76
Strachan, Alex, 69–70, 87
strategic essentialism, 28–9
Stroumboulopoulos, George, 58
synecdoche, 48–53, 62–4

That '70s Show (television show),
130–1
theory, 12–13
Thorne, Rev. William (character), 46,
100–2, 106, 109–10; and ecumenism, 112, 123, 139–40; introduction,
107–9; redemption, 110–13; and
Sarah Hamoudi, 114–19. See also
religion as culture
Tinic, Serra, 97, 148n7
Toronto International Film Festival,
37
Toronto, Ontario, 5, 8, 34, 39–40, 43,
46, 71, 75–7, 84, 107, 112
Toronto Star, 3, 86
Trailer Park Boys, 5, 42
translation studies, 11–12; and agent-
oriented approach, 12
Tupper, Fred (character), 46–7, 76–7,
123, 132, 135, 147n11, 150n1; and
critics, 71
TV2 Zebra. See Norway

Usman, Azhar, 134

Vellani, Aliza. See Siddiqui, Layla
(character)

Wente, Margaret, 68, 72, 147n8
WestWind Pictures. See Darling,
Mary; Donnelly, Clark; Leo, Anton
Whoopi (television show), 130–2
Wilcox, David, 123
Will & Grace (television show), 28
Writers Guild of America, 36

Zahn, Paula, 83–6, 148n5

CULTURAL SPACES

Cultural Spaces is an interdisciplinary book series that examines cultural practices and social relations through bold, new investigations of the contemporary world. Authors are invited to explore themes and subjects including, but not limited to: citizenship, indigeneity, migration, ecology, environment, violence, difference and desire. Studies may take the form of cultural, literary, visual, political, sociological, or ethnographic analyses.

General Editor: Jasmin Habib, University of Waterloo
Editorial Advisory Board:
Lauren Berlant, University of Chicago
Homi K. Bhabha, Harvard University
Hazel V. Carby, Yale University
Richard Day, Queen's University
Christopher Gittings, University of Western Ontario
Lawrence Grossberg, University of North Carolina
Mark Kingwell, University of Toronto
Heather Murray, University of Toronto
Elspeth Probyn, University of Sydney
Rinaldo Walcott, OISE/University of Toronto

Books in the Series:
Peter Ives, *Gramsci's Politics of Language: Engaging the Bakhtin Circle and the Frankfurt School*
Sarah Brophy, *Witnessing AIDS: Writing, Testimony, and the Work of Mourning*
Shane Gunster, *Capitalizing on Culture: Critical Theory for Cultural Studies*
Jasmin Habib, *Israel, Diaspora, and the Routes of National Belonging*

Serra Tinic, *On Location: Canada's Television Industry in a Global Market*
Evelyn Ruppert, *The Moral Economy of Cities: Shaping Good Citizens*
Mark Coté, Richard J.F. Day, and Greg de Peuter, eds., *Utopian Pedagogy: Radical Experiments against Neoliberal Globalization*
Michael McKinnie, *City Stages: Theatre and the Urban Space in a Global City*
David Jefferess, *Postcolonial Resistance: Culture, Liberation, and Transformation*
Mary Gallagher, ed., *World Writing: Poetics, Ethics, Globalization*
Maureen Moynagh, *Political Tourism and Its Texts*
Erin Hurley, *National Performance: Representing Quebec from Expo 67 to Céline Dion*
Lily Cho, *Eating Chinese: Culture on the Menu in Small Town Canada*
Rhona Richman Kenneally and Johanne Sloan, eds, *Expo 67: Not Just a Souvenir*
Gillian Roberts, *Prizing Literature: The Celebration and Circulation of National Culture*
Lianne McTavish, *Defining the Modern Museum: A Case Study of the Challenges of Exchange*
Misao Dean, *Inheriting a Canoe Paddle: The Canoe in Discourses of English-Canadian Nationalism*
Sarah Brophy and Janice Hladki, eds, *Embodied Politics in Visual Autobiography*
Robin Pickering-Iazzi, *The Mafia in Italian Lives and Literature: Life Sentences and Their Geographies*
Claudette Lauzon, *The Unmaking of Home in Contemporary Art*
Kyle Conway, Little Mosque on the Prairie *and the Paradoxes of Cultural Translation*